# E[X]TREME DEMOCRACY

## edited by
## MITCH RATCLIFFE
## JON LEBKOWSKY

# Preface
## In the midst of history

Politics is changing. The sudden relevance of Howard Dean's campaign for the 2004 Democratic presidential nomination, which broke all records for fund-raising by a Democratic candidate, has transformed political professionals and journalists' perception of the Internet as a tool for organizing. Groups like MoveOn.org on the left and Grassfire.org on the right have pioneered issues-based activism, challenging older special interest operations for supremacy on their respective wings of the political spectrum. The rise of blogs and email discussions, to name just a couple applications of the Internet to discourse, have produced new pundits and centers of political influence in hyperspeed, as audiences and communities of interest form as quickly as headlines break. In every level of government, from cities accepting payments for traffic tickets or counties offering business and vehicle registration over the Net to state and federal agencies disclosing their activities through Web sites and email lists, the transformation to a digital government is underway. Public debate about the direction government should take has reached a critical mass that could transform the very notion of democratic systems, if citizens take the initiative and seize the reins of power from the professionals struggling to regain control of the process.

Indeed, politics is *always* changing as society incorporates new technology for disseminating information and connecting people. We have to be optimistic about the trend toward increasingly sophisticated use of technology in government and politics, since it is an inevitable aspect of history. From smoke signals to the press, local canvassing by candidates to nationally televised debates, the acceleration of political discourse through communications technology has been a faithful disruptor of accepted wisdom throughout human history.

Let's get something straight from the very beginning: Technology is disruptive because of the uses people put it to, it is not disruptive in an of itself, because if it is left unused it has no influence on the organization of society. Technology's social and political meaning is discovered through its use, as humans experience the way a technical

6

hack changes the flow of information and power in a system. Think about any new technology introduced in the workplace during the past 30 years and it is plain that, while the inventor may have had an inkling of the way a product could change an organization, the actual scope and impact of organizational change is the result of people arguing over, evangelizing about, and stumbling to new arrangements of people and resources in a company, an industry or an economy.

People change history and they use tools to do it. This is an important supposition when considering what will happen to politics because of the Internet. The adoption of application software and physical and logical protocols is deeply related to the availability of resources to bring these investments to fruition. Even as the Internet reshapes the communications universe a second and, probably, more powerful movement is preparing the ground for a new crop of tools that are based on open source technology that can be shared at low cost and modified by any user to create new features or emphasize certain functionality. As the global economy becomes increasingly interconnected, the availability to low-cost information technology — for we are moving from the early adoption phase of the information economy, when every new feature came at a high price, to a time when hundreds of millions of people have the basic skills that allow them to piece together an information technology-based solution to myriad communications, logistical and organizational challenges. The mechanics are taking over, bringing computational wizardry to the masses and, as a result, the masses are poised to take over the public discourse for the first time since Walter Cronkite set the national water-cooler agenda with his comments after the Tet Offensive that turned the tide of American opinion about the Vietnam War:

> To say that we are closer to victory today is to believe, in the face of the evidence, the optimists who have been wrong in the past. To suggest we are on the edge of defeat is to yield to unreasonable pessimism. To say that we are mired in stalemate seems the only realistic, yet unsatisfactory, conclusion. On the off chance that military and political analysts are right, in the next few months we must test the enemy's intentions, in case this is indeed his last big gasp before negotiations. But it is increasingly clear to this reporter that the only rational way out then will be to negotiate, not as victors, but as an honorable people who lived up to their pledge to defend democracy, and did the best they could.

This is Walter Cronkite. Good night.[1]

Since February 27, 1968, television reigned supreme as the national forum for political debate. In the meantime, the concentration of ownership of television stations has continued unabated, so that today fewer than a half dozen corporations frame the political questions of the day, and mostly in terms of a horse race or a tabloid scandal.

Today, the television networks are struggling to stay in control of the political debate as hundreds of thousands of Web sites, weblogs and mailing lists recast what has been a relatively uniform view of events into a kaleidoscopic debate. And, as the number of hues of political information increases, the power of the television networks can be decreased exponentially; if bloggers and online pundits and debating societies in mailing lists decide not to follow the basic script from television that describes every political encounter of a winner and a loser, who's up, who's down and what the extremes of public opinion add up to at the end of each day.

Alexis de Tocqueville, the French aristocrat who surveyed the young American democracy in the 1830s would understand quite clearly what is at stake today. It is far too convenient to believe that today's technology is something utterly new or that it makes something utterly new possible for the first time. Consider this statement by author Rebecca Blood, an avid blogger[2]:

> A weblog is something fundamentally new. Something no one can quite put their finger on, not yet. And those who try to define the phenomenon in terms of current institutions are completely missing the point.
>
> Consider the average weblog. Maintained by an unpaid enthusiast, this site will be updated perhaps a dozen times a day with links to interesting news stories and entries on other weblogs, accompanied by a few lines - or paragraphs - of commentary. A blogger interested in current events may include links to several accounts of one event,

---

[1] Reporting Vietnam, Part One, p. 582

[2] The revolution should not be eulogised, by Rebecca Blood. The Guardian Unlimited, December 18, 2003. URL: http://www.guardian.co.uk/online/weblogs/story/0,14024,1108306,00.html

noting differences in tone or detail, another may post the occasional recipe or pictures from a recent trip. A blogger may have a thousand readers, but more likely a few hundred or a couple of dozen, some of whom will offer comments of their own, right on the site. The weblog is at once a scrapbook, news filter, chapbook, newsletter, and community.

This is not passive news consumption. Neither is it broadcasting. The average blogger has time to surf the web, but no resources to report stories. Some bloggers will follow a news story to the end, some may lose interest after a few days. Commentary will range from the fully-formed to the random blurt and can freely mix the public and the personal.

All this represents something new: participatory media. And it matters. Not because of its resemblance to familiar institutions, but because of its differences from them.

We believe participatory media is something significant and important, an opportunity society should not pass by, that should not be missed after the 30 year pause in individual thinking represented by television's ascendancy. But, participatory media is nothing new, we are merely being given another shot at taking up the challenge of participating in the public debate about what events of the day mean to the individual, the state and society. Tocqueville describes exactly the same phenomena in the United States during the 1830s[3]:

> In the United States printers need no licenses, and newspapers no stamps or registration; moreover, the system of giving securities is unknown.
>
> For these reasons it is a simple and easy matter to start a paper; a few subscribers are enough to cover expenses, so the number of periodical or semiperiodical productions in the United States surpasses all belief. The most enlightened Americans attribute the slightness of the power of the press to this incredible dispersion; it is an axiom of political science that there the only way to neutralize the effect of newspapers is to multiply their numbers. I cannot imagine why such a self-evident truth has not been more commonly accepted among us. I can easily see why those bent on revolution through the press try to see that it should have only a few powerful organs; but the official partisans of the established order and the natural supporters of existing laws should

---

[3] de Tocqueville, Alexis. Democracy in America, Perrenial Classics Edition, HarperCollins, New York, 2000. p. 184

think that they are reducing the effectiveness of the press by concentrating it — that is something I just cannot understand. Faced by the press, the governments of Europe seem to me to behave as did the knights of old toward their enemies; they observed from their own experience that centralization was a powerful weapon, and they want to provide their enemy herewith, no doubt to win greater glory by resisting him.

Rebecca Blood's "something new" is Tocqueville's "axiom of political science," that the proliferation of sources of news and analysis decreases the power of a dominant source of information. A bit later in Democracy in America, Tocqueville describes the blogging writing style unmistakably as characteristic of democratic media[4]:

Then there comes the long catalog of political pamphlets, for in America the parties do no publish books to refute each other, but pamphlets which circulate at an incredible rate, last a day, and die.... By and large the literature of a democracy will never exhibit the order, regularity, skill, and art characteristic of aristocratic literature; formal qualities will be neglected or actually despised. The style will often be strange, incorrect, overburdened, and loose, and almost always strong and bold. Writers will be more anxious to work quickly than to perfect details. Short works will be commoner than long books, wit than erudition, imagination than depth. There will be a rude and untutored vigor of thought with great variety and singular fecundity. Authors will strive to astonish more than to please, and to stir passions rather than to charm taste.

This isn't to say that the potential for the Internet to change the political landscape is diminished in any way, rather it suggests that we could very well make something extraordinary happen to political discourse globally now that we are presented an opportunity to use a medium that can be accessed from any home, office or café, which supports a wide range of publishing and communications channels, and transcends the one-way media of the past 100 years with a truly interpersonal venue for debate and the discovery of common interests and compromise.

The whole history of democracy and technology has set the stage for what happens next. This book is about how to make the most of the

---

[4] ibid, pp. 470 and 474

opportunity, for, as we said before, our humanity compels us to be optimistic about the growing dependence of governments, governance and political debate on new technologies of communication. — *M.R.*

# The Founding Documents

As the presidential campaign cycle in the United States ground into gear in early 2003, several notable essays describing a new approach to politics were posted on the Internet. Visionary and evangelical, they sparked widespread discussion amongst netizens and programmers who would become leaders in the Dean for America campaign and other online projects that have transformed political fund-raising and organizing.

Viewed today, just a year later, the raw intellectual energy is tempered by the reader's awareness of the rapid progress in campaign strategy that has embraced and begun to use the Internet effectively. There is still a long way to go, giving these essays an idealistic color that is more pronounced in retrospect. Just as we read Common Sense and other colonial pamphlets, these essays will remain informative and important to understand the paths democrats as political thinking evolves.

# Emergent Democracy
## by Joichi Ito

We thought it would be useful to introduce *Emergent Democracy* with a note about the collaborative process that produced the paper. Joichi ("Joi") Ito is an intensely hip world-traveling venture capitalist based in Japan but also in cyberspace; he is also the nexus of a loose global community of social software entrepreneurs and hackers , tech-focused academics, writers and miscellaneous travelers who hang out online in his IRC chat room, and who converse asynchronously via weblog posts and comments. Ito is a force of nature carried from conference to dinner table around the world; he surely has as many frequent flier miles as he does megabytes of connectivity, as he turns up everywhere and meets everyone he finds interesting to add to his understanding about where the world is headed.

In March 2004 Ito started thinking about the potential relationship of weblogs to grassroots or (as Ross Mayfield of SocialText called it) *emergent* democracy. He invited anyone reading his weblog to join a "happening," a teleconference augmented by a chat room (for visual feedback) and a wiki (for collaborative note-taking and annotation). The first happening led to a second, and to the composition of this essay drafted and circulated by Joi and through collaboration with several others at Joi's collaborative workspace or wiki. Someone else posted it to a system called Quicktopic, which includes a forums-based document review capability. Ito encouraged anyone to review the document at either place and post comments and revisions.

In all this the idea was to use an open process online to create a document about social software and democracy.

There are two ways to look at this. First, as a publishing phenomenon. Weblogs are simple content management systems for publishing to the web, and political weblogs could be compared to the tracts published by early activists like Tom Paine. Second, weblogs are conversations and not like published documents. There's a lot of call and response among bloggers, between blogs and through embedded systems for posting comments on individual blogs. As platforms for conversation, weblogs can support the kind of discussion and debate that are so crucial to democratic systems.

The essay is the result of an experiment, but it is also a good overview of then-current thinking about social software and its relevance to political life. It's even more interestinig given the nature of the virtual community that produced it. Ito is international (he was raised and schooled in both the United States and Japan), and he spends much of his life online establishing casual friendships with other cyberspace denizens who are spread around Japan, the United States, and other countries. When he thinks of democracy, he is thinking of h the United States, Japan and how it can be applied worldwide, since he has spread his roots so widely during his life.

I was involved in the process of creating the essay and have revised the version included here to enhance readability and clarify some assumptions that were left hanging in the original. An earlier version is posted at http://joi.ito.com/static/emergentdemocracy.html. — J.L.


## Introduction

Developers and proponents of the Internet have hoped to evolve the network as a platform for intelligent solutions which can help correct the imbalances and inequalities of the world. Today, however, the Internet is a noisy environment with a great deal of power consolidation instead of the level, balanced democratic Internet many envisioned.

In 1993, author Howard Rheingold wrote in *The Virtual Community*[5]:

We temporarily have access to a tool that could bring conviviality and understanding into our lives and might help revitalize the public sphere. The same tool, improperly controlled and wielded, could become an instrument of tyranny. The vision of a citizen-designed, citizen-controlled worldwide communications network is a version of technological utopianism that could be called the vision of "the electronic agora." In the original democracy, Athens, the agora was the marketplace, and more — it was where citizens met to talk, gossip, argue, size each other up, find the weak spots in political ideas by debating about them. But another kind of vision could apply to the use

---

[5] Rheingold, Howard. (1993) Virtual Community. Retrieved February 18, 2003, from http://www.rheingold.com/vc/book/

of the Net in the wrong ways, a shadow vision of a less utopian kind of place — the Panopticon.

Rheingold has been called naïve,[6] but it is clear that the Internet has become a global agora, or gathering place. Effective global conversation and debate is just beginning. We are on the verge of an awakening of the Internet, an awakening that may facilitate the emergence of a new democratic political model (Rheingold's revitalization of the public sphere). However it could also enable the corporations and governments of the world to control, monitor and influence their constituents, leaving the individual at the mercy of and under constant scrutiny by those in power (an electronic, global Panopticon).

We must influence the development and use of these tools and technologies to support democracy, or they will be turned against us by corporations, totalitarian regimes and terrorists. To do so, we must begin to understand the process and implications necessary for an Emergent Democracy. This new political model must support the basic characteristics of democracy and reverse the erosion of democratic principles that has occurred with the concentration of power within corporations and governments. New technologies can enable the emergence of a functional, more direct democratic system which can effectively manage complex issues. Viable technologies for direct democracy will support, change or replace existing representative democracies. By direct democracy, we don't mean simple majority rule, but a system that evolves away from the broadcast style of managed consensus to a democratic style of collective consensus derived from "many-to-many" conversations.

### Democracy

The dictionary defines democracy as "government by the people in which the supreme power is vested in the people and exercised directly by them or by their elected agents under a free electoral system." With the Gettysburg Address, Abraham Lincoln gave us a more eloquent definition, government "of the people, by the people, and for the people."

---

[6] Rheingold, Howard. (2001) MIT Press. 2001 Edition of The Virtual Community. Chapter 11, "Rethinking Virtual Communities," pp 323-

A functional democracy is governed by the majority while protecting the rights of minorities. To achieve this balance, a democracy relies on a competition of ideas, which, in turn, requires freedom of speech and the ability to criticize those in power without fear of retribution. In an effective representative democracy power must also be distributed to several points of authority to enable checks and balances and reconcile competing interests.

## Competition of ideas

Democracy is itself an incomplete and emergent political system, and must, by its nature, adapt to new ideas and evolving social standards. A competition of ideas is essential for a democracy to embrace the diversity of its citizens and protect the rights of the minority, while allowing the consensus of the majority to rule.

This foundation was considered so fundamental to the success of democracy, that the First Amendment to the United States Constitution enumerates three rights specifically to preserve the competition of ideas: the freedoms of speech, of the press, and of peaceable assembly.

## The Commons[7]

Effective debate requires a shared set of references and metaphors. The expansion of culture and knowledge depends on linguistic and conceptual shorthand based on shared knowledge and experience. Collaborative, innovative discussion is impossible if every item must be expanded and reduced to so-called first principles. This body of knowledge, experience and ideas has come to be known as a commons.

If nature has made any one thing less susceptible than all others of exclusive property, it is the action of the thinking power called an idea, which an individual may exclusively possess as long as he keeps it to himself; but the moment it is divulged, it forces itself into the possession of every one, and the receiver cannot dispossess himself of it. Its peculiar character, too, is that no one possesses the less, because every other possesses the whole of it. He who receives an idea from me, receives

---

[7] Lessig, Lawrence. (2002). The Future of Ideas. Retrieved February 16, 2003, from http://cyberlaw.stanford.edu/future/

instruction himself without lessening mine; as he who lights his taper at mine, receives light without darkening me.

That ideas should freely spread from one to another over the globe, for the moral and mutual instruction of man, and improvement of his condition, seems to have been peculiarly and benevolently designed by nature, when she made them, like fire, expansible over all space, without lessening their density in any point, and like the air in which we breathe, move, and have our physical being, incapable of confinement or exclusive appropriation. (Thomas Jefferson)

Another aspect: the Internet may be considered a commons or public network, though there is persistent threat of enclosure (transferring resources from the commons to individual ownership) based on enforcement of intellectual property and distribution rights. However no one owns the Internet, and no single national entity has jurisdiction, so it remains an open, accessible platform for all kinds of activity, including the evolution of the social commons described above.

*Emerging Limits on Debate*

The competition of ideas requires critical debate that is widely heard, and open to a diverse set of participants. Although we have many tools for conducting such debate, increasingly there are barriers to our engaging in it at all.

Even though ideas are not, in theory, subject to copyright, trademark or patent protection, increasingly draconian intellectual property legislation practically limits the scope and meaning of fair use and the flow of innovation, thereby having the same effect as if ideas were property owned and controlled by corporations. This includes the code inside computers and networks, which controls the transmission or reproduction of information. It includes spectrum allocation, determining whether it is shared by individuals or allocated to large corporations broadcasting protected intellectual property.[8] The effect of

_____

[8] For more information see: Frankston, Reed, and Friends. The Intellectual Property Meme. Retrieved February 16, 2003, from http://www.satn.org/archive/2003_01_26_archive.html - 90254497

these laws is broad, especially given the chilling effect in the fear of lawsuits.

As the notion of intellectual property continues to grow in scope, more and more of what was one part of common knowledge is becoming the property of corporations. As the infrastructure for communication becomes more tuned to the protection of property than the free spread of ideas, the capacity for critical debate is severely constrained.

## The Role of Media

The competition of ideas has evolved as technology has advanced. For example, the printing press made it possible to provide more information to the masses and eventually provided the people a voice through journalism and the press. Arguably, this has been replaced by the voice of mass media operated by large corporations. As a result, there is less diversity and more internalization of the competition of ideas.

Weblogs are Web sites that include links and personal commentary published in reverse chronological order. Often called "blogs" for short, weblogs have become a standard for online micropublishing and communication, thanks to the development of several simple content management systems that support the weblog format.[9] In *The Weblog Handbook,* Rebecca Blood catalogs several types of weblogs, noting that the classic type is the filter, a type of weblog that filters web content by some criterion (often the weblog author's interest), essentially a collection of links that point to web pages and web sites, and a usually brief description of the link and why it is interesting. Weblogs and other forms of filtering, coupled with many of the capture and transmission technologies discussed by Steve Mann, author of "Wearable Computing: Toward Humanistic Intelligence"[10] may provide a better method of capturing and filtering relevant information. At the same time, they may suppress information where the privacy damage exceeds the value to the public.

---

[9] *Microcontent News* has a good overview of weblog systems at http://www.microcontentnews.com/articles/ blogware.htm.

[10] Steve Mann, "Wearable Computing: Toward Humanistic Intelligence." IEEE Intelligent Systems, May-June 2001, p. 12.

An example of weblogs exceeding the ability of the mass media to identify relevant information is the case of Trent Lott. The national media covered briefly his racist comments during Strom Thurmond's 100th birthday party. After the national media lost interest, the weblogs continued to find and publicize evidence of Lott's hateful past until the mass media once again took notice and covered the issue in more depth.[11]

The balance between what's relevant and what's not relevant is culturally biased and difficult to sustain. We need mechanisms to check filters for corruption and weighted perspectives. A variety of checks and balances and a diversity of methods and media can provide the perspectives we need for a balanced view of current events.

Blogs may be evolving to become more than filters; they may be replacing traditional news sources, according to journalist Jay Rosen:

"Blogs are undoing the system for generating authority and therefore credibility of news providers that's been accumulating for well over 100 years. And the reason is that the mass audience is slowly, slowly disappearing. And the one-to-many broadcasting model of communications — where I have the news and I send it out to everybody out there who's just waiting to get it — doesn't describe the world anymore. And so people who have a better description of the world are picking up the tools of journalism and doing it. It's small. Its significance is not clear. But it's a potentially transforming development... I like [it] when things get shaken up, and when people don't know what journalism is and they have to rediscover it. So in that sense I'm very optimistic."[12]

## Privacy

Whether a system is democratic or otherwise, people or groups with power or wealth often see no benefit in keeping the general population well informed, truly educated, their privacy ensured or their discourse

---

[11] Shachtman, Noah. "Blogs Make the Headlines". Wired News. Retrieved February 18, 2003, from
http://www.wired.com/news/culture/0,1284,56978,00.html

[12] Jay Rosen interviewed by Christopher Lydon, October 4, 2003.
http://blogs.law.harvard.edu/lydon/2003/10/04

uninhibited. Those are the very things that power and wealth fear most. Old forms of government have every reason to operate in secret, while denying just that privilege to subjects. The people are minutely scrutinized while the powerful are exempt from scrutiny.[13] (Dee Hock) We can't expect support where power and wealth are concentrated, beyond lip service, for greater, truly meaningful citizen participation in governance. Greater democracy requires that we work constantly to build and sustain structures for effective democratic participation.

In addition to the technical and legal ability to speak and engage in critical debate, citizens must be allowed to exercise this ability without fear of retribution from government or from other institutions where power and wealth are concentrated (e.g. corporate entities). In the increasingly sophisticated world of massive databases and systematic profiling of individuals, the protection of those citizens willing to question and challenge power must be assured. In a networked society where each individual's data has value, we should consider a definition of rights by which each individual owns and manages data relevant to his identity.

It is essential to understand the difference between personal privacy and transparency. While individuals have a right to privacy, powerful institutions must operate transparently, so that abuses of power are not concealed by veils of secrecy.

In one of the earliest critiques of a national ID card proposal (January 1986), Professor Geoffrey de Q Walker, now dean of law at Queensland University, observed:

One of the fundamental contrasts between free democratic societies and totalitarian systems is that the totalitarian government [or other totalitarian organization] relies on secrecy for the regime but high surveillance and disclosure for all other groups, whereas in the civic culture of liberal democracy, the position is approximately the reverse. [14]

---

[13] Hock, Dee, founder of Visa International whose work on organization theory is described in the book *The Birth of the Chaordic Age.*

[14] Davies, Simon. http://wearcam.org/envirotech/simon_davies_opposition_to_id_card_sche mes.htm

Steve Mann presents the notion of sousveillance[15] as a method for the public to monitor the established centers of power and provide a new level of transparency. Traditionally, this has been the role of the press, but the press is decreasingly critical and vigilant, instead focusing on sensational stories, propaganda, and "infotainment."

## Direct Democracy and Scale

The concept of direct democracy, where citizens are directly responsible for their own governance - originated in Athens, Greece, around the fifth century. Though Athenian democratic governance was direct, it was also limited. Only males born of an Athenian mother and father participated. According to Professor Paul Cartledge, "the citizen body was a closed political elite."[16] Of a population of 250,000, an average of 30,000 were eligible to participate, i.e. a mere 12%, a relatively small group with little diversity.

Common supposition is that direct democracy is not feasible for large, diverse populations. There are practical and technical issues: how do you coordinate ongoing large-scale decision-making that is effective for a broad populace? How can the general population digest and comprehend the complexities involved in running a large state requiring deep understanding of the issues, specialization, and a division of labor. Representative democracy, wherein elected representatives of the people are chosen through a voting mechanism, is considered by most to be the only possible way to manage a democracy of significant scale.

Democratic nations generally adopt republican form of representative democracy, formed in reaction to governments where leadership was hereditary (monarchy). The hereditary model was abandoned and leaders were periodically appointed under a constitution. Republics now tend to be representative democracies, where leaders are periodically elected by citizens, and all adults with few exceptions have an opportunity to vote. Representative democracy allows leaders to specialize and focus on the complex issues of governance, which an

---

[15] Mann, Steve. "Sousveillance, not just surveillance, in response to terrorism". Retrieved February 18, 2003, from http://www.chairetmetal.com/cm06/mann-complet.htm

[16] Cartledge, Paul, "The Democratic Experiment." BBCi, January 1, 2001. http://www.bbc.co.uk/history/ancient/greeks/greekdemocracy_03.shtml

uneducated and uninterested general population could not be expected to grasp. Representative democracy is considered more practical than direct democracy, which becomes increasingly difficult with larger and more diverse populations.

The failure of democracy to scale is easy to understand. The founding fathers of the United States, the "égalité, fraternité and liberté" of France, and most other liberals who moved society toward freedom and liberty in the 1700's, could not foresee the accelerated population growth over the following two centuries. The couldn't predict the radical evolution of science, the rapid development of technology and the pronounced increases in mobility of information, money, goods, services and people. Nor could they know or visualize the topography of countries such as the United States, Canada, and China, or continents such as Africa, Northern Europe, Russia, or Latin America. Evolving nations were laid out on maps that bore little resemblance to the reality of the environment, and were not predictive of the huge increases in scale of population, commerce, and government. In the main, no one foresaw a need for the right to self-organize — to adjust scale and degrees of separation as such increases occurred.[17]

As the issues facing government have become more complex, social technologies have emerged that enable citizens to self-organize more easily. These technologies may eventually enable democracies to scale and become more adaptable and direct.

As the voting mechanism becomes more organized and the difficulty of participating in critical debate increases, forms of influence are increasingly relevant and detrimental to the balance of power. Elected representatives attend more readily to those who have the power to influence the voting mechanism and the public debate; these are often minorities who have more financial influence or the ability to mobilize large numbers of motivated people through ideological or religious channels. Extremists and corporate interests can become dominant, and

---

[17] Hock, Dee. Email to Joichi Ito. March 8, 2003. Retrieved from http://joi.ito.com/archives/2003/03/10/an_email _from_dee_hock_about_the_emergent_democracy_ paper.html

a "silent majority" may have little input into the selection of representatives or the critical debate.[18]

A variety of groups have been successful in polling the silent majority and amplifying its opinions to provide support for moderate politicians on policy issues. One such group , One Voice[19], conducts telephone and internet polls of average Israeli and Palestinians, most of whom are in favor of peace.. The organization amplifies their opinions by publishing poll results in reports and the mass media. This method of bypassing the traditional methods of influencing representatives is a form of direct democracy, which is becoming increasingly popular and important as technology makes such polling easier.

Generally, polling, as a form of direct democracy is effective for issues which are relatively simple. and about which the silent majority have an opinion that is under-represented. For more complex issues, such direct democracy is criticized as populist and irresponsible.

To address this issue, Professor James S. Fishkin, Director of Stanford University's Center for Deliberative Democracy, has developed a method called deliberative polling. Deliberative polling combines deliberation in small group discussions with scientific random sampling to increase the quality and depth of the understanding of the participants, while maintaining a sampling that reflects the actual distribution of opinion in the population, rather than the distribution of political power. Deliberative polling has been used successfully to poll people about relatively complex issues such as tax policies.

## Emergence

Emergence is a term relevant to the study of complex systems. Emergence is what you have when the relatively simple interactions of relatively simple parts of a system yield complex results over time. Emergent behaviors are behaviors that are not directed by systems of command and control, but emerge from subtle, complex interactions.

---

[18] Ito, Joichi. (2002). Rebuilding Modern Politics: Can the System Fix Itself? Joi Ito's Web. Retrieved February 16, 2003, from http://joi.ito.com/archives/2002/09/23/rebuilding_modern_politics_can_the_system_fix_itself.html

[19] ; http://www.silentnolonger.com/

Common examples are flocks of ducks or birds that act in concert but with no specific leader, or colonies of ants that establish routes for collecting food based on group experience reinforced by pheromones.

In the book *Emergence*[20], Steven Johnson writes about harvester ant colonies, which exhibit an amazing ability to solve difficult problems, including geometry. The following exchange is from an interview with Deborah Gordon who studies ants.

She says, "Look at what actually happened here: they've built the cemetery at exactly the point that's furthest away from the colony. And the midden is even more interesting: they've put it at precisely the point that maximizes its distance from both the colony and the cemetery. It's like there's a rule they're following: put the dead ants as far away as possible, and put the midden as far away as possible without putting it near the dead ants."

Johnson explains that there is no single ant in charge. The ants' solving of such problems is emergent behavior resulting from simple rules and diverse interactions with immediate surroundings and neighbors.

The complex human fetus develops from simple cells through this same principle: following a simple set of rules encoded in DNA. When the first cell divides into two, one half becomes the head side and the other the tail. The next time it divides, the quarters determine whether they are to be the head or the tail, and they become the head of the head, or the tail of the head, and so on. This division and specialization continues until in very short order the cells have created a complex human body. The liver cells know to turn into liver cells by sensing that their neighbors are also liver cells and "reading" the DNA. There is no omniscient control, just a growing number of independent cells following rules and communicating with and sensing the state of their neighbors[21]

---

[20] Johnson, Steven. *Emergence: The Connected Lives of Ants, Brains, Cities, and Software.* Scribner, 2002.

[21] Johnson, Steven. *Emergence: The Connected Lives of Ants, Brains, Cities and Software.* New York: Scribner, September 10, 2002.

In *The Death and Life of Great American Cities*, Jane Jacobs argues that urban planning in America tends to fail when top-down plans to change the nature of neighborhoods are implemented. Most large projects designed to increase the quality of ghetto areas by building large apartment projects have not succeeded in their aim. Conversely, neighborhoods that have thrived have done so through a kind of emergence. She argues that the interaction between people on the sidewalks and streets creates a street culture and intelligence more suitable than central control for managing neighborhoods in cities, and that instead of bulldozing problems, city planners should study neighborhoods that work and try to mimic the conditions that produce the positive emergent behavior.[22]

Can citizens self-organize to deliberate on, and to address, complex issues democratically, without any one citizen required to know and comprehend the whole? This is the essence of emergence, the way that ant colonies can "think" and cellular DNA can evolve complex human bodies. If information technology could provide tools for citizens in a democracy to participate and interact in a way that facilitates self-organization and emergent understanding, we can evolve a form of emergent democracy that would resolve complexity and scalability issues associated with democratic governance.

In complex systems the role of the leader is not about determining direction and controlling followers. The leader maintains integrity, mediates the will of the many, influencing and communicating with peers and with other leaders.[23] The leader becomes more of facilitator (or hub), and custodian of the process, than a power figure. She is the catalyst or manager of critical debate, or the representative of a group engaged in critical debate.[24] The leader is often the messenger delivering the consensus of a community to another layer or group. As leadership

[22] Jacobs, Jane. (1961). Random House, Inc. The Death and Life of Great American Cities.

[23] Hock, Dee. (1999). Leader-Follower. Future Positive. Retrieved February 16, 2003, from http://futurepositive.synearth.net/stories/storyReader$173

[24] Ito, Joichi. (2003). Leadership in an emergent democracy. Joi Ito's Web. Retrieved February 16, 2003, from http://joi.ito.com/archives/2003/02/16/leadership_in_an_emergent_democracy.html

becomes necessary to manage the development of an opinion or idea about a complex issue, information technology can enable quick and ad hoc leader selection and representation of consensus opinion in a larger debate.

## Weblogs and emergence

In *Emergence*, Steven Johnson writes:

The technologies behind the Internet — everything from micro-processors in each Web server to the open-ended protocols that govern the data itself — have been brilliantly engineered to handle dramatic increases in scale, but they are indifferent, if not down-right hostile, to the task of creating higher-level order. There is, of course, a neurological equivalent of the Web's ratio of growth to order, but it's nothing you'd want to emulate. It's called a brain tumor.

*Emergence* was written in 2001. A change has taken place on the Internet since 2000. Weblogs, which we have defined as personal web sites with serial content posted in reverse chronological order, have begun to grow in number and influence. Weblogs exhibit a growing ability to manage a variety of tasks, and emergent behavior is evident because of changes in the way weblogs are managed.

Johnson's explanation for the inability of web pages to self-organize is,

Self-organizing systems use feedback to bootstrap themselves into a more orderly structure. And given the Web's feedback-intolerant, one-way linking, there's no way for the network to learn as it grows, which is why it's now so dependent on search engines to rein in its natural chaos.

He also describes how, in the example of the ants, the many simple, local, random interactions of the ants helped them exhibit emergent behavior.

Weblogs are different from traditional web pages in several ways. Weblogs involve the use of content management tools, which make it much easier to add entries, with a resulting increase in the number and frequency of items posted. The posts are generally small items with a variety of information types - e.g. text, photographs, audio, and video referred to as micro-content.[25] Weblog culture encourages bloggers (people who run weblogs) to comment on entries in other weblogs and link to the source. Some systems have a protocol that supports interactive linking: i.e. when a blogger posts an item with a link to another weblog, a link to his new item is created on that weblog. In addition to HTML content, weblogs often generate XML[26] files based on a standard protocol for syndication called RSS[27], which allows computers to receive updates to weblogs through special clients aggregating syndicated content - such as Feedreader[28] for Windows and NetNewsWire[29] for the Macintosh. These news aggregators constantly scan the users' favorite weblogs for new posts.

When new entries are posted to a weblog, a notification may also be sent to services such as weblogs.com[30], which keep track of weblog updates in near real-time. This information is also used by a variety of new services to generate meta-information about weblogs. These new information sites include Blogdex[31], which scans weblogs for quoted articles and ranks them according to the number of weblog references,

---

[25] Weinberger, David. Small Pieces Loosely Joined. Retrieved February 18, 2003, from http://www.smallpieces.com/

[26] "Extensible Markup Language (XML) is a simple, very flexible text format derived from SGML ( ISO 8879 ). Originally designed to meet the challenges of large-scale electronic publishing, XML is also playing an increasingly important role in the exchange of a wide variety of data on the Web and elsewhere." Retrieved February 16, 2003, from http://www.w3.org/XML/ - intro

[27] "RSS is a Web content syndication format. Its name is an acronym for Really Simple Syndication. RSS is dialect of XML. All RSS files must conform to the XML 1.0 specification, as published on the World Wide Web Consortium (W3C) website. At the top level, a RSS document is a <rss> element, with a mandatory attribute called version that specifies the version of RSS that the document conforms to." Retrieved February 16, 2003, from http://backend.userland.com/rss

[28] http://www.feedreader.com/

[29] http://ranchero.com/software/netnewswire/

[30] http://www.weblogs.com/

[31] http://blogdex.media.mit.edu/

and Technorati,[32] which ranks weblogs by tracking inbound and outbound links to specific weblogs and/or weblog posts.

Technorati's results in particular look like diagrams of small-world networks.33 Weblog links are governed by much the same rules. They represent a scale-free network of weblogs where friends generally link to friends, but some weblogs serve as hubs with many more connections, including links to whole other clusters of weblogs, and to other content within the Internet. (It would be interesting to see how the pattern of weblog links looks relative to linking patterns in the web overall. Are weblogs an organizing structure of the web, or merely another cluster within the web?)

In addition to linking articles between weblogs, bloggers link to each other via blogrolls, marginal lists of personal favorite weblogs. Services such as blogrolling.com[34] help bloggers manage their blogrolls and see who is blogrolling them. Services such as blogstreet[35] provide a method of viewing the "neighborhood" of a blogger by following and analyzing blogroll links.

In this way, the structure of weblogs addresses the problem that Johnson raised when he suggested that the Web is not self-organizing. Through the feedback and two-way linking we have described, weblogs show emergent self-organization.

### The Power Law

With the appearance of the World Wide Web, proponents hoped that the low barriers to entry (inexpensive web hosting, ease of setting up a web page) would dramatically increase the number of people publishing their thoughts, and that this would lead to a diverse and decentralized system. What happened instead was that portals and search engines

---

[32] http://www.technorati.com/

[33] Watts, Duncan and Steven H. Strogatz, "Collective dynamics of 'small-world' networks." Nature, Volume 393, June 1998, pp. 440-2.

[34] http://www.blogrolling.com/

[35] http://www.blogstreet.com/

captured much of the traffic and an attention economy[36] formed as attention became a scarce resource for which various commercial entities competed. Users focused on portals first to help them find what they were looking for. Then they went to the large ecommerce and news sites that appeared during the Internet boom. These sites provided a sense of order, a variety of products, and high quality information. A minority of web surfers landed on smaller, less prominent sites. This attention economy created a value in site traffic, which was purchased from more popular sites in the form of paid advertisements and sponsored links. This is still the primary income model for search engines and portal sites today.

In a widely distributed and linked paper, Clay Shirky argues that weblogs are exhibiting a sort of order now because the community is still small. As the community increases in size, he contends, this order will fragment, as it did for online communities in the past, such as Usenet news groups, mailing lists and bulletin boards. In his paper, "Power Laws, Weblogs, and Inequality,"[37] Shirky shows that an analysis of inbound links for weblogs shows a standard power law distribution. The power law distribution is a distribution where the value of any unit is $1/n$ of its ranking. The second place weblog has $1/2$ of the inbound links of the top ranking weblog, the third place weblog has $1/3$ of the inbound links and so on.

This power law distribution can be counterintuitive. Shirky argues that the top-ranking weblogs will eventually become mass media, while the weblogs at the bottom of the curve will have difficulty gaining any attention. As a result, these weblogs will appear as nothing more than local conversations with friends. He suggests that it will be increasingly difficult to displace the high-ranking sites, and his power law distribution data for weblogs supports his claims.

---

[36] Goldhaber, Michael. (1997) "The Attention Economy and the Net". First Monday. Retrieved February 16, 2003, from http://www.firstmonday.dk/issues/issue2_4/goldhaber/

[37] Shirky, Clay. (2003). Power Laws, Weblogs, and Inequality. Clay Shirky's Writings About the Intenet. Retrieved February 16, 2003, from http://www.shirky.com/writings/powerlaw_weblog.html

Shirky's analysis may be missing important factors, however. Weblogs form a scale-free network where some nodes are hubs, i.e. more heavily linked than others, and this does suggest a power law distribution. However there may be dynamism that the power law doesn't capture. Subnetworks of weblogs may become linked, for instance, as during the Iraqi war, when warbloggers (a subset or subnetwork of bloggers supporting the war) debated antiwar bloggers, thereby forming links between the two networks. This has resonance with the concept of emergent communities of interest espoused by Valdis Krebs, which demonstrates how subnetworks may be linked through affinity points.[38]

## Mayfield's Ecosystem

Ross Mayfield, CEO of the social software company SocialText, proposed an alternative view of the political economy of weblogs. Mayfield points out that not all links have equal value. He explains that there are three different types of networks developing among weblogs: creative, social, and political networks.

A creative network is a flat network of a production-oriented group of close associates with deep trust and dense inter-linking. It is said that 12 people is the optimum number for holding a dinner conversation or a tight team.[39]

A social network is the traditional weblog form. The Law of 150[40] is a theory that people can maintain an average of 150 personal relationships. The Law of 150 is a bell-shaped distribution where some weblogs receive more attention than others, but the distribution fairly represents the quality of the weblogs.

---

[38] Krebs, Valdis. "The Social Life of Books: Visualising Communities of Interest via Purchase Patterns on the WWW." Orgnet.com, 1999. http://www.orgnet.com/booknet.html.

[39] Gladwell, Malcolm. *The Tipping Point: How Little Things Can Make a Big Difference.* Newport Beach, California: January 2002.

[40] Law of 150: Robin Dunbar, British Anthropologist, Professor of Psychology, University of Liverpool: R.I.M Dunbar, "Neocortex size as a constraint on group size in primates," Journal of Human Evolution (1992), vol. 20, pp. 469-493

A political network follows Shirky's power law and is similar to a representative democracy where weblogs receive links from thousands of other weblogs. Each link may be thought of as a vote. The weblogs at the top of this power curve have a great deal of influence.

## The Strength of Weak Ties

In "The Strength of Weak Ties," Mark Grano-vetter[41] describes the value of weak ties in networks. Strong ties are your family, friends and other people you have strong bonds to. Weak ties are relationships that transcend local relationship boundaries both socially and geographically. A study by Granovetter demonstrates that people are more likely to find employment through their weak ties than their strong ties.

It is the ability to operate in all three of Mayfield's clusters, and to transcend boundaries between them that make weblogs so potentially powerful. A single weblog and even a single entry in a weblog can have an operational purpose, a social purpose, and an impact on the political network. Recall that emergence seems predicated on many mechanisms of communication between ele-ments. For instance, when I blog something about Emergent Democracy, I may be speaking creatively to the small group of researchers working on this paper; socially to a larger group of friends who are thinking along with me and trying to get a handle on the concept; and on a political level to readers I don't know, but who I'm hoping to influence with my talk about a new kind of politics.

Many bloggers create their weblogs in order to communicate with their strong-tie peers, linking to and communicating within this small group at the creative level. At some point, someone in the peer group will discover some piece of information or point of view which resonates with the next, social level. Then a larger number of social acquaintances will pick up those entries that they believe may be interesting to others in their individual social networks. In this way, a small group focusing on a very specific topic can trigger a weak-tie connection carrying useful information to the next level. If this information resonates with even more bloggers, the attention given the source will increase rapidly. The individual or group who created the original comment or post will also

---

[41] Granovetter, Mark. (1973). "The Strength of Weak Ties." American Journal of Sociology, 78 (May): 1360-1380

continue to participate in the conversation, since they can be aware, through technorati or blogdex, of all of the links to the original piece of information as they propagate.

Weblogs create a positive feedback system, and with tools for analysis like technorati, we can identify the importance of information at the political level by tracking its movement across the weak ties between networks and network levels.

Noise in the system is suppressed, and signal amplified. Peers read the operational chatter at Mayfield's creative network layer. At the social network layer, bloggers scan the weblogs of their 150 acquaintances and pass the information they deem significant up to the political networks. The political networks have a variety of local maxima which represent yet another layer. Because of the six degrees phenomenon, it requires very few links before a globally significant item has made it to the top of the power curve. This allows a great deal of specialization and diversity to exist at the creative layer without causing disruptive noise at the political layer. The classic case, already mentioned above, was the significant chatter at the creative level when Trent Lott praised Strom Thurmond's 1948 segregationist campaign for the presidency, though conventional journalists had ignored the comment. The story escalated to influential bloggers and there was a real impact at the political level, leading to Lott's resignation.

### The brain and excitatory networks

For a couple years now, software engineer Peter Kaminski of SocialText [42] has been working on the hypothesis that the process that governs the way we thinkdescribed by neurobiologist author William Calvin[43] as the "emergent properties of recurrent excitatory networks in the superficial layers of cerebral cortex," scales up in a similar fashion to the way people

---

[42] http://www.istori.com/peterkaminski/

[43] Calvin, William. *How Brains Think: Evolving Intelligence, Then and Now.* New York: Basic Books, 1997.

work together in groups, and groups of groups — and ultimately, up to direct democracy.[44]

Calvin notes that the cerebral cortex is made up of columns of neurons, which are tightly interlinked and analogous to the creative network. These columns resonate with certain types of input. When they are excited, they excite neighboring columns. If the neighboring columns resonate with the same pattern, they also excite their neighbors. In this way, the surface of the cerebral cortex acts as a voting space, with each column of neurons, when excited by any of a variety of different patterns (thoughts), selectively resonating and then exciting their neighbors. When a significant number of the columns resonate with the same pattern, the thought becomes an understanding. Sensory organs provide the inputs to the various columns and the brain as a whole drives output to other organs based on the understanding.

Calvin's model of human thought process suggests that the brain uses emergence, the strength of weak ties, and a neighbor excitation model for resolving thoughts. The structure of the brain is similar to Mayfield's system. One of the keys is that the columns only excite their neighbors. This self-limiting factor is also one of the factors that Johnson describes in creating the emergent behavior of ants. The influence of weblogs is similarly constrained by the ability of individuals to read only a limited number of weblog entries per day and the tendency to focus, not on the weblogs with a high political ranking, but on the creative and social weblogs of interest. This dampening feedback is essential in maintaining the volume of interaction in the important zone of maximum emergence between completely random noise and completely useless order.

## Trust

Another important aspect of understanding the relationship between the components of the network and the nature of emergent behavior in human networks is the issue of trust.

Francis Fukuyama, in his book *Trust*[45], says that it was the nations that managed to create a layer of trust larger than the family unit and smaller

---

[44] Kaminski, Peter. (2003) Self-similar Scaling and Properties of Recurrent Excitatory Networks. Retrieved February 16, 2003, from http://www.istori.com/log/archives/00000237.html

than the nation that were able to build large and scalable organizations. In pre-industrial Germany, it was the guilds, in early Japan it was the *iyemoto* (feudal families which allowed new members), and in the US, it was a variety of religious groups.

Behavioral psychologist Toshio Yamagishi[46] distinguishes between assurance and trust.[47] Yamagishi argues that, in a closed society, people do not base their social expectations on trust. Rather, behavioral standards derive from the inability of the individual to escape from the community, and the fear of punishment. Conversely in open communities where people are free to come and go, trust and trustworthiness are essential to creating collaborative organizations. Yamagishi provides data showing that closed societies such as Japan have a lower percentage of people who trust others than open societies, such as the United States, where trust between individuals is necessary.

Yamagishi conducted an experiment using a market simulation where participants were classified as buyers or sellers. They bought and sold items within their groups. The sellers could lie about the quality of the items that they were selling. In the closed market scenario where sellers' behaviors were associated with their identities, the quality of the transactions was naturally high. In a completely anonymous system, the quality was low. When participants were allowed to change their identities and only negative reputation was tracked, the quality started high but diminished over time. When the participants were allowed to change their identities and only positive reputation was tracked, the quality started low but increased over time and approached the quality of transactions in the closed network.[48]

---

[45] Fukuyama, Francis. *Trust: Human Nature and the Reconstitution of Social Order.* New York: Free Press, 1996.

[46] http://lynx.let.hokudai.ac.jp/members/yamagishi/english.htm

[47] Yamagishi, Toshio. (1999) Tokyo: Chuo Koron Shinsha. From assurance based society to trust based society: Where is the Japanese system heading? (In Japanese)

[48] Yamagishi, Toshio and Matsuda, Masafumi. (2002) "Improving the Lemons Market with a Reputation System: An Experimental Study of Internet Auctioning". Retrieved February 18, 2003, from http://joi.ito.com/archives/papers/Yamagishi_ASQ1.pdf

As networks become more open and complex, the closed networks which rely on the ability to punish members and the ability to exclude unknown participants becomes extremely limiting. The dynamic open networks, which rely on the ability of members to trust each other and identify trustworthiness through reputation management, are scalable and flexible. Links between weblogs, the ability to view the histories of individuals through their weblogs and the persistence of the entries enhances greatly the ability to track positive reputation. Trust and reputation build as the creative, social and political networks harbor mutual respect recognized and illustrated through linking and reciprocal linking, particularly in blogrolling behavior and secondarily in linking and quoting. Another factor in maintaining a high level of trust is to create an ethic of trustworthiness. Trustworthiness comes from self-esteem, which involves motivation through trusting oneself rather than motivation through fear and shame. [49]

## The toolmakers

After the Internet bubble a great number of talented programmers and architects were no longer focused on building components for large projects, which were often doomed by the basic top-down nature of hastily built business plans concerned more with investor appeal than anything else. These talented programmers and architects are now more focused on smaller projects to build tools and design architectures for themselves, instead of creating innovative technologies for imagined customers in imagined markets for investors imagining valuations and exits. These toolmakers are using tools they have created to communicate, discuss, and design new infrastructures. They are sharing information, setting standards, and collaborating on compatibility. The community of toolmakers for weblogs and associated technology is vibrant, similar to the Internet Engineering Task Force (IETF) during the early days of the Internet, when independent programmers were first allowed to write networking software and enter the domain previously controlled by large hardware companies and telecommunications firms.

The weblog developer community, which initially developed tools for personal use, now has significant impact and influence on mass media, politics, and classic business networking. This inspires hope that we will

---

[49] Vasconcellos, John. University of California Press. The Social Importance of Self-Esteem.

discover how to scale the weblog network in a way that will allow bloggers to play an increasingly important role in society.

## Where are we today?

There are several million weblogs on the Internet. However, the tools are still difficult for many people to use, and weblogs are still an obscure phenomenon, especially for those who spend little or no time online. However more weblogs appear every day, and what started as an American phenomenon is rapidly beginning to appear in other countries.

One aspect of weblogs that has increased their value over traditional web pages is the frequency and immediacy of discussion. Recently, a group of bloggers, including myself, have started to organize "Happenings",[50] which involve a live voice conference, a chat room for parallel conversation and for moderating the voice conference, and a Wiki' a tool that allows any number of people to easily create and edit plain-text web pages ) in order to provide a space for collaboration. Weblogs by their nature can be updated as fast as email, but chat and voice provide faster and more personal levels of communication as the discussion of an issue expands and escalates from the creative to the political level.

With the increase in wireless mobile devices like cameras and phones, mobile weblogging, or "moblogging"[51] (posting photos and text from mobile phones and other mobile devices) is gaining popularity. As location information becomes available for the mobile devices, moblogging will be a way to annotate the real world, allowing people to leave information in locations or search for information about specific locations. Although moblogging has privacy issues, its ability to contribute to Steve Mann's vision of sousveillance is significant. Sousveillance, French for "undersight," is the opposite of surveillance. Examples of sousveillance include citizens keeping watch on their government and police forces, student evaluations of professors, shoppers keeping tabs on shopkeepers.[52]

---

[50] http://radio.weblogs.com/0114726/2003/02/15.html - a291

[51] http://radio.weblogs.com/0114939/outlines/moblog.html

[52] Mann, Steve. "Sousveillance." http://wearcam.org/sousveillance.htm.

All of these new developments are components that are being tied together with open standards and a community of active architects and programmers. A dialog, tools, and a process to manage this dialog is emerging.

This paper was written using this process. A variety of people were engaged in conversations on weblogs about democracy, weblog tools, critical debate, the war in Iraq, privacy and other issues discussed in this paper. As these ideas were linked across weblogs, a group of people resonated with the idea of emergent democracy. I asked people to join me in a telephone call and we had an initial voice conference call of about twelve people where we identified some of the primary issues. Ross Mayfield called it a "happening."

We scheduled another call, which included 20 people, and many of the people from the first call provided tools to support the happening, including a Wiki; a trackback weblog[53], which tracked entries in different weblogs about emergent democracy; a chat; and a teleconference that was open for anyone to call and join the discussion. The second happening moved the discussion to the next level of order, and, as a result, I was able to organize some of the thoughts into the first draft of this paper.

I posted the draft of this paper on my weblog[54] and received a great number of comments and corrections, which sparked another email dialog about related topics. Much of this feedback has been integrated into this version of the paper, which is my version of a community dialog on the Internet, and could not have been written without this community's input and access to the social tools described above.[55]

---

[53] http://topicexchange.com/t/emergent_democracy/

[54]

http://joi.ito.com/archives/2003/02/16/emergent_democracy_paper_draft.html

[55] Special thanks to all of the people who participated in the happening, sent me suggests and commented on my weblog regarding this paper. These people include: Clay Shirky, Ross Mayfield, Pete Kaminski, Gen Kanai, Liz Lawley, Sébastien Paquet, Flemming Funch, Adina Levin, Edward Vielmetti, Greg Elin, Stuart Henshall, Jon Lebkowsky, Florian Brody, Mitch Ratcliffe, Kevin Marks, George Por, Dan Gillmor, Allan Karl, Rich Persaud , George

## Conclusion

We have explored the concepts of democracy and emergence, how they are related, and how practical applications of the two concepts are supported by social technologies. The authors feel that the emergent democracy provides an effective next step toward a more participatory form of government that leverages the substantial advances in communications technology that we've seen over the last century. Traditional forms of representative democracy can barely manage the scale, complexity and speed of the issues in the world today. Representatives of sovereign nations negotiating with each other in global dialog are limited in their ability to solve global issues. The monolithic media and its increasingly simplistic representation of the world cannot provide the competition of ideas necessary to reach informed, viable consensus. The community of developers building social software and other tools for communication should be encouraged to consider their potential positive effect on the democratic process as well as the risk of enabling emergent terrorism, mob rule and a surveillance society.

We must protect the availability of these tools to the public by protecting the electronic commons. We must open communications spectrum and make it available to all people, while resisting increased control of intellectual property, and the implementation of architectures that are not inclusive and open. We must work to provide access to the Internet for more people by making tools and infrastructure cheaper and easier to use, and by providing education and training.

Finally, we must explore the way this new form of democratic dialog translates into action and how it interacts with the existing political system. We can bootstrap emergent democracy using existing and evolving tools and create concrete examples of emergent democracy, such as intentional blog communities, ad hoc advocacy coalitions, and activist networks. These examples will create the foundation for understanding how emergent democracy can be integrated into society generally.

---

Dafermos, Steve Mann, Karl-Friedrich Lenz , Toph, Chris Case and Howard Rheingold.

# The Second Superpower
# Rears its Beautiful Head
# by James F. Moore

As the United States government becomes more belligerent in using its power in the world, many people are longing for a "second superpower" that can keep the US in check. Indeed, many people desire a superpower that speaks for the interests of planetary society, for long-term well-being, and that encourages broad participation in the democratic process. Where can the world find such a second superpower? No nation or group of nations seems able to play this role, although the European Union sometimes seeks to, working in concert with a variety of institutions in the field of international law, including the United Nations. But even the common might of the European nations is barely a match for the current power of the United States.

There is an emerging second superpower, but it is not a nation. Instead, it is a new form of international player, constituted by the "will of the people" in a global social movement. The beautiful but deeply agitated face of this second superpower is the worldwide peace campaign, but the body of the movement is made up of millions of people concerned with a broad agenda that includes social development, environmentalism, health, and human rights. This movement has a surprisingly agile and muscular body of citizen activists who identify their interests with world society as a whole — and who recognize that at a fundamental level we are all one. These are people who are attempting to take into account the needs and dreams of all 6.3 billion people in the world — and not just the members of one or another nation. Consider the members of Amnesty Inter-national who write letters on behalf of prisoners of conscience, and the millions of Americans who are participating in email actions against the war in Iraq. Or the physicians who contribute their time to Doctors Without Borders/ Medecins Sans Frontieres.

While some of the leaders have become highly visible, what is perhaps most interesting about this global movement is that it is not really directed by visible leaders, but, as we will see, by the collective, emergent action of its millions of participants. Surveys suggest that at least 30 million people in the United States identify themselves this way — approximately 10% of the US population. The percentage in Europe is undoubtedly higher. The global membership in Asia, South America, Africa and India, while much lower in percentage of the total population, is growing quickly with the spread of the Internet. What makes these numbers important is the new cyberspace-enabled interconnection among the members. This body has a beautiful mind. Web connections enable a kind of near-instantaneous, mass improvisation of activist initiatives. For example, the political activist group Moveon.org, which specializes in rapid response campaigns, has an email list of more than two million members. During the 2002 elections, Moveon.org raised more than $700,000 in a few days for a candidate's campaign for the US senate. It has raised thousands of dollars for media ads for peace — and it is now amassing a worldwide network of media activists dedicated to keeping the mass media honest by identifying bias and confronting local broadcasters.

New forms of communication and commentary are being invented continuously. Slashdot and other news sites present high quality peer-reviewed commentary by involving large numbers of members of the web community in recommending and rating items. Text messaging on mobile phones, or texting, is now the medium of choice for communicating with thousands of demonstrators simultaneously during mass protests. Instant messaging turns out to be one of the most popular methods for staying connected in the developing world, because it requires only a bit of bandwidth, and provides an intimate sense of connection across time and space. The current enthusiasm for blogging is changing the way that people relate to publication, as it allows realtime dialogue about world events as bloggers log in daily to share their insights. Meta-blogging sites crawl across thousands of blogs, identifying popular links, noting emergent topics, and providing an instantaneous summary of the global consciousness of the second superpower.

The Internet and other interactive media continue to penetrate more and more deeply all world society, and provide a means for instantaneous personal dialogue and communication across the globe. The collective power of texting, blogging, instant messaging, and email across millions of actors cannot be overestimated. Like a mind constituted of millions of inter-networked neurons, the social movement is capable of astonishingly rapid and sometimes subtle community consciousness and action.

Thus the new superpower demonstrates a new form of "emergent democracy" that differs from the participative democracy of the US government. Where political participation in the United States is exercised mainly through rare exercises of voting, participation in the second superpower movement occurs continuously through participation in a variety of web-enabled initiatives. And where deliberation in the first superpower is done primarily by a few elected or appointed officials, deliberation in the second superpower is done by each individual — making sense of events, communicating with others, and deciding whether and how to join in community actions. Finally, where participation in democracy in the first superpower feels remote to most citizens, the emergent democracy of the second superpower is alive with touching and being touched by each other, as the community works to create wisdom and to take action.

How does the second superpower take action? Not from the top, but from the bottom. That is, it is the strength of the US government that it can centrally collect taxes, and then spend, for example, $1.2 billion on 1,200 cruise missiles in the first day of the war against Iraq. By contrast, it is the strength of the second superpower that it could mobilize hundreds of small groups of activists to shut down city centers across the United States on that same first day of the war. And that millions of citizens worldwide would take to their streets to rally. The symbol of the first superpower is the eagle — an awesome predator that rules from the skies, preying on mice and small animals. Perhaps the best symbol for the second superpower would be a community of ants. Ants rule from below. And while I may be awed seeing eagles in flight, when ants invade my kitchen they command my attention.

In the same sense as the ants, the continual distributed action of the members of the second superpower can, I believe, be expected to eventually prevail. Distributed mass behavior, expressed in rallying, in voting, in picketing, in exposing corruption, and in purchases from particular companies, all have a profound effect on the nature of future society. More effect, I would argue, than the devastating but unsustainable effect of bombs and other forms of coercion.

Deliberation in the first superpower is relatively formal — dictated by the US constitution and by years of legislation, adjudicating, and precedent. The realpolitik of decision making in the first superpower — as opposed to what is taught in civics class — centers around lobbying and campaign contributions by moneyed special interests — big oil, the military-industrial complex, big agriculture, and big drugs — to mention only a few. In many cases, what are acted upon are issues for which some group is willing to spend lavishly. By contrast, it is difficult in the US government system to champion policy goals that have broad, long-term value for many citizens, such as environment, poverty reduction and third world development, women's rights, human rights, health care for all. By contrast, these are precisely the issues to which the second superpower tends to address its attention.

Deliberation in the second superpower is evolving rapidly in both cultural and technological terms. It is difficult to know its present state, and impossible to see its future. But one can say certain things. It is stunning how quickly the community can act — especially when compared to government systems. The Internet, in combination with traditional press and television and radio media, creates a kind of "media space" of global dialogue. Ideas arise in the global media space. Some of them catch hold and are disseminated widely. Their dissemination, like the beat of dance music spreading across a sea of dancers, becomes a pattern across the community. Some members of the community study these patterns, and write about some of them. This has the effect of both amplifying the patterns and facilitating community reflection on the topics highlighted. A new form of deliberation happens. A variety of what we might call "action agents" sits figuratively astride the community, with mechanisms designed to turn a given social movement into specific kinds of action in the world. For example, fundraisers send out mass appeals, with direct mail or the Internet, and if they are tapping into a live issue, they can raise money very quickly. This money in turn can be used to support activities consistent with an emerging mission.

The process is not without its flaws and weaknesses. For example, the central role of the mass media — with its alleged biases and distortions — is a real issue. Much news of the war comes to members of the second superpower from CNN, Fox, and the New York Times, despite the availability of alternative sources. The study of the nature and limits of this big mind is just beginning, and we don't know its strengths and weaknesses as well as we do those of more traditional democracy. Perhaps governance is the wrong way to frame this study. Rather, what we are embarked on is a kind of experimental neurology, as our communication tools continue to evolve and to rewire the processes by which the community does its shared thinking and feeling. One of the more interesting questions posed to political scientists studying the second superpower is to what extent the community's long-term orientation and freedom from special interests is reinforced by the peer-to-peer nature of web-centered ways of communicating — and whether these tendencies can be intentionally fostered through the design of the technology.

Which brings us to the most important point: the vital role of the individual. The shared, collective mind of the second superpower is made up of many individual human minds — your mind and my mind — together we create the movement. In traditional democracy our minds don't matter much — what matters are the minds of those with power of position, and the minds of those that staff and lobby them. In the emergent democracy of the second superpower, each of our minds matters a lot. For example, any one of us can launch an idea. Any one of us can write a blog, send out an email, create a list. Not every idea will take hold in the big mind of the second superpower — but the one that eventually catches fire is started by an individual. And in the peer-oriented world of the second superpower, many more of us have the opportunity to craft submissions, and take a shot.

The contrast goes deeper. In traditional democracy, sense-making moves from top to bottom. "The President must know more than he is saying" goes the thinking of a loyal but passive member of the first superpower. But this form of democracy was established in the 18th century, when education and information were both scarce resources. Now, in more and more of the world, people are well educated and informed. As such, they prefer to make up their own minds. Top-down sense-making is out of touch with modern people.

The second superpower, emerging in the 21st century, depends upon educated informed members. In the community of the second superpower each of us is responsible for our own sense-making. We seek as much data — raw facts, direct experience — as we can, and then we make up our own minds. Even the current fascination with "reality television" speaks to this desire: we prefer to watch our fellows, and decide ourselves "what's the story" rather than watching actors and actresses play out a story written by someone else. The same, increasingly, is true of the political stage — hence the attractiveness of participation in the second superpower to individuals.

Now the response of many readers will be that this is a wishful fantasy. What, you say, is the demonstrated success of this second superpower? After all, George Bush was almost single-handedly able to make war on Iraq, and the global protest movement was in the end only able to slow him down. Where was the second superpower?

The answer is that the second superpower is not currently able to match the first. On the other hand, the situation may be more promising than we realize. Most important is that the establishment of international institutions and international rule of law has created a venue in which the second superpower can join with sympathetic nations to successfully confront the United States. Consider the international effort to ban landmines. Landmines are cheap, deadly, and often used against agrarian groups because they make working the fields lethal, and sew quite literally the seeds of starvation. In the 1990s a coalition of NGOs coordinated by Jody Williams, Bobby Muller and others managed to put this issue at the top of the international agenda, and promote the establishment of the treaty banning their use. For this, the groups involved were awarded the 1997 Nobel Peace Prize. While the United States has so far refused to sign the treaty, it has been highly isolated on the issue and there is still hope that some future congress and president will do so.

At the Kyoto meetings on global climate change, a group of NGOs coordinated by Nancy Keat of the World Resources Institute joined with developing nations to block the interests of the United States and its ally, big oil. The only way for the United States to avoid being checkmated was to leave the game entirely. In the World Trade Organization, the second superpower famously shut down the Seattle meeting in 1999, and later helped to force a special "development round" focused on the needs of poor countries. That round is currently underway — and while the United States and others are seeking to subvert the second superpower agenda, the best they have achieved to date is stalemate.

And finally, while George Bush was indeed able to go to war with Iraq, the only way he could do so was to ignore international law and split with the United Nations. Had he stayed within the system of international institutions, his aims likely would have been frustrated. The French and the Germans who led the attempt to stop him could not, I believe, have done what they did without the strength of public opinion prodding them — the second superpower in action.

Now we all know that the Bush administration has decided to undermine, in many cases, the system of international law. Some argue that by pulling out, the administration has fatally damaged the international system, and ushered in a new era where the United States determines the rules — hub and spoke style — through bilateral deals with other nations. The result, some will say, is that the second superpower no longer has a venue in which to meet the first effectively. In my view this is an overly pessimistic assessment — albeit one that members of the second superpower need to take seriously and strive to render false by our success in supporting international institutions.

International law and institutions are not going away. Too many parties want and need them. First, individuals around the world are becoming more globally aware, and more interested in international institutions. Global media, travel, and immigration all contribute to citizens being aware of the benefits of consistent approaches to everything from passport control to human rights. It is striking, for example, that up until the final days before the war, a majority of the US population wanted the president to deal with Iraq in concert with the United Nations. Second, business organizations want global rule of law. Global trade is now central to a vast majority of businesses and almost all nations — and such trade requires rules administered by multilateral bodies. Third, most nations want a global legal system. In particular, European nations, wary of war, outclassed in one-on-one power confrontations with the United States, have become strongly committed to a post-national world. They are pouring collective national resources of enormous magnitude into continuously strengthening the international system.

The key problem facing international institutions is that they have few ways to enforce their will on a recalcitrant US government. And this is where the second superpower is a part of the solution. Enforcement has many dimensions. When the United States opts to avoid or undermine international institutions, the second superpower can harass and embarrass it with demonstrations and public education campaigns. The second superpower can put pressure on politicians around the world to stiffen their resolve to confront the US government in any ways possible. And the second superpower can also target US politicians and work to remove at the polls those who support the administration's undercutting of international law.

Longer term, we must press for a direct voice for the second superpower in international institutions, so that we are not always forced to work through nations. This means, as a practical matter, a voice for citizens, and for NGOs and "civil society" organizations. For example, the Access Initiative of the World Resources Institute is working to give citizens' groups the ability to influence environmental decisions made by international organizations such as the World Bank. The Digital Opportunity Task Force of the G8 group of nations included a formal role for civil society organizations, as does the United Nations Information and Communications Technology Task Force.

Overall, what can be said for the prospects of the second superpower? With its mind enhanced by Internet connective tissue, and international law as a venue to work with others for progressive action, the second superpower is starting to demonstrate its potential. But there is much to do. How do we assure that it continues to gain in strength? And at least as important, how do we continue to develop the mind of the second superpower, so that it maximizes wisdom and goodwill? The future, as they say, is in our hands. We need to join together to help the second superpower, itself, grow stronger.

First, we need to become conscious of the "mental processes" in which we are involved as members of the second superpower, and explore how to make our individual sense-making and collective action more and more effective. This of course means challenging and improving the mass media, and supporting more interactive and less biased alternatives. But more ambitiously, we will need to develop a kind of meta-discipline, an organizational psychology of our community, to explore the nature of our web-enabled, person-centered, global governance and communication processes, and continue to improve them.

Second, and ironically, the future of the second superpower depends to a great extent on social freedoms in part determined by the first superpower. It is the traditional freedoms — freedom of the press, of assembly, of speech — that have enabled the second superpower to take root and grow. Indeed, the Internet itself was constructed by the US government, and the government could theoretically still step in to restrict its freedoms. So we need to pay close attention to freedom in society, and especially to freedom of the Internet. There are many moves afoot to censor the web, to close down access, and to restrict privacy and free assembly in cyberspace. While we generally associate web censorship with countries like China or Saudi Arabia, tighter control of the web is also being explored in the United States and Europe. The officials of the first superpower are promoting these ideas in the name of preventing terrorism, but they also prevent the open peer-to-peer communication that is at the heart of the second superpower. We need to insist on an open web, an open cyberspace, around the globe, because that is the essential medium in which the second superpower lives.

Third, we must carefully consider how best to support international institutions, so that they collectively form a setting in which our power can be exercised. Perhaps too often we attack institutions like the World Bank that might, under the right conditions, actually become partners with us in dealing with the first superpower. International institutions must become deeply more transparent, accessible to the public, and less amenable to special interests, while remaining strong enough to provide a secure context in which our views can be expressed.

And finally, we must work on ourselves and our community. We will dialogue with our neighbors, knowing that the collective wisdom of the second superpower is grounded in the individual wisdom within each of us. We must remind ourselves that daily we make personal choices about the world we create for ourselves and our descendants. We do not have to create a world where differences are resolved by war. It is not our destiny to live in a world of destruction, tedium, and tragedy. We will create a world of peace.

# Power Laws, Weblogs and Inequality
## by Clay Shirky

A persistent theme among people writing about the social aspects of weblogging is to note (and usually lament) the rise of an A-list, a small set of webloggers who account for a majority of the traffic in the weblog world. This complaint follows a common pattern we've seen with MUDs, BBSes, and online communities like Echo and the WELL. A new social system starts, and seems delightfully free of the elitism and cliquishness of the existing systems. Then, as the new system grows, problems of scale set in. Not everyone can participate in every conversation. Not everyone gets to be heard. Some core group seems more connected than the rest of us, and so on.

Prior to recent theoretical work on social networks, the usual explanations invoked individual behaviors: some members of the community had sold out, the spirit of the early days was being diluted by the newcomers, et cetera. We now know that these explanations are wrong, or at least beside the point. What matters is this: Diversity plus freedom of choice creates inequality, and the greater the diversity, the more extreme the inequality.

In systems where many people are free to choose between many options, a small subset of the whole will get a disproportionate amount of traffic (or attention, or income), even if no members of the system actively work towards such an outcome. This has nothing to do with moral weakness, selling out, or any other psychological explanation. The very act of choosing, spread widely enough and freely enough, creates a power law distribution.

### A Predictable Imbalance

Power law distributions, the shape that has spawned a number of catch-phrases like the 80/20 Rule and the Winner-Take-All Society, are finally being understood clearly enough to be useful. For much of the last century, investigators have been finding power law distributions in human systems. The economist Vilfredo Pareto observed that wealth follows a "predictable imbalance", with 20% of the population holding 80% of the wealth. The linguist George Zipf observed that word frequency falls in a power law pattern, with a small number of high frequency words (I, of, the), a moderate number of common words (book, cat cup), and a huge number of low frequency words (peripatetic, hypognathous). Jacob Nielsen observed power law distributions in web site page views, and so on.

We are all so used to bell curve distributions that power law distributions can seem odd. The shape of Figure 1, several hundred blogs ranked by number of inbound links, is roughly a power law distribution. Of the 433 listed blogs, the top two sites accounted for fully 5 percent of the inbound links between them. (They were InstaPundit and Andrew Sullivan, unsurprisingly.) The top dozen (less than three percent of the total) accounted for 20 percent of the inbound links, and the top 50 blogs (not quite 12 percent) accounted for 50 percent of such links.

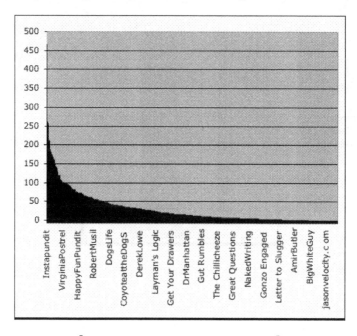

Figure 1: 433 weblogs arranged in rank order by number of inbound links[56]

---

[56] The data is drawn from N.Z Bear's 2002 work on the blogosphere ecosystem. The current version of this project can now be found at http://www.myelin.co.nz/ecosystem/.

The inbound link data is just an example: power law distributions are ubiquitous. Yahoo Groups mailing lists ranked by subscribers is a power law distribution. (see Figure 2) LiveJournal users ranked by friends is a power law. (see Figure 3) Jason Kottke has graphed the power law distribution of Technorati link data. The traffic to this article will be a power law, with a tiny percentage of the sites sending most of the traffic. If you run a website with more than a couple dozen pages, pick any time period where the traffic amounted to at least 1,000 page views, and you will find that both the page views themselves and the traffic from the referring sites will follow power laws.

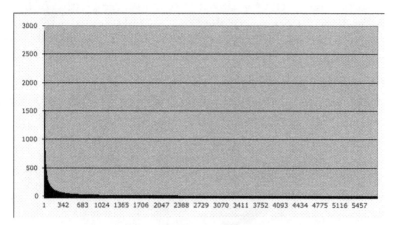

Figure #2: All mailing lists in the Yahoo Groups Television category, ranked by number of subscribers (Data from September 2002.)

50

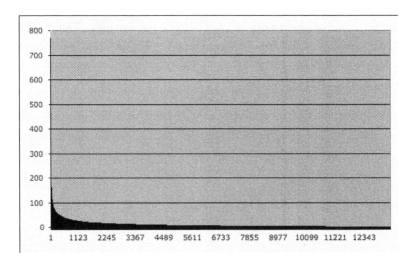

## Rank Hath Its Privileges

The basic shape is simple: In any system sorted by rank, the value for the Nth position will be $1/N$. For whatever is being ranked — income, links, traffic — the value of second place will be half that of first place, and tenth place will be one-tenth of first place. There are other, more complex formulae that make the slope more or less extreme, but they all relate to this curve. We've seen this shape in many systems. What've we've been lacking, until recently, is a theory to go with these observed patterns.

Now, thanks to a series of breakthroughs in network theory by researchers like Albert-Laszlo Barabasi, Duncan Watts, and Bernardo Huberman among others, breakthroughs being described in books like Linked, Six Degrees, and The Laws of the Web, we know that power law distributions tend to arise in social systems where many people express their preferences among many options. We also know that as the number of options rise, the curve becomes more extreme. This is a counter-intuitive finding; most of us would expect a rising number of choices to flatten the curve, but in fact, increasing the size of the system increases the gap between the Number One spot and the median spot.

A second counter-intuitive aspect of power laws is that most elements in a power law system are below average, because the curve is so heavily weighted towards the top performers. In Figure 1, the average number of inbound links (cumulative links divided by the number of blogs) is 31. The first blog below 31 links is 142nd on the list, meaning two-thirds of the listed blogs have a below-average number of inbound links. We are so used to the evenness of the bell curve, where the median position has the average value, that the idea of two-thirds of a population being below average sounds strange. (The actual median, 217th of 433, has only 15 inbound links.)

## Freedom of Choice Makes Stars Inevitable

To see how freedom of choice could create such unequal distributions, consider a hypothetical population of a thousand people, each picking their 10 favorite blogs. One way to model such a system is simply to assume that each person has an equal chance of liking each blog. This distribution would be basically flat — most blogs will have the same number of people listing it as a favorite. A few blogs will be more popular than average and a few less, of course, but that will be statistical noise. The bulk of the blogs will be of average popularity, and the highs and lows will not be too far different from this average. In this model, neither the quality of the writing nor other people's choices have any effect; there are no shared tastes, no preferred genres, no effects from marketing or recommendations from friends.

But people's choices do affect one another. If we assume that any blog chosen by one user is more likely, by even a fractional amount, to be chosen by another user, the system changes dramatically. Alice, the first user, chooses her blogs unaffected by anyone else, but Bob has a slightly higher chance of liking Alice's blogs than the others. When Bob is done, any blog that both he and Alice like has a higher chance of being picked by Carmen, and so on, with a small number of blogs becoming increasingly likely to be chosen in the future because they were chosen in the past.

Think of this positive feedback as a "preference premium." The system assumes that later users come into an environment shaped by earlier users; the thousand-and-first user will not be selecting blogs at random, but will rather be affected, even if unconsciously, by the preference premiums built up in the system previously.

Note that this model is absolutely mute as to why one blog might be preferred over another. Perhaps some writing is simply better than average (a preference for quality), perhaps people want the recommendations of others (a preference for marketing), perhaps there is value in reading the same blogs as your friends (a preference for "solidarity goods," things best enjoyed by a group). It could be all three, or some other effect entirely, and it could be different for different readers and different writers. What matters is that any tendency towards agreement in diverse and free systems, however small and for whatever reason, can create power law distributions.

Because it arises naturally, changing this distribution would mean forcing hundreds of thousands of bloggers to link to certain blogs and to de-link others, which would require both global oversight and the application of force. Reversing the star system would mean destroying the village in order to save it.

### Inequality and Fairness

Given the ubiquity of power law distributions, asking whether there is inequality in the weblog world (or indeed almost any social system) is the wrong question, since the answer will always be yes. The question to ask is "Is the inequality fair?" Four things suggest that the current inequality is mostly fair.

The first, of course, is the freedom in the weblog world in general. It costs nothing to launch a weblog, and there is no vetting process, so the threshold for having a weblog is only infinitesimally larger than the threshold for getting online in the first place.

The second is that blogging is a daily activity. As beloved as Josh Marshall (TalkingPointsMemo.com) or Mark Pilgrim (DiveIntoMark.org) are, they would disappear if they stopped writing, or even cut back significantly. Blogs are not a good place to rest on your laurels.

Third, the stars exist not because of some cliquish preference for one another, but because of the preference of hundreds of others pointing to them. Their popularity is a result of the kind of distributed approval it would be hard to fake.

Finally, there is no real A-list, because there is no discontinuity. Though explanations of power laws (including the ones here) often focus on numbers like "12 percent of blogs account for 50 percent of the links", these are arbitrary markers. The largest step function in a power law is between the Number One and Number Two positions, by definition. There is no A-list that is qualitatively different from their nearest neighbors, so any line separating more and less trafficked blogs is arbitrary.

## The Median Cannot Hold

However, though the inequality is mostly fair now, the system is still young. Once a power law distribution exists, it can take on a certain amount of homeostasis, the tendency of a system to retain its form even against external pressures. Is the weblog world such a system? Are there people who are as talented or deserving as the current stars, but who are not getting anything like the traffic? Doubtless. Will this problem get worse in the future? Yes.

Though there are more new bloggers and more new readers every day, most of the new readers are adding to the traffic of the top few blogs, while most new blogs are getting below average traffic, a gap that will grow as the weblog world does. It's not impossible to launch a good new blog and become widely read, but it's harder than it was last year, and it will be harder still next year. At some point (probably one we've already passed), weblog technology will be seen as a platform for so many forms of publishing, filtering, aggregation, and syndication that blogging will stop referring to any particularly coherent activity. The term "blog" will fall into the middle distance, as "home page" and "portal" have, words that used to mean some concrete thing, but which were stretched by use past the point of meaning. This will happen when head and tail of the power law distribution become so different that we can't think of J. Random Blogger and Glenn Reynolds of Instapundit as doing the same thing.

At the head will be webloggers who join the mainstream media (a phrase which seems to mean "media we've gotten used to.") The transformation here is simple - as a blogger's audience grows large, more people read her work than she can possibly read, she can't link to everyone who wants her attention, and she can't answer all her incoming mail or follow up to the comments on her site. The result of these pressures is that she becomes a broadcast outlet, distributing material without participating in conversations about it.

Meanwhile, the long tail of weblogs with few readers will become conversational. In a world where most bloggers get below average traffic, audience size can't be the only metric for success. LiveJournal had this figured out years ago, by assuming that people would be writing for their friends, rather than some impersonal audience. Publishing an essay and having three random people read it is a recipe for disappointment, but publishing an account of your Saturday night and having your three closest friends read it feels like a conversation, especially if they follow up with their own accounts. LiveJournal has an edge on most other blogging platforms because it can keep far better track of friend and group relationships, but the rise of general blog tools like Trackback may enable this conversational mode for most blogs.

In between blogs-as-mainstream-media and blogs-as-dinner-conversation will be Blogging Classic, blogs published by one or a few people, for a moderately-sized audience, with whom the authors have a relatively engaged relationship. Because of the continuing growth of the weblog world, more blogs in the future will follow this pattern than today. However, these blogs will be in the minority for both traffic (dwarfed by the mainstream media blogs) and overall number of blogs (outnumbered by the conversational blogs.)

Inequality occurs in large and unconstrained social systems for the same reasons stop-and-go traffic occurs on busy roads, not because it is anyone's goal, but because it is a reliable property that emerges from the normal functioning of the system. The relatively egalitarian distribution of readers in the early years had nothing to do with the nature of weblogs or webloggers. There just weren't enough blogs to have really unequal distributions. Now there are.

**Addendum:** *David Sifry, creator of the Technorati.com, has created the Technorati Interesting Newcomers List, in part spurred by this article. The list is designed to flag people with low overall link numbers, but who have done something to merit a sharp increase in links, as a way of making the system more dynamic. [Editors' note: The Interesting Newcomers List no longer exists, but you can still find many references to it, and perspectives on it, if search for "Technorati interesting newcomers."]*

# Section One:
# Politics and Change

# Extreme Democracy:
## Deep confidence in the people
## Mitch Ratcliffe

Human society evolves. For millennia it has proceeded toward a more scalable and widely distributed form of social control, toward egalitarian politics and markets, toward democracy. From the first tiny democracies in Greek city-states, in which a few citizens controlled the fate of populations of free and enslaved men, women and children to today's continental democracies, the history of human civilization has drifted toward greater participation by people in the decisions that affect their lives. And society is still only halfway, if that far, along the path to egalitarian participation in social decision-making.

The first decade of the 21$^{st}$ century represents a unique moment in history, as the economic sphere of life has leapt far ahead of the civil sphere and a correction, a great catching up, is at hand. This is a book for people who want to use technology to make that correction happen, to place control of society firmly in the hands of citizens.

Expectations about the availability of information and the right to express an opinion among citizens around the world have been transformed by the availability of ubiquitous mass media and the Internet. In advanced economies, activist organizations like MoveOn.org have brought two million progressive contributors to bear on far ranging issues, from censuring President Clinton to the Bush-Cheney energy bill of 2004. Howard Dean's campaign for president transformed the limits of fund-raising early in presidential campaigns. Around the world in 2002 and 2003, people organized protests for and (primarily) against the U.S. invasion of Iraq through email, mailing lists and text messaging, bringing millions into the streets in an unprecedented expression of public sentiment. In the developing world, radio and small presses are changing the flow of information as individual citizens call in to talk about what they've read and seen that affects their lives. Internet, when it is widely available in Africa and Central Asia, could replace bullets as revolutionary tools.

At the same time, citizens of the developed and underdeveloped world are impatient as they have never been before for change and opportunity. People have come to expect instant gratification of their economic desires while the processes of government have, by comparison, remained largely unresponsive. Yet for centuries, technology of religious and civic governance preceded innovation in the economic sphere. The priest and the king were the models for the organization of the master-and-slave and feudal economic systems; early corporations developed on the council model of the Italian republic; the modern corporation's ability to scale was built on the experience of Prussian governmental organizations. Government led the way until very recently in history, the last few seconds in the timeframe of human civilization.

With the invention of the mass media, privately owned newspapers began to reorganize the process of policy-making through public debate, a trend amplified by television, which sped the delivery of, and public deliberation about, news about events. Since then government has increasingly adopted the pace and priorities of the private sector rather than leading the way. Computation and the Internet, which have accelerated the process of innovation in the private sector while introducing a radically decentralized approach to decision-making, are about to revolutionize public governance, as well.

What happens when people deal with their own problems? The tools available today and that are just over the governmental horizon deliver on the dreams of liberals and conservatives — though each come at it from a different perspective. Liberals would like people to have their government organize to provide sustenance to the needy and address social problems that hold back portions of the population; conservatives would like to see people organize their own solutions, and when government needs to play a part in those solutions, it can, if led by the people. In a densely networked world, citizens can organize to address social problems; they can use the mechanisms of government to finance the filling of potholes or providing universal healthcare, allowing for new ideas to come from anywhere. In an extreme democracy, every citizen is a potential leader, not just a voter.

"Extreme democracy" is a political philosophy of the information era that puts people in charge of the entire political process. It suggests a deliberative process that places total confidence in the people, opening the policy-making process to many centers of power through deeply networked coalitions that can be organized around local, national and international issues. It emphasizes the importance of tools designed to break down barriers to collaboration and access to power, acknowledging that political realities can be altered by building on rapidly advancing generations of technology and that human organizations are transformed by new political expectations and practices made possible by technology.

Extreme democracy is not direct democracy, which assumes all people must be involved in every decision in order for the process to be just and democratic. Direct democracy is inefficient, regardless of the tools available to voters, because it creates as many, if not more, opportunities for obstruction of social decisions as a representative democracy. Rather, we assume that every debate one feels is important will be open to participation; that governance is not the realm of specialists and that activism is a critical popular element in making a just society. Extreme democracy can exist alongside and through co-evolution with the representative systems in place today; it changes the nature of representation, as the introduction of sophisticated networked applications have reinvented the corporate decision-making process.

Rather than debate how involved a citizen should be or fret over the lack of involvement among citizens of advanced democracies, the extreme democracy model focuses on the act of participation and assumes that anyone in a democracy is free to act politically. If individuals are constrained from action, they are not free, not citizens but subjects.

The basic unit of organization in an extreme democracy is the activist, a citizen engaged with an issue of concern about which they are willing to invest their time and effort to evolve relevant policy, whether at the local, state, national or international level. They engage their fellow citizens seeking support rather than demanding it at the point of a gun. Small groups of activists have changed the world repeatedly and at every stage in history. Martin Luther was an ecclesiastical political activist and Martin Luther King was a civil rights activist. Gandhi was a political activist, just like Benjamin Franklin and Nelson Mandela, though Franklin finally advocated a violent break with England and Mandela laid his guns down before he successfully ousted the apartheid government of South Africa.

Activists, like citizens, may become representatives or they may, having achieved success, go home until the next issue they care about comes to public debate. The key idea is that activism and citizenship are on a continuum that describes both active and passive citizenship; for the most part, people do not take action in politics, choosing to vote on issues raised by others, but at any time they are free and able, using the tools available to all citizens, to become activists. One might be an activist about a single issue or many; the principal of extreme democracy is that when one cares about an issue, they should be free to become deeply involved in public decisions about that issue.

Extreme democracy, taking a cue from the recent evolution of software development towards a practice known as "extreme programming," anticipates a politics based on lowered friction in communication that increases the diversity of ideas and opinions that can be brought to bear on the development of public policy. Using the communications channels available to people in advanced economies today, activists can form teams locally or across the globe to develop new options and policy alternatives, for example an idea about financing public schools or road repairs in a small city or an energy and conservation policy for the United States. Extreme democracy is predicated on the belief that policy can be developed by small groups based on simple steps and extensive communication among affected parties and those responsible for carrying out policy. Finally, based on the experience of extreme programming, which ships an incomplete but sufficient software release and draws on the experience of real people using it to roll out a series of improvements, extreme democracy argues that policy and governmental systems, instead of remaining relatively rigid for decades, can be improved constantly through feedback and re-calibration.

At the same time, extreme democracy recognizes that there are challenges inherent in unbridled communications. The more people brought into contact the greater the potential for conflict and the more difficult it becomes to reach a compromise or even recognize commonality across large groups of people. A densely networked society can be infected by vile ideas about race, faith and class that unleash tyrannies that claim to be "populist" and patriotic while justifying the killing or jailing or enslavement of millions. It has happened dozens of times in the past century. Those with unqualified faith in tools for doing politics need to open their eyes to the potential for abuse and its consequences.

When I told my 10-year-old about this book, he said, "You mean the more we change democracy, the more we have to change?" Indeed, it's that simple, but history and politics are always more complex because they deal with the details of many lives. To begin, we have to understand politics and its role in human life.

"Politics" in current usage sounds like a curse upon our houses. "I think the country is tired of people playing politics all the time in Washington. And I believe that they're holding this man's nomination up for political purposes. It's not fair, and it's not right," President George W. Bush said of the nomination of Judge Charles Pickering to the federal court in the spring of 2002[57] and accusations of "politics" are rampant in the national dialogue. These charges come from all sides of the political conversation.

The value of political change is usually determined by the way people feel about politics in the first place. Dissatisfaction drives change, so the political process is strewn with the disgruntled. Many Americans, indeed, many people around the world, believe politics is "broken".[58] This, however, is like arguing that the human circulatory system is designed wrong. Politics is a reflection of the times and the people, and today, in the United States, the populace is split very evenly between the political parties. Public discourse is the process humans have used to organize themselves and worked out their differences for all time. Since politics is a process and not an artifact, this human process changes over time and never breaks or requires replacement — getting rid of or replacing politics with another process would be tantamount to a shop clerk deciding she has a bad heart and trying to do a transplant herself, starting by murdering the first person who walks into the shop because they seemed like a good choice for a donor heart. The body politic cannot be put on bypass while a new political system is installed. We're part of an evolving system and have to live through it.

---

[57] "President Calls on Senate to Stop Playing Politics," Remarks by President George W. Bush during a photo opportunity, March 6, 2002.
http://www.whitehouse.gov/news/releases/2002/03/20020306-5.html

[58] "Politics is broken. We are left with a de-moralized populace, and a power-hungry elite." Bill Bradley,
http://www.antidote.org.uk/html/transformativecitizenship.htm

Politics is simply the debate about society's options that seeks to refine the quality of life through the allocation of resources, rights, responsibility and opportunity; embracing politics as an essential aspect of our humanity invigorates existence. Anyone who has had the experience of participating in a political campaign in which they were listened to and engaged in real debate about what the campaign or candidate should stand for knows the thrill. When Democrats talk of Howard Dean's having "revitalized the party," they really mean that the Dean campaign was the venue in which many people first experienced the rush of political participation. It feels good, like sex does, because it is how we participate in making our world.

"Politics" is the "science and art of government; the science dealing with the form, organization, and administration of a state or part of one, and with the regulation of its relations with other states," as well as "the branch of moral philosophy dealing with the state or social organism as a whole," according to the *Oxford English Dictionary*. In other words, politics is the practice of participating in the making of a direction for society. It does 2,500 years and more of human history an injustice to denigrate politics. "Politics" made its appearance in the English language in the $16^{th}$ century and, in fact, it was a derogatory description of human action ("he's playing politics") before it was referred to as simply a science, the practice of governing. The practice of politics, though, predates the first English judgments of its meaning by more than 2000 years.

Pericles, in his funeral oration over the Athenian dead after the first year of the Peloponnesian War, laid out the complete confidence that the city had in its people to rule themselves when he said "Although a few may originate a policy, we are all able to judge it." The democracy in Athens did not survive the war. The idea did survive, and has informed every democratic movement since. It is emblematic of a long debate about the best political order for a society, as elites have contested with egalitarians over who is fit to rule, which has provided the two extreme poles of political philosophy since. In *The Discourses*, Machiavelli describes the debate in simple terms, that of the ability of a people to reason:

The demands of a free populace, too, are very seldom harmful to liberty, for they are due either to the populace being oppressed or to the suspicion that it is going to be oppressed, and, should these impressions be false, a remedy is provided in the public platform on which some man of standing can get up, appeal to the crowd, and show it is mistaken. And though, as Tully remarks, the populace may be ignorant, it is capable of grasping the truth and readily yields when a man, worthy of confidence, lays the truth before it.

The people's judgment is where a democrat's confidence rests and, if the people are well informed by a responsible government and press, if they are socialized to value participation, it is a confidence well placed. Democracy is government by the people, simple as that. And it may be applied to a narrow set of social questions or very broadly, depending on the degree of choice available in society and the competing institutions, such as the market, for making social choices.

As Machiavelli knew, it is a mistake to think that exercising total power is the sole end of politics — his notorious advice to the prince was to balance the use of raw power with strategic concessions to the people and rivals. When absolute power guides politicians, politics is a metaphorical war for absolute control and not a mechanism for a plurality of ideas and opinions to inform public policy.

Unfortunately, the pursuit of absolute power is the rule of the day in politics and it is tearing the middle ground out from under the people as the rise of a networked society begins. As the potential number and range of connections available between people are increasingly dense and varied, the political center should be expanding to accommodate more perspectives; instead it is being eaten away by extremists who are shearing off constituencies from the center. If every one of these factions treats politics as a zero-sum game, where no compromise is possible, networked politics will lead to unending strife.

As citizens organize to address very specific needs or issues through the networks growing around them, the necessity for a new perception of political practice is increased by orders of magnitude, becoming more pressing with every geometric increase in the number of connections available within society. The borders and barriers to cooperation based on the pokey and expensive communications of the steam ship and telegraphic era are falling for obvious and visible reasons.

---

[59] Niccolo Machiavell, The Discources, Penguin Books, New York, 1998, pp. 114-115

Change begins with the actions of individuals, who organize, collaborate and plan, forming groups that coalesce into movements. That is, politics and parties have played an essential role in the aggregation of resources and reservoirs of influence that can be applied from one election cycle to the next. The permanent infrastructures of political parties may not disappear, but they will be altered irrevocably by the rise of the networked society.

What President Bush is attacking when he talks about "playing politics" is partisanship, which has concerned American presidents since the administration of George Washington, who condemned political parties as one of the greatest threats to the nascent United States. Politics is only a Bad Thing for someone on the losing end of a policy decision, without anything to show for their efforts; zero-sum politics leaves a lot of folks feeling this way and provides a handy bludgeon for the party in power to use against opponents. As evidenced by the account[60] of Vice President Cheney's comment that the Bush Administration could slash taxes because the Republicans had won the midterm election in 1992 — "This is our due," he said — President Bush practices the most extreme zero-sum politics the United States has ever seen while denouncing it.

Partisan debate conducted with respect for all parties rather than disdain, however, has been the foundation of discourse about the broad brush strokes that describe American history. Without Thomas Jefferson's Republican Party's (the direct ancestor of today's Democratic Party) militancy on behalf of yeoman farmers and Westerners, some say the United States would have become a monarchy. Abraham Lincoln helped to bring the Republican Party into being over the issues of slavery and a national identity that transcended regional differences. Theodore Roosevelt first converted the Republican Party, then the nation, to a program of governmental power on behalf of the citizen in contrast to the corporations that dominated the "Gilded Age." Woodrow Wilson and the Democrats set the United States on a course as the guardian of freedom that prepared the country to fight Nazism and Communism. Franklin Roosevelt's New Deal altered the role of government and placed the welfare of the individual citizen at the epicenter of social investment through government. Ronald Reagan challenged the notion of a welfare state and introduced a concept of patriarchal state that

---

[60] Ron Suskind, The Price of Loyalty, Simon & Schuster, New York, 2004.

defends Judeo-Christian values with the ferocity once reserved for Communists. And, because partisan perspective does inform everything, there is something for everyone to object to in this description of important sea changes in American politics. Political parties have served an important purpose in that they have helped a large and barely connected society retain networks of activists and patronage that were necessary to sustain power across large regions over long periods of time.

Political parties are very much like corporations were before the advent of the networked computer. They are hierarchical and rigid with leadership that is hard to displace or enter on any terms other than those laid down by the longest serving veterans. As the networked computer broke down the old boys' networks within companies and opened the membrane surrounding senior management, not to mention unleashing a wave of outsourcing and exporting of formerly core assets to partners and overseas, the Internet is about to hollow out the major political parties.

What had been the preserve of the national and state organizations — voter records management, fund-raising and allocation of support and funds — can be handled at the periphery of the political system for the first time, allowing many smaller organizations to exert influence and trade for support with other groups. Because people now can come together through networks to work together on issues of common concern or to trade support on issues, the parties will likely migrate to purely national campaigns that must activate networks of support that are superfluous at the local and state level.

As more people connect and learn through the Internet, public debate about the direction government should take has reached a critical mass that could transform the very notion of democratic systems. This transition will not end differences of opinion, nor will it abolish ideology from public debate. It will simply make the debate more fluid, with many more specific perspectives represented, because the massive party infrastructures are becoming more porous. The Howard Dean campaign, where it was possible to find far-left Democrats hoping to stop the war in Iraq working together with moderate and center-right Republicans angry about runaway deficits, demonstrates how an extremely democratic technology can bring together many perspectives. Its massive fund-raising success of the during 2003 and early 2004, which built a war chest of $45 million for a candidate who began his quest for the White House as an asterisk, is the proof point for the transformation of politics via network. That campaign failed for a variety of reasons, but the example is a clear statement about people's willingness to work together despite their differences when they see a clear opportunity to make a difference.

Citizens can make this a watershed era by taking the initiative and seizing the reins of power from the professionals struggling to regain control of the process and working with them to restructure campaign strategy. The decades ahead could mark a profound break in political history, if people understand and act on this opportunity.

# Building on experience
## by Mitch Ratcliffe

How change in society happens is a mystery that seems clear only in retrospect. In politics, the actual moments when change happens or policy becomes inevitable are the subject of guesswork, and campaign strategy is developed based on past experience that can be proved starkly inadequate in the face of current events. Building tools for doing politics based on the experience of the recent past, particularly the Dean campaign, requires a critical approach that separates the novelty of political engagement from the realities of the political process as it changes and evolves.

Calls for a revolution in politics based on new tools for communicating with other activists will lead to enduring changes that happen in small steps. Political reality has a way of attenuating idealism. It is far more likely that by examining human nature and the ideas about "emergent democracy" in circulation today we can find the bridges between established and novel practices to build on and solidify changes for the better. Trying overthrow the whole system would bring down much more than the political parties and create a dangerous environment in which demagogues could use networked political tools to call for violent reactions to existing and previous inequities.

John Adams, revolutionary and America's first conservative president, wrote to his longtime political rival and friend Thomas Jefferson of their shared experience of the break with England: "What do we mean by revolution? The war? That was no part of the revolution; it was only an effect and consequence of it. The revolution was in the minds of the people, and this was effected from 1760 to 1775, in the course of fifteen years, before a drop of blood was shed at Lexington."[61] The revolution in the colonies began on August 5, 1735, in New York, when the trial of John Peter Zenger got underway. Zenger was charged with publishing seditious libels after he criticized the colonial governor in print. Despite the governor's successful effort to pack the jury with his own cronies, Zenger was acquitted based on the argument that printing the "just

---

[61] Adams, John, The Works of John Adams, Vol. 10, Little, Brown, Boston, 1956, p. 85.

complaints of of a number of men" is an essential form of free speech. Instead of pleading "Not Guilty," Zenger's lawyer turned the law on its head and admitted Zenger was the publisher of the language in question, and that publishing the charges against the governor was justifiable because it brought a truth to light, a concept that did not exist in Britain. While there were many more steps before the break with England was inevitable, a simple twist on the law ignited the spark that burned all the way to 1776.

In the colonies, the common man had access to the press for the first time. Zenger and his contemporary, Ben Franklin, were communicating across the settled regions of North America. It was the first time egalitarian communication took place on that scale; the French experience shows that the same phenomenon in a society steeped in power and privilege can ignite a wave of vengeance. The tools we build must be applied thoughtfully, in synchrony with the times and used for just ends.

The term "emergent democracy" has appeared to describe the potential for change that exists in the interregnum between the time political professionals were surprised by the new dynamics of the Internet and when they regain management of the national agenda. Emergence is a phenomenon first described by complexity theorists that has been popularized in recent years as describing spontaneous intelligence that appears in a system, whether it is a society, an anthill or a neural network.

"Emergent democracy" is a misapplication of terms, since it implies that political results are emergent properties that rise from the political system rather than a result of contending sources of power in society debating, negotiating and, ultimately, agreeing on a direction that will be shared by all members of society. What I believe emergence theories of social activity are really proposing is that the policies that will structure the activity of society cannot be planned once and executed without any changes to produce a just and engaging world. Flexibility, the hallmark of the networked enterprise, the venue in which most information toolmakers learn their craft, is necessary, though not sufficient, for a living process to be initiated and thrive. The closest anyone has ever come to this ideal in politics were the framers of the U.S. Constitution, a document just flexible enough to provide rule of law within a rapidly changing society for 215 years, so far.

Put emergence together with democracy and what do you get? There is no authoritative definition of "emergent democracy." The phrase has been used to describe self-organizing movements with no apparent leaders, governance based on the input and self-organized projects of the governed, and political action based on groups forming around issues and taking responsibility for enacting policy. All of these phenomena exist in democracy or have existed at moments in history; the real difference between democracy and emergent democracy is the sense of dynamism that erupts at the earliest stages of group formation, what I call "the entrepreneurial moment" when a group of people decide to throw their lots together and try to change the world. It is an entrepreneurial moment due to the huge risks everyone involved must recognize and accept. Will the people at the table with you betray you? Will you hold together in the face of opposition or is there a weak link in the group on whom you cannot count, placing your efforts and reputation at risk for nothing?

These same questions apply whether a movement begins in a cave, a meeting room or an online chat room. They are human questions with as many answers as there are combinations of people. You cannot simply engineer a tool and wipe away these uncertainties. In fact, overcoming the fear of these uncertainties, whether through faith in your comrades or actual experience that proves the mettle of everyone you work with on a campaign — for dogcatcher or president — is an important part of the socialization process that happens within groups.

Because much of the group forming taking place today happens virtually, there is a sense that political boundaries have exploded and that it will be a long time before there is an "establishment" holding the reins of history. Let's, nonetheless, try to put some boundaries around the concept of emergent democracy to provide a starting point for readers new to the idea.

"Democracy" is defined by the *Oxford English Dictionary* as "Government by the people; that form of in which the sovereign power resides with the people as a whole, and is exercised either directly by them (as in the small republics of antiquity) or by officers elected by them. In modern use often more vaguely denoting a social state in which all have equal rights, without hereditary or arbitrary differences of rank or privilege." To some degree, this definition adds to the fuzziness, since democracy has come to stand for pluralism and egalitarianism as well as government by the people.

Perhaps the adjective "emergent" can lend some clarity? According to the *OED*, "emergent" is used to describe something that rises out of the surrounding medium, that is in the process of issuing forth or that emerges unpredictably as the result of an evolutionary process. If one understands "democracy" to mean a system of governance in which people propose competing policies, conduct informed debate and, after a suitable period of deliberation, negotiation and compromise, arrive at a final policy that may or may not bear a strong resemblance to the original proposal, democracy has always been emergent in nature because one could never be sure what would come out of the meat grinder, even when the inputs are clearly understood. Human deliberation remakes ideas and policies, just as evolution redesigns dinosaurs into birds and gives the mammals a turn at dominance. The addition of the Internet to the democratic equation doesn't add any particular virtues or certainties to democracy, instead it accelerates the rate at which ideas can be disseminated and groups coalesce around ideas to ignite activism.

Emergent democracy has attracted a fair amount of attention for its contention that democratic mechanisms must be found to "rectify the imbalance and inequalities of the world.... [as] basic attributes of democracy ...have eroded as power has become concentrated within corporations and governments," according to Japanese venture capitalist and activist Joichi Ito. His article, "Emergent Democracy," along with another paper posted on the World Wide Web, "The Second Superpower Rears its Beautiful Head," by James F. Moore, a fellow at Harvard's Berkman Center for Internet & Society, have crystallized the idea that an activist population can have a tremendous and trans-national impact on policy and economics. Moore, in particular, has emphasized the post-national qualities of this movement, which is only possible because of the Internet's instant communication features. "The Internet and other interactive media continue to penetrate more and more deeply all world society, and provide a means for instantaneous personal dialogue and communications across the globe. The collective power of texting, blogging, instant messaging, and email across millions of actors cannot be overestimated," Moore wrote. He continued:

Like a mind constituted of millions of inter-networked neurons, the social movement is capable of astonishingly rapid and sometimes subtle community consciousness and action. Thus the new superpower demonstrates a form of "emergent democracy" that differs from the participative democracy of the US government. Where political participation in the United States is exercised mainly through rare exercises of voting, participation in the second superpower movement occurs continuously through participation in a variety of web-enabled initiatives. And where deliberation in the first superpower is done primarily by a few elected or appointed officials, deliberation in the second superpower is done by each individual — making sense of events, communicating with others, and deciding whether and how to join in community actions. Finally, where participation in democracy in the first superpower feels remote to most citizens, the emergent democracy of the second superpower is alive with touching and being touched by each other, as the community works to create wisdom and to take action.

How does the second superpower take action? Not from the top, but from the bottom. That is, it is the strength of the US government that it can centrally collect taxes, and then spend, for example, $1.2 billion on 1,200 cruise missiles in the first day of the war against Iraq. By contrast, it is the strength of the second superpower that it could mobilize hundreds of small groups of activists to shut down city centers across the United States on that same first day of the war. And that millions of citizens worldwide would take to their streets to rally. The symbol of the first superpower is the eagle — an awesome predator that rules from the skies, preying on mice and small animals. Perhaps the best symbol for the second superpower would be a community of ants. Ants rule from below. And while I may be awed seeing eagles in flight, when ants invade my kitchen they command my attention.

Moore is heavily influenced by the work of sociobiologist E. O. Wilson, whose work with ants is well known and who single-handedly launched several fields of biological research and the notion of an empirical and philosophical continuity between the physical and social sciences. Wilson melds ecology with sociology and psychology in order to show how basic laws can extend across the boundary between the "hard sciences" and "soft" social sciences. However, the theories of behavioral biology are "riddled with semantic ambiguity. Like buildings constructed hastily on unknown ground, they sink, crack, and fall to pieces at a distressing rate for reasons seldom understood by the architects."[62] This is a very apt description of the problem of erecting an explanation for how society might be changing, as emergent democracy aspires to. Moore previously authored a business book, *The Death of Competition*, which applied Wilson's ideas to business for the first time. In that book, Moore drew on the ecological metaphor, explaining "executives need to think of themselves as part of organisms participating in an ecosystem in much the same way that biological organisms participate in a biological ecosystem." Now, he is extending many of these ideas to politics, as well, and ants are a key metaphor for Moore and other emergent democracy theorists.

If it is hard to find satisfactory definitions of emergent democracy and the ideas themselves are, at this point, a "hypothesis in need of confirmation,"[63] it is even harder to avoid sweeping generalizations about human and physical nature when talking about emergent democracy. The metaphors offered by emergence and emergent democracy theorists should be taken with a saltshaker rather than one grain of skepticism. It is very easy to confuse biology with the complex interactions of society, divorcing the "socio-" Wilson added to the root "biology" in order to make a metaphor crystalline. Metaphors unfortunately often ignore the details of life to capture the sense of events and so it is with emergence and ants.

Ant metaphors and discussions of emergence frequently tread into the dicey territory of over-simplification, where individual volition and acts of leadership are discounted.

A lot of people loathe E. O. Wilson because he had the audacity to combine the social and biological in an attempt to draw a complete picture of the factors that drive the development of species, including *Homo Sapiens*. During early public discussions of sociobiology in the 1970s, Wilson was attacked and, on one occasion, doused with ice water by angry scientists, because people believed he was arguing for biological determinism that prevents the exercise of free will. Biologist Stephen J.

---

[62] Edward O. Wilson, Sociobiology, The Abridged Edition, The Belknap Press of Harvard University Press, Cambridge, Mass. 1980, p. 15

[63] Email correspondence with Mitch Ratcliffe, from David S. Isenberg Ph.D., January 5, 2004

Gould remained a lifelong and vociferous rival of Wilson's, accusing Wilson of reducing all human potential to outcomes based on the random combination of DNA. Actually, Wilson has repeatedly refuted that he advocates a biological determinism. In *On Human Nature*, Wilson wrote "cultural change is the statistical product of the separate behavioral responses of large numbers of human beings who cope as best they can with social existence."[64] In other words, while you can assess the behavior of populations statistically and make predictions about what will happen to that society, the free will of individuals decides the actual contours of history.

At the same time, a little determinism is a good thing and we live comfortably in a largely deterministic world. Philosopher Daniel Dennett argues that the fact our options are bounded by past decisions and, in part, because of our genetic heritage, we enjoy a profound freedom of action, since a largely deterministic world allows us to assess options and expected outcomes with a high degree of confidence[65]. If sheep occasionally flew or water unexpectedly passed through the face of a dam, deciding about future allocation of resources among, and the rights and responsibilities of, citizens would be far less organized.

The very idea of a deterministic world offends many people for all the wrong reasons. If genetics did not determine the combinations of cells produced in the womb, would Christians be satisfied to give birth to

---

[64] Edward O. Wilson, On Human Nature, Harvard University Press, Cambridge, Mass., 1978, p. 78

[65] Daniel Dennett, Freedom Evolves, Viking, New York, 2003, p. 25: "Determinism is the thesis that "there is at any instance exactly one physically possible future" (Van Inwagen 1983, p. 3). This is not a particularly difficult idea, one would think, but it's amazing how often even very thoughtful writers get it flat wrong. First, many thinkers assume that determinism implies inevitability. It doesn't. Second, many think it is obvious that indeterminism—the denial of determinism—would give us agents some freedom, some maneuverability, some elbow room, that we just couldn't have in a deterministic universe. It wouldn't. Third, it is commonly supposed that in a deterministic world, there are no *real* options, only apparent options. This is false. Really? I have just contradicted three themes so central to discussions of free will, and so seldom challenged, that many readers suppose I am kidding, or using these words in some esoteric sense. No, I am claiming that the complacency with which these theses are commonly granted without argument is itself a large mistake."

marmosets? If the laws of physics in the dimensions we inhabit were broken with the same ease they are in several quantum dimensions, would there be civilization or fire to cook our food and heat our homes, if those homes would even stand up? If God were to offer to reverse time, allowing the ultimate victory of Islam over Christianity in the 10th century, would an observant Muslim living in Mecca today be willing to forego his very existence (and all the eternal rewards that go with it) because that triumph wiped out his family and nullified any chance of his birth a thousand years before? A nondeterministic world is the world of science fiction, the scariest science fiction, where nothing can be predicted and clear-cut choices intended to create paradise land us in Hell.

The largely deterministic world costs us, too. From the moment we are born to the day we die we have to make decisions that involve forgoing one opportunity in pursuit of another. This is not a world made for people who can't get over buyer's remorse, yet it is filled with ideologues who argue that they have not, in fact, missed opportunities and only made the right decisions along the way.

Since time's arrow flies the way it does and we have a limited number of opportunities for instigating change in a human lifetime, leadership is particularly important in getting political movements underway. Someone somewhere has to get people moving in the same direction. Not so with theories of emergence that claim order emerges from chaotic behavior among members of a society. E. O. Wilson and Bert Hölldobler went to great lengths to counter the tendency of previous researchers to anthropomorphism when describing ant societies. Yet, because their book, *The Ants*, is considered one of the foundational texts of social emergence, their work has been used to justify an ant metaphor for human behavior that presumes there is no leadership in the ant world.

Ants are an important example for Joichi Ito and the emergent democracy group he formed, as well. Ito quotes author Steven Johnson, who draws heavily on other ant studies to describe emergent phenomena:

> In the book Emergence, Steven Johnson writes about harvester ant colonies, which exhibit an amazing ability to solve very difficult

problems including geometry problems. The following exchange is from an interview with Deborah Gordon who studies ants.

She says, "Look at what actually happened here: they've built the cemetery at exactly the point that's furthest away from the colony. And the midden is even more interesting: they've put it at precisely the point that maximizes its distance from both the colony and the cemetery. It's like there's a rule they're following: put the dead ants as far away as possible, and put the midden as far away as possible without putting it near the dead ants."

Johnson explains that there is no ant in charge. The ants' solving of such problems is emergent behavior that comes from their following very simple rules and having several ways to interact with their immediate surroundings and neighbors.

The human fetus develops into a higher level of order through this principle of following a set of rules and interacting with its immediate neighbors. When the first cell divides into two, one half becomes the head side and the other the tail. The next time it divides, the quarters determine whether they are to be the head or the tail, and they become the head of the head, or the tail of the head, and so on. This division and specialization continues until in very short order the cells have created a complex human body. The liver cells know to turn into liver cells by sensing that their neighbors are also liver cells and reading the DNA code to understand exactly what it is supposed to do. There is no omniscient control, but just a huge number of independent cells following rules and communicating with and sensing the state of their neighbors.

There is a two-fold paradox in the emergent democracy movement, largely because it is focused on the mechanisms and outcomes of democracy rather than the inputs to the system, i.e. human action. The paradox hinges on the notion that activity in non-human systems, such as nature (though we are very much a part of nature, only living in mental exile from it), is random and miraculously gives rise to coherent emergent behavior.

Virtually every ant metaphor ignores the role of power or leadership, the very essence of politics. In fact many proponents of the idea of emergent democracy dismiss these qualities and insist there is no leader and no power at the individual level, that, in fact, power resides only with the group. Yet, Wilson and Bert Hölldobler's *The Ants* makes plain that the activity of ants is not in the slightest bit random, it is highly stylized and clearly intentional. An individual ant does a variety of things with its body — in fact, it is equipped with an arsenal of glands and sensors that are used to communicate — to interact with other ants.

The reality is that each ant is at any moment a potential leader. In Moore's memorable and accurate phrase, "Ants rule from the bottom up." They find some food and lay down a path of pheromones back to the nest, which others can follow to retrieve more food. Each successive ant to follow various trails makes changes, contributing to complex outcomes like the location of the midden (the trash heap) relative to the colony. Little acts that are simply too simple for us to attribute intelligence to add up to recognizably organized systems. We want to impose an order on what is produced, but the order is the product of many small intentions.

Emergence, to a great degree, is simply what we didn't plan. How to arrive at the best possible unplanned outcome is what emergent democracy is about. This is what is meant when people talk about "the edge taking charge" or "decision-making at the edge of the network." Instead of centralized planning, emergent democracy describes being involved in a conversation with ideas coming from many more quarters than in a slow analog debate where a central figure filters most ideas before presenting them to the community and few in the community have an opportunity to contribute their perspective.

The atomic actions of human society are more complex, at least they seem so to us humans, but most of our decisions are unplanned and not based on the goals or milestones of overarching rational plan. We become unconstructively reductive when we say that ant behavior is random because it is unlike how we organize ourselves, since there is undoubtedly some form of society among ants. The tools we use to link up as people engaged in collective action are metaphorically like the substances that cellular units of the brain or an ant colony or any collectively intelligent aggregate of non-intelligent (in the human sense) use to communicate. Yet the minds sitting in front of the screen at a node in the network are much more complex than ants or brain cells, blending as they do genetic and sociological factors in every decision.

During one emergent democracy "happening" (the term Ross Mayfield applied to Joi's multi-channel meetings that included telephone, Web chat and wiki interfaces), it was suggested that people want to know about other people so that they can vet the credentials of those who are attempting to lead them, even in the case of a "smart mob" such as the Philippine crowd action that led to the end of the scandal-ridden presidency of Joseph Estrada. Author Howard Rheingold coined the term "smart mob" to describe how a self-organizing group using text messaging on wireless phones coalesced into a second instance of "People Power" ending a Filipino regime. A colleague on the call responded "Isn't the point that there is no leader?" Well, no.

Each citizen is a potential leader in a democracy; in an extreme democracy citizens needn't only join a great campaign for president or governor, but will have the tools that those campaigns have had at their fingertips to address local and international issues from a networked computer. They'll have a printing press, a campaign database that draws on public information to build voter lists quickly and accurately, the technology to support discussion and policy debates, to interact with other activists and blend their efforts, and to raise funds. Each citizen will have the choice to lead when the issue is one they care about passionately.

Leadership is essential to coordinated action, whether it is in political, economic, social, theological or military matters. What we must keep in mind when exploring the ideas of emergent democracy is that the ease of communication today is just one factor in the changing panorama of political evolution. At each moment a different person might be leading the way.

Emergent democracy, then, is a way of describing the experience of the democratic process at the speed of the information age, but it is not a comprehensive political philosophy. Just as business processes and fads carried by electronic media can sweep through an organization or a teenaged population, respectively, an idea can change the world more quickly than ever before. Today, ideas and movements can come from any quarter of society and spread through activists and mavens to influence great ships of state. It feels new, because it is such raw experience of the power of democratic activism, but the processes are as familiar and human as the stories we tell our children about better worlds and their ability to achieve their dreams.

A political philosophy must incorporate more than the experience of participation. An analysis of power, definite ideas about the role of the citizen and the government, and the principles society will embrace about the value of the individual are required, as well. Extreme democracy seeks to provide these foundational ideas to place the thrill of emergent organizations into socio-political context.

Traditional ideas of political organization are based on concentric spheres of democratic action, from the direct to the representative, because democracy does not scale smoothly from small to large societies. A village or organization in which members can talk together frequently can practice a form of direct democracy while a small city will require some system of representation to keep abreast of the many issues, from school funding and filling potholes to providing funding for police and licensing businesses and automobiles. What works in a city will grind to a halt when applied to a region or nation, because of the variety of functions government fulfills across large geographic areas.

Networked society, however, is not constrained by geography. A group can spring up around a common need or idea without regard to the distance between members. The most profound political changes have been wrought by groups that found bonds or maintained bonds across great distance to forge movements, but it was slow and much more difficult to maintain a critical level of engagement when each passage in a debate could take weeks to reach all participants. Even after the appearance of electronic communications, like radio, political communication has taken place at a slower pace than normal conversation — it was encrypted or, to hide the fact that communication was taking place.

Extreme democracy takes place in real-time. Power is diffused because the traditional gatekeepers are dethroned. Ironically, the press, the institution that has contributed most to the disruption of power in recent history, is on the receiving end of the disruption represented by emergent democracy. The power to make oneself or one's organization heard has never been so available. Let us refer to this as the power of promotion. Each citizen still has a single vote, but they can by publishing on the Web amplify their opinions to reach the public attention more frequently than ever. As the Howard Dean campaign demonstrated, the power of the press to set the agenda of the campaign was undermined by a distributed organization; as a corollary to the power of promotion, the Dean campaign also shows that with promotional tools a campaign can collect more money faster, from smaller donors, than ever before. By organizing through networks, massive movements can be manufactured by a few dedicated individuals without — for the first time — having to have the wherewithal to travel to conduct organizing activity.

To understand the impact of the obliteration of geography, we have to take some time with the idea of network theory, a relatively new science that seeks to describe how ideas and influence travel across society through recognizable interconnections between groups; your most engaging friend is likely one of these interconnections, as skilled communicators are frequently the most responsible for spreading ideas.

Networks and their effects on human relationships have been the subject of intense study for only a few years, but theorists propose a wide range of rules that describe the behavior of connected people, networked groups and organizations. These laws are double-edged blades for the aspiring social theorist since a "law" in the scientific sense when applied to groups of people is an appeal to reason in nature that may not exist in the population one is describing; people can act irrationally or inconsistently in similar circumstances, defying the "law" apparently at will. Despite the fact that the mathematics of networks are generally couched in value-neutrality, the absence of influence and the notion of frictionless transaction, they are projected onto a value-filled social networks of influence characterized by many forms of friction. Network theory is useful, however, because it highlights the singular importance of influence and leadership within social and political networks.

The issue of scale[66], which in mathematics describes the place of any numerical expression relative to a chosen base, is applicable in social and political networking. For example, a base ten system, the scale describing any value is demarcated by 10s; think of a topological map, on which a mountain range's height can be determined by counting the number of lines, each line representing a hundred or 1,000 feet, from the base elevation and multiplying the steps by the number of feet they represent. In social situations, we can think of scale as the number of steps it takes to accomplish a goal, how many people in city hall do you have to talk to in order to get your sidewalk repaired? How many people can fit into

---

[66] Barabåsi, Albert-Låzlo, Linked, How Everything Is Connected to Everything Else and What It means for Business, Science, and Everyday Life, Plume Penguin, 2003. P. 70.

the local Starbucks before you have to build another one? Scaling issues are very important to any investment of social, political or economic capital, yet they are disorienting, too, because the limits of human networks only become evident when they are reached, the point of diminishing returns when progress is halted or each additional step becomes more expensive than the one before. The critical mistake for many investors and managers working at Internet companies during the bubble years was assuming that any investment would pay itself back in multiples, when, in fact, many of the steps companies took led to unprofitable customers who weren't willing to pay a premium for the convenience of, for example, buying dog food on the Web.

In political networks, limits make themselves known in two ways, as a negative, the void that opens when a community no longer scales efficiently, and in extraordinary exceptions to the limits that prove the rule in all other circumstances.

Failure to scale is evident when people feel disenfranchised, when they no longer have sufficient contact or interaction with their government to see their wishes reflected in its actions. Another form of negative experience of limits is the self-dealing that takes place when a politician no longer feels accountable to constituents. We are familiar with and react against the notion of power as it is exercised by individuals for their own benefit — perhaps a mayor starts dealing local favors to statewide interests to gain leverage in an upcoming election or perhaps someone just sells their vote for money; at these times, individual politicians impose limits on group action by sucking away resources for themselves. Everyone has a story of a politician who, seeing only their own well-being, sacrificed the common good to maintain their power and privilege. Everyone knows someone who has monopolized connections for their benefit at the expense of others; it happens in business, churches and school, as well as in politics.

British anthropologist Robin Dunbar suggests a "rule of 150," a scale that explains how our brains are hardwired to deal effectively with no more than 148.4 people. [67] This idea, that we are not capable of exceeding these numbers of relationships over long periods, is borne out

---

[67] R. I. M. Dunbar, "Neocortex size as a constraint on group size in primates," Journal of Human Evolution, 1992, vol. 20, pp. 469-493.

by experience, as most people find their group of friends and colleagues changing over time.

The other experience of scale is intimately tied to these types of networking limits. It is only the very industrious, like President George H. W. Bush, who wrote notes to thousands of people annually in order to sustain social obligations, that seem able to marshal large networks of social relationships to political ends, to burst through limits that confine others. Historian Kevin Phillips demonstrates how exceptions to social rules, like the rule of 150, can thrive, writing of both presidential Bushes: "Father and son also had a striking ability to remember people's names and faces and to memorize things, especially baseball batting orders, starting lineups, and fraternity members. For both — and apparently for [George H.W.'s father] Prescott Bush and Great-grandfather Bush, too — unusual memory was a great asset, both in retail politicking and in retaining data and information."[68] The exception proves the rule, as simply being able to remember and manage more than 150 relationships can have huge social results. A memory for facts alone would be largely useless socially, in fact it generally alienates people from others because they are perceived as know-it-alls. But a memory for faces and names is a social tool that can be used to flatter and coax cooperation from others.

In smaller groups, such as among close-knit groups or a successful team, the numbers of intense relationships a person can maintain are more restricted. For many years social researchers emphasized these tighter social ties, or "strong ties," when trying to assess the optimum size of a group. Then, along came a social researcher named Marc Granovetter, who was intrigued by studies conducted by psychologist Stanley Milgram. During a string of groundbreaking research projects during the 1960s, Milgram unearthed evidence of "small world" relationships among very large networks of people.

Stanley Milgram's famous, though not most infamous, experiment on social ties, in which he asked people to try to get a letter to one of several targets by going through a network of acquaintances to find a personal connection to the target, provided the well-worn concept of "six degrees of separation." This is the idea that, on average, each person

---

[68] Kevin Phillips, American Dynasty, Viking, New York, 2003, p. 44

is approximately six social steps away from anyone else in the world. By asking a friend if they know a friend of someone we'd like to meet, according to this idea, we would find that the target was between four and eleven introductions away, with the average being six steps, or degrees. Milgram's 1967 experiment, which identified the "small world problem" (after the "It's a small world" uttered by people who learn they have an acquaintance in common) as a field ripe for investigation, was the basis of another breakthrough piece of research by Mark Grannovetter, who established that "weak ties," those ties that are not central to the function of groups but happen to link clusters of people, are the primary vectors of the experience of small worlds. It is the person who is able to leap barriers between two groups who is critical to the success of a six-degrees chain. This explains the political success of the otherwise singularly uninspiring Bush family, which, as Kevin Phillips points out "have produced no college presidents or stonemasons, no scientists or plumbing contractors — generally speaking, their progeny have become almost exclusively financial entrepreneurs." [69]

Scale issues can be managed using the carefully composed messages in a heavily mediated society, where most policy issues are experienced as events on television and abstracted from day-to-day life, people become inured to abuses and cynical about them. When the news leads each day with bad news, common sense suggests that people tend to remember bad news more often than good behavior.

But in politics, when people are engaged, when they feel there is something at stake, whether it's their local school district or a national campaign for president, the opposite is true: A few small positives will outweigh a lot of bad news. In gambling, another human practice as old as society and probably older than politics, in a lottery or at the craps table people focus on the few moments of good luck. You've seen people win in Las Vegas, even though the vast majority of people lose in Las Vegas? You remember those moments more than the losses, because we want to win or see people win; we want the best for others or we might envy their success. Casinos, like the mediascape, are designed to enhance the impression of success. When a player at the craps table is handed the dice, the chances are only 2.675 percent that they will be able to set a point on the first role and throw a seven to win on the

---

[69] Phillips, American Dynasty, p. 45

subsequent roll.[70] Awful chances, but the room is open and carries sound well in order to broadcast the sound of success from one of the hundred tables in the casino (where the odds suggest, someone will be winning almost all the time), along with the ringing bells of slot machines, all to reinforce the sense that everyone wins at least some of the time. This reduces the sense that the odds are against you, just as intense media coverage of stories of the party you support winning, good works, luck and profit (especially the state lottery, which features a winner on the weekly drawing, but ignores the millions of losers). Television news is a casino, with enough good news and distractions (squirrels that water ski) to inure the viewer to the bad news, that they lost the school levy vote or that their candidate isn't being covered. News directors don't design the news for this effect, rather it is what they are told works by the people who own the television networks, who study places like Las Vegas to figure out how to hold people's attention.

And, in politics, there is legitimately good news to report; good people do step up regularly and volunteer to benefit others, school levies pass and heroic sacrifices are made by police officers, teachers and even politicians, so there is enough good news to make most people who feel disenfranchised feel pretty good about humans. Cincinnatus, a patrician farmer, was called to be dictator of Rome and set the example for the office, which held total power, by finishing the task of defending Rome and foregoing power to return to his farm. Livy relates this act thousands of years later and it seems extraordinary, but people make these kinds of selfless sacrifices in many ways all the time.

---

[70] Krigman, Alan, Why It's Easy to Believe Rare Events Happen All the Time, Casino City Times, July 8, 2003.
http://krigman.casinocitytimes.com/articles/6106.html: "The likelyhood that a shooter will establish a point and throw a seven on the subsequent roll is 24/36 multiplied by 6/36. This equals 11.11 percent. In round numbers, it's 11 chances out of 100 for any shooter. And the probability it'll take place several times in a row is 12 out of 1,000 for two, 14 out of 10,000 for three, and 15 out of 100,000 for four. Chances are lower of Come bettors getting up on three numbers in consecutive rolls, then striking out on the fourth. Probability is 2.675 percent. This is roughly 27 chances out of 1,000 for any shooter, 7 out of 10,000 for two in a row, and 2 out of 100,000 for a terrible trifecta."

Total power is in our hands on many occasions, over life and death, promotion and being stuck in a dead-end job, and the ability to make life better or worse for others while our privileged situation is unaffected. Manipulation or, more benignly, management of perception has everything to do with the use to which we put our networks, and that is what is missing from the analysis by most network theories. That is what is changing most with the rise of the networked society as the cost of communication and managing information falls dramatically each year.

Now the Internet has given a voice to concerns that political systems are no longer producing the results that keep the people happy or, at least, pacified, and this has taken the political world by surprise. The speed and ease of making connections, while fleeting, can produce substantial emotional and political momentum. The persistent network of weak ties George H. W. Bush accomplished through sheer determination and tens of thousands of pens and uncounted reams of notepaper the ordinary citizen can accomplish using email lists, blog and simple syndication technology, It still requires determination and persistence, but is much more efficient. Inflamed passions, like the outrage felt by Sims who believe they have been denied the right to free speech, can catalyze decisive political action. The Howard Dean campaign focused a broad-based frustration with the George W. Bush administration.

In Korea, Roh Moo-hyun, a failed national assembly candidate in 2000, and 300 supporters, allegedly used the Internet to raise $1 billion from 180,000 Koreans and win the 2002 presidential election on a wave of reform messages. Roh promised that "If I am elected, I will put an end to the old politics and usher in a new Korea and a new era of politics in Korea. The old politics, the 20th Century politics, the Three-Kim (Kim Young Sam, Kim Dae Jung, and Kim Jong Pil) conservativism, regionalism, cronyism, factionalism, confrontational conflicts, and corruption in high places shall be no more. Instead, a new political era of pan-national cohesion, true participatory democracy, people-centered government, clean government, and a brand-new 21st Century government will be ushered in." The passions of Koreans were ignited and Roh swept into office. During 2003, Roh was revealed to have accepted large donations from corporations and to have hidden the donations.[71] As voters seek Net-savvy candidates, they need to be aware that the billing isn't always as good as it is with the show playing behind the door.

Speed politics and new technology meet the greatest resistance at the walls of the old system. During the 1990s, politicians routinely discounted email input from the public, saying privately that it took little investment of time or thought to create an electronic message compared to the investment required to write a letter and mail it. When the Clinton administration introduced its White House email addresses, the first in history, it said: "Initially, your e-mail message will be read and receipt immediately acknowledged. A careful count will be taken on the number received as well as the subject of each message. However, the White House is not yet capable of sending back a tailored response via electronic mail. We are hoping this will happen by the end of the year."[72]

The White House experimented with a number of automated systems for tallying public input, but did not actually read individual messages for content, instead treating them like votes in a poll. This isn't significantly different than postal mail or faxes sent to the White House, but the expectation of people sending messages to the White House is that their words will be read and absorbed. Writing an email may take as long as writing a letter, but because an email could easily be copied and sent a thousand times at virtually no cost, White House or Congressional staff discounted the value of each email received.

According to a Clinton Administration official who worked on the email project, there were several important barriers to email's acceptance as a valid reflection of public sentiment. At first, in 1993 and 1994, the White House assumed that, based on the rather elite demographics of Internet users at the time, that email reflected only a fragment of society. But that changed rapidly as companies like America Online and Prodigy

---

[71] Na Jeong-ju, "'Roh aware of Illegal Funds,'" The Korea Times, December 29, 2003.
http://times.hankooki.com/lpage/200312/kt2003122917280610440.htm

[72] Office of Presidential Correspondence, Letter from the President and Vice President in announcement of White House electronic mail access, June 1, 1993

"were forced to open pipes to the Internet so that customers could directly access www.whitehouse.gov as well as send email directly to President Clinton."[73] Government, in addition to being impacted by technology, can lead the way toward wider adoption of technology.

Behind the fence at the White House, however, there was a cadre of career staff that resisted email, because they had spent many years processing constituent messages via postal mail and telephone calls. This was the main source of the "it takes greater commitment of time and effort to pen a letter" sentiment that often seeped out to the public and that Web activists glommed onto as a consistent sore point. "I'm sure the percentage of ranting and the [ratio] of frivolous to the sober and the thoughtful was comparable among all avenues of communication," the official said. He related how when President Clinton gave a major speech he helped man the telephone lines since no such effort was needed for email input. A drunken caller took 15 minutes of his time, allowing him time to take only a few calls that evening — the total number of calls handled was in the hundreds, while the White House received more than 20,000 emails a day at the time.

By 2001, most U.S. federal government agencies had a Web site to promote policy to the public and almost 95 percent of local governments were coming online with their own sites.[74] The impact of public input via the Web was virtually nil, as most email was simply ignored in many government offices. At the White House, a sampling of emails is provided to the President for review, but only a summary view is possible. The Congressional Management Foundation suggested that representatives are being buried in what are, because they come from non-constituents, extraneous emails: "The public's expectation to receive responses from Members who do not represent them is like their showing up at the town hall meeting and demanding to be treated like a constituent. Members' inefficient and unresponsive e-mail practices are akin to keeping constituents waiting in long lines for hours before letting them into the town hall meeting. Instead of fostering democracy, these conflicting practices and expectations of all the parties are fostering

---

[73] From private email, information provided by former Clinton aide on a background basis

[74] International City/Council Management Association

cynicism and eroding trust."[75] Granted, blaming activists for using cheap and easy email to make as much noise as possible is rather missing the point, that when people have an opportunity to be heard they take it. The result was an immediate and almost total neutering of individual email as a form of political expression.

Activists realized that email could be used to exert political force in the aggregate and, often, in forms of contact with political representatives that are relatively old-fashioned. One of the first substantial protests coordinated by email was MoveOn.org's Virtual March on Washington on February 26, 2003, when more than a half million people phoned and faxed Congress with messages demanding an alternative to the invasion of Iraq. The protest was highly coordinated, with individuals assigned specific times to call.[76] OpenDemocracy, a U.K.-based group, developed coordinated mailing and calling campaigns in Europe and helped activist establish physical gatherings in support of peaceful solutions to the Iraq showdown and the Israeli-Palestinian conflict, among other international campaigns. Tying up government phones is an extremely effective way to get attention, even if it doesn't stop wars — this is very early action in a new political strategy.

In the United Kingdom, the government of Prime Minister Tony Blair has launched an aggressive program, called "The Big Conversation," to bring parliamentarians and bureaucrats into a dialogue with citizens. This is an important departure from the notion that email is a form of polling. The Big Conversation depends on citizens submitting policy suggestions for discussion among Labour Party members — the old process of building a party platform, in which many of the important compromises necessary to build a broad coalition are hammered out, is being reborn on the Web.

Individual insurgents, too, have found the Web is better than owning a press in the revolutionary era. When Senator Trent Lott stood up at retiring Senator Strom Thurmond's 100th birthday party and said, ""I

[75] "E-mail Overload in Congress," A report of the Congress Online Project, a partnership of the Congressional Management Foundation and George Washington University, http://www.congressonlineproject.org/email.html

[76] Alan Elsner, "'Virtual' War Protest Jams Congressional Phones," Reuters, February 26, 2003.

want to say this about my state: when Strom Thurmond ran for President, we voted for him. We're proud of it. And if the rest of the country had followed our lead, we wouldn't have had all these problems over all these years, either," the press at large ignored the statement, but a number of bloggers, people publishing their ideas on a Web page arranged in reverse-chronological order (the last posting appears at the top and others are arranged by descending date order on pages that can go on for many screens worth of data), offended at this endorsement of segregation, were enraged. Bloggers like InstaPundit Glenn Reynolds and Josh Marshall of Talking Points Memo compiled documentary evidence that Lott, who immediately apologized for the comments, had actually been saying exactly the same thing for decades. If Lott was sorry now, why was he repeating himself after having said the same thing about Thurmond, who argued in the 1948 presidential election, when he ran as a third-party "Dixiecrat" candidate that federal law and troops "cannot force the Negro into our homes, schools, our churches," several times between 1965 and 2002? Refusing to let the story die, the bloggers forced a national debate that resulted in Lott's resignation as Senate Majority Leader.

In the case of Trent Lott, the public led the pundits. As CNN reported:

> If Lott didn't see the storm coming, it was in part because it was so slow in building. The papers did not make note of his comments until days after he had made them. But the stillness was broken by the hum of Internet "bloggers" who were posting their outrage and compiling rap sheets of Lott's earlier comments. It took a few more days before Democrats denounced Lott and demanded a censure.[77]

That a few people with Web presence and, comparatively speaking, small audiences, though very large social networks, could carry such weight in national politics was a stark reminder of the role of the press in the American Revolution, when a few key publishers repeated the messages that ignited an insurrection. Bloggers are powerful conduits for ideas because, like George H. W. Bush and his personal note-based network, connections can be activated with a few well-chosen words. This ability to build a social network that is available when an issue of importance

---

[77] Dan Goodgame and Karen Tumulty, Lott: Tripped up by history, cnn.com, December 16, 2002.
http://www.cnn.com/2002/ALLPOLITICS/12/16/timep.lott.tm/

arises is as important today as the power of the press in the pre-Revolutionary era in America and France, when wits and ideologues like Benjamin Franklin, Thomas Paine and Jean-Paul Marat could inflame regions with a publication that, if it found success with local audiences was recirculated across the entire country. Likewise, the samizdat press of Soviet Russia and Eastern Europe, which operated on a network of readers who passed along mimeographed and photocopied pamphlets, toppled a totalitarian government by keeping ideas alive and circulating. Focal points in society like these bloggers can, if supported by action, produce dramatic results.

As Mohandas K. Gandhi said, "One cannot unite a community without a newspaper or journal of some kind." These separate trends of individual expression through blogs, an egalitarian journalism, and or+ganized online activism are waking unrecognized communities of interest that will confound a political system designed for representation of geographic constituencies. A concerted effort by the peoples of the world can transform the perception of the means and ends of government. Meanwhile, politics, the art of participation in social decision-making and a practice closely related to being "polite," which means to achieve refinement, continues to function essentially as it has throughout history, through debate and compromise among people.

An answer to the continuing debate about political process will be based on the integration of many, though not all, threads in recent human development into an expanded concept of the individual as the basis for the concept of sovereignty and the redefinition of the role of government institutions in order to revitalize political processes. A political philosophy must incorporate more than the experience of participation. An analysis of power, definite ideas about the role of the citizen and the government, and the principles society will embrace about the value of the individual are required, as well. Extreme democracy seeks to provide these foundational ideas to place the thrill of emergent organizations into socio-political context.

# Two ways to emerge, and how to tell the difference between them
## by Steven Johnson

Four years ago, when I first started writing about emergence and political movements, it was much easier to find instances of self-organizing behavior in ant colonies and video game simulations than it was in the world of political struggle. But you could sense even then that the times were changing. The bottom-up communities that had emerged on the web over the preceding years were a clear sign of things to come: if the Slashdot demographic could coalesce into such a powerful collective force in a matter of years, it was easy to see how a group organized around political values rather than Linux could arise without the usual building blocks of money and infrastructure to support it. Indeed, some of this had already been visible on the streets of Seattle and other cities, thanks to the anti-globalization protests of the late nineties, which deliberately modeled themselves on swarm systems. I ended my 2001 book, *Emergence*, with a hopeful look at those protestors:

To some older progressives, steeped in the more hierarchical tradition of past labor movements, those diverse "affinity groups" seemed hopelessly scattered and unfocused, with no common language or ideology uniting them. It's almost impossible to think of another political movement that generated as much public attention without producing a genuine leader — a Jesse Jackson or Cesar Chavez — if only for the benefit of the television cameras. The images that we associate with the anti-globalization protests are never those of an adoring crowd raising its fists in solidarity with an impassioned speaker on a podium. That is the iconography of an earlier model of protest. What we see again and again with the new wave are images of disparate groups: satirical puppets, black-clad anarchists, sit-ins and performance art — but no leaders. To old-school progressives, the Seattle protestors appeared to be headless, out of control, a swarm of small causes with no organizing principle — and to a certain extent they're right in their assessment. What they fail to recognize is that there can be power and intelligence in a swarm, and if you're trying to do battle against a distributed network like global capitalism, you're better off becoming a distributed network yourself.

*Emergence*, as it happened, was released in early September, 2001. It was, needless to say, an interesting time to have made a prediction about the liberating power of decentralized, cell-structure political movements. What I'd imagined a blueprint for future grassroots struggle turned out to be a remarkably apt description of the organizational strategies used by Al Qaeda. I had imagined emergent political movements as the last great hope for democracy, and here they were being hijacked by deeply reactionary, anti-democratic terrorists. Post 9/11 it was impossible to read those closing pages of my book, and not think of global terror, and in fact, I began hearing somewhat unnerving reports that the book was being widely read in the Defense Department and Homeland Security. Books invariably have a life of their own, where they depart from their author's intentions in all sorts of unusual ways, but this was a particularly cruel twist. My little manual for creating emergent political movements was being used to better understand how to shut them down.

But as 9/11 began to have less of a stranglehold on the American consciousness, and we began attacking old-fashioned, top-down dictatorships, another model of emergent political organization began to dominate the news: the leaderless activism of moveon.org, the instant collectives of meetup.com, and of course the revolutionary — if ultimately unsuccessful — Presidential campaign of Howard Dean. Swarm systems stopped being a strategy for overthrowing the Great Satan, and became a tool for "taking back democracy." Which was where I'd imagined them to be all along.

Watching the Dean campaign's meteoric rise and fall helped me to see some of my original ideas about emergence with a new clarity, particularly as they related to collective behavior among humans. I think now that I was really forcing two kinds of emergence to coexist under a single umbrella term. Imagine it as the difference between clustering and coping. Some simpler emergent systems are good at forming crowds; other, more complex ones, are good at regulating the overall state of the system, adapting to new challenges, evolving in response to opportunities. Sometimes, I suspect, it's helpful to blur the distinctions between clustering and coping for simplicity's sake. But when you subject them to the intense scrutiny and pressure of a national political campaign, the fault lines inevitably appear. Right now, emergent politics is brilliant at clustering, but clustering is not enough to get a national candidate elected. In fact, without the right coping mechanisms in place, clustering can sometimes work against your interests. You need crowds to get elected to public office, but without more complex forms of self-regulation, crowds can quickly turn into riots. And riots don't win elections.

## Clustering

One of the funny things about the literature of emergence is that it is strangely obsessed with slime. Slime *mold*, to be precise, thanks to researchers who have investigated this strange creature's capacity to oscillate between one organism and many: hundreds of free-floating cells that under the right circumstances will gang up together and become a single unit. For a long time, experts believed that there had to be a single "pacemaker" cell that initiated the clustering activity, a general calling the troops into formation. But researchers now believe that the clustering is a self-organizing phenomenon: no single cell is in charge of the slime mold system. Instead, the cells signal to each other using deposits of pheromone; in certain circumstances, the cells will follow pheromone trails, and when those trails reach a certain density — a tipping point — the cells begin to cluster together into a single unit. There are now wonderful computer simulations of slime model behavior available where you can experiment with different lengths and persistence of pheromone trails. Within a certain range, the cells remain free-floating agents, roaming aimlessly across the screen. But make the trails long enough, or make them decay at a slower rate, and the slime mold cells will quickly start to group together in large bodies.

When you see these clusters emerge for the first time, there's something undeniably magical in the sight. The brain somehow wants to find a leader in the collective, despite the fact that it knows intellectually that the pattern is forming via the laws of self-organization. Clusters of this sort can take a number of forms: the flocking patterns of birds (or boids, as in their computer doppelgangers), the orderly, single-file lines of ants marching across a picnic blanket. Behind each formation lies a shared group logic: following simple rules of signaling, systems of individual agents can organize themselves into higher-level shapes without any individual agent calling the shots. For the most part, these systems rely on the runaway amplification of positive feedback: create a pheromone trail strong enough to attract another ant, who lays down another layer of pheromone, thus making the trail strong enough to attract two ants, who then thicken the trail even more. Positive feedback loops are often the turbines of biological growth, and all emergent systems rely on them at least in part. But they lack a certain subtlety, a certain responsiveness. They're great at conjuring up crowds. But they're lousy at coping.

## Coping

The collective behavior of the social insects — ants, bees, termites — is so marvelously orchestrated that many observers have suggested that the colony itself should be considered the organism proper, with the individual ants or termites functioning as so many cells in a body. (Hence the term supra-organism, sometimes used to describe colonies of social insects.) A swarm of social insects has far more personality and agility than a simple self-organizing cluster. Clusters just mass together in a big lump; colonies solve problems. They manage food resources through feast and famine; they allocate tasks with an almost Taylorite efficiency. As anyone who has ever battled termites know, they pull off dazzling — if destructive — feats of engineering, building nests out of the most unlikely of materials. Most importantly, perhaps, colonies are adaptive to changing circumstances. I don't mean "adaptive" in the sense of having evolved as a product of natural selection, though they are certainly that too. I mean "adaptive" in the sense of being able to respond quickly and effectively to new situations, to both opportunities and threats. Distribute three pieces of food within a few feet of a harvester ant colony, and the ants will 1) locate all three items, and 2) dedicate resources to collecting the nearest food first, followed by the second-nearest, and then ending with the most remote food. Try it again with food dispersed in different locations, and they'll solve the puzzle all over again.

This kind of emergent behavior is crucial to an organism's — or a group's — homeostasis, its ability to keep itself intact and healthy in unpredictable environments. Clustering is, ultimately, a more dynamic version of the beautiful crystal shapes generated by snowflakes: amazing patterns generated out of simple rules. Coping systems, on the other hand, have the spontaneity and intelligence of life: they seem to learn from experience; they probe and explore the environments; they keep themselves healthy and well-fed in sometimes hostile conditions. To do this, they require two key elements that are not necessary in clustering systems. First, they need a relatively complex semiotic code to communicate between agents. E. O. Wilson estimates that the pheromone signaling system used by ants contains as much as two dozen "words": "food this way," "danger," "help wanted," etc. The second key ingredient is in a sense built out of the first: coping systems need meta-information about the state of the collective. Traditionally this information is conveyed via indirect means, precisely because the system itself lacks a command control apparatus that can broadcast data to the entire swarm. Task allocation, for instance, seems to emerge through individual ants tracking the frequency with which they encounter other ants doing specific tasks. Instead of a system-wide alarm announcing that there are too many foragers, individual ants sense indirectly that there may be too many foragers by counting the ratio of foragers-to-nest-builders, and changing their activity if the ratio gets too far out of whack. Instead of the runaway amplifications of positive feedback, you get a system of checks and balances, driving the system towards an equilibrium point, even as it encounters unforeseen situations.

## The Madness Of Crowds

How does the opposition between clustering and coping map onto emergent politics? I would argue that almost all the tools we've developed — and almost all the tools exploited by the Dean campaign — were fundamentally about clustering: new ways of forming crowds, whether online or off. Meetup.com is of course the ultimate example of this. As Clay Shirky adroitly suggests, Meetup is fundamentally about "lowering the cost of organizing real-world gatherings." That's not a bad way of describing the evolutionary strategies of systems that self-organize into clusters. In the case of our slime molds, the lowered cost comes in the form of not having to evolve a higher-level intelligence capable of assessing the entire state of the collective and making an executive decision to form a cluster. There's an evolutionary cost in creating a central nervous system, and the simple positive feedback mechanism of the cluster enabled the slime mold collective to avoid that cost. In the case of the Dean campaign, of course, Meetup enabled Dean supporters to organize themselves without requiring the headquarters in Vermont to arrange and keep track of all those gatherings, which in itself creating a higher-level form of positive feedback: it became a national news story that all those groups were spontaneously forming all over the country, which led directly to the formation of new, and larger, clusters.

There was, to be sure, meta-information about the overall state of the Dean supra-organism flowing through the system, but that information

94

primarily took the form of two key indices: people and dollars. The main Dean site — mirrored cheerfully by big media reporters and op-ed writers — was a constant barrage of stats about the number of Meetups held during the past week, and the latest staggering fundraising numbers. All of which created a powerful autocatalytic set, one that seemed likely to propel Dean to the nomination by the time early January rolled around. But as we've seen, clustering usually isn't enough when the environment gets more difficult. You need more responsive, more homeostatic tools to deal with sudden change and challenges. The system needs more than just a positive feedback loop, more than an attractor. It needs to be able to steer.

I'll reserve judgment on what the ultimate cause was behind the Dean campaign's loss in Iowa. The downward spiral of negative campaigning, wasted television ads, a "vast moderate media conspiracy" — choose your poison, the end result was in late January the Dean campaign suddenly had to confront a new reality. It had to cope and not just cluster. It needed information about vulnerabilities in the system, and feedback mechanism that would enable the system to correct itself. But those tools weren't built into the emergent system of the Dean campaign; the tools of the Dean campaign were all about generating increasing amounts of energy: more people, more dollars. They weren't about responding to new challenges, and altering the direction of the supraorganism accordingly.

You could see this limitation most clearly by following the main Dean blog at blogforamerica.com. For months, the blog had actually been a reliable source of information about the state of the Dean campaign: new meetups and fundraising records, the latest polls, advance word about media appearances, summaries of op-eds about the Governor and the primary race. Spending time at the Dean blog at once made you feel part of a community and at the same time actually gave you relevant news. It was as informative as any political news wire, but it had a grassroots authenticity to it as well. But as it turned out, that authenticity was entirely predicated on a certain external environment: one in which Dean was the frontrunner, and almost all of the news — whether fundraising or polling or media coverage — was positive. When the dynamics of the campaign shifted literally overnight, and the external world began serving up genuinely bad news about Dean's prospects as a candidate, the Dean blog quickly became yet another campaign PR site: willfully ignoring the steady stream of dismal numbers and declining support. The authenticity of the site disappeared, because the authenticity had ultimately been the product of a positive feedback cascade. When the external environment turned negative, all that was left was spin.

It's entirely possible that the Dean campaign could have righted itself in the weeks after January, but I suspect that correction would have only come via a top-down process, not an emergent one, because the tools developed to support Dean were clustering in nature, not coping. (Dean seems to have hit upon the same insight during that period, in his famous call for a more centralized campaign after Trippi's departure.) A clustering emergent system is ultimately focused on doing more of what the system is already doing: how can we get a bigger crowd? How can we raise even more money? A coping system is just as often about patching holes — looking for weaknesses and figuring out ways to compensate for them. When Dean fared so poorly in Iowa — even before the Scream — there was no way for the system to make an assessment about what went wrong, and institute the proper repairs.

I suspect that such a system may well be fundamentally incompatible with the necessary structure of a national political campaign, at least for the foreseeable future. Emergent systems that excel at coping do so out of truly local information; they take their random walks through their neighborhoods and record patterns in what they find. National campaigns, on the other hand, work at a macro scale, and they are necessarily wedded to the broadcast amplifications of the national media. Whatever local disturbances or opportunities they discover are quickly uploaded to the world of network TV and satellite feeds, where they undergo all sorts of distortions. And national campaigns, by definition, have to have leaders, at least in the form of the politicians themselves. From my perspective, at least, one of the crucial failings of the Dean campaign is that the energy unleashed by the clustering tools distracted both the country and the campaign from problems in the candidate himself, problems which ultimately became visible when voters actually sat down to decide who to vote for.

Is there an emergent politics capable of a more subtle form of self-regulation? If there is, I think it will first take shape, not as a political campaign, but as a more local, day-to-day affair: more *polis* than politics. With the right tools, local communities should be able to create emergent systems that help govern and shape their own development in

96

new kinds of ways: the "eyes on the street" that Jane Jacobs celebrated in her classic works on urbanism, now amplified by the communications and pattern-recognition tools of the networked age. Just as the ants find their way to new food sources and switch tasks with impressive flexibility, our community tools should help us locate and improve troubled schools, up-and-coming playgrounds, areas lacking crucial services, areas with an abundance of services, blocks that feel safe at night and blocks that don't — all the subtle patterns of community life now made public in a new form. That kind of politics — the kind built from the ground up, without leaders — is truly within our grasp right now, if we can just build the right tools. To me, that's the real promise of emergent democracies, and not the dream of collaboratively steering a politician to the White House. Think local, act local.

It has taken 10 years of talk about "new media" for a critical mass to understand that every computer desktop, and now every pocket, is a worldwide printing press, broadcasting station, place of assembly, and organizing tool — and to learn how to use that infrastructure to affect change.

Previous technologies allowed users only to communicate one-to-one (telephones) or few-to-many (broadcast and print media). Mobile and deskbound media such as blogs, listservs and social networking sites allow for many-to-many communication. This provides opportunities and problems for progressive political activists in three key areas: Gathering and disseminating alternative and more democratic news; creating virtual public spheres where citizens debate the issues that concern democratic societies; and organizing collective political action.

### The new news

Blogs and moblogs, such as the international network of Independent Media Centers, South Korea's influential OhMyNews and MoveOn.org's misleader.org are signs of what *San Jose Mercury-News* columnist Dan Gillmor calls an emerging "we journalism." Each of these sites offers up-to-the-minute news alerts, provided by a combination of citizen-reporters and trained staff. While the owners and administrators of such sites range widely — from passionate individuals to collectives to upstart nonprofits — these blogs are markedly more democratic than their corporate-run, top-down brethren.

Internal and external forces, however, threaten to undermine "we journalism" before its impact is fully realized.

Misinformation, disinformation, incredulity and magical thinking all are problems on the supply side of these new reporting modes. Aggregators of blog postings — which rank blog listings by popularity, similar to Google's page rank technology — already serve as a filter for this flood of amateur journalism. And reputation systems, filters and syndication services also could develop into useful tools for assessing the veracity of information sites. But political activists and those who sponsor progressive projects also have a role: For "we journalism" to have long-term credibility and lasting impact, progressives must fund, staff and promote media literacy — teaching users to create and consume this new journalism.

Activists also have a role in turning back corporate attacks that seek to privatize the Internet by regulating content and limiting amateurs' ability to produce cultural works that compete with media conglomerates.

Today, a small number of broadband Internet providers, such as Comcast and Viacom, are pushing for regulations that would enable them to pick and choose the content that travels over their part of the network. The courts also are coming to bear in this fight, as companies work to extend copyright far beyond its original intent and establish digital rights schemes that make it difficult to produce or distribute digital content not authorized by the entertainment industry.

The consolidation of media ownership in the hands of a small number of individuals or cartels — who exchange political funding for legislative and regulatory favors — is being fought by organizations such as the Electronic Frontier Foundation. But activists who have not been involved in technology or media issues need to join in this battle, because communication media under dispute are profoundly political tools. In coming decades, Internet-based media will exert more and more influence over what people know and believe and how they can organize and assemble for collective action.

## The electronic town square

Network TV news and talk radio are hardly examples of the reasoned debate philosopher Jürgen Habermas had in mind when he described the public sphere as central to the life of a democracy. Indeed, they are an example of the manipulation of public opinion via popular media that he warned about.

Online and many-to-many technologies can shift the locus of the public sphere from a small number of powerful media owners to entire populations. The value of Internet discourse in this effort has not been proven, however, perhaps because the literacy around this use of media has not had sufficient time to mature — the World Wide Web is barely 10 years old, and has been gaining uninitiated users each year.

Now, for better and worse, citizens are arguing with each other — with varying degrees of civility — and sometimes marshaling evidence to buttress logic in countless blogs, listservs, chat rooms and message boards. The quality and level of know-how and the willingness of a significant portion of the population to adopt and self-enforce online etiquette will determine whether reasoned debate will flourish online or be drowned out by surlier forms of argument. Activists and journalists must take a leading role in determining the success of this outcome by wielding these technologies skillfully and purposively.

## Organizing collective action

Only recently have political activists successfully used many-to-many media to mobilize large-scale collective action such as street demonstrations and protests, electoral fundraising, get-out-the-vote campaigns and legislative lobbying. Technologies and methodologies are developing very rapidly at this point, and so are the political moves to neutralize them.

In the United States, Howard Dean's presidential campaign has mobilized the self-organizing capabilities of blogs. Meetup.com and online fundraising propelled this underdog to front-runner status. If Dean wins, 2004 will be the watershed political event for the Internet that the Kennedy-Nixon debates were for television in 1960. In a few years, MoveOn.org also has grown from a Web site protesting the Clinton impeachment to an effective lobbying movement that influences legislation and elections. MoveOn.org played an important part in the recent effort to lobby Congress to overturn the FCC's deregulation of media cross-ownership.

Innovations aren't confined to the United States. Neither ex-President Estrada of the Philippines nor newly elected President Roh in South Korea would be in their present positions if smart mobs had not worked so effectively. In the Philippines, a million citizens used SMS to organize street demonstrations that helped topple the Estrada regime. In South Korea, the cyber-generation, seeing their favored candidate losing in exit polls, used a Web site to organize a get-out-the-vote campaign involving 800,000 personal e-mails and uncounted SMS messages, turning the tide in the election's final hours.

Activists should now concentrate their efforts in this last sphere — technology-amplified collective action. The above examples are just the beginning. The capabilities of media are multiplying, the number of people who use their mobile phones as Internet connections and text-messaging media is growing explosively. And activists are only beginning to experiment with ways to multiply their ability to organize collective action.

Influencing elections and legislation is the sine qua non of effectiveness. In the next few years, peer-to-peer, self-organized, citizen-centric movements enabled by smart mob media will either demonstrate real political influence, be successfully contained by those whose power they threaten, or recede as a utopian myth of days gone by. What progressives know now, and what we do soon, will decide which of those scenarios unfolds.

# The dead hand of modern democracy: Lessons for emergent post-modern democrats
## by Ken White

Let us not be too hasty to bury the present; it's not dead yet, and a pre-mortem might provide some useful information. Those of us moving ahead ought to remember Santayana's famous dictum, and meditate — deeply — on what, and whom, we might leave behind.

Emergent democracy can augment and, perhaps, even gradually supplant outmoded forms of self-governance, but *only* if we appreciate why those forms were once "moded" — suited to their times and uses. After all, Democracy 2.0 (if we consider Athens "1.0") has enjoyed a pretty good 220-year run, even with all its failings.

Considering which critical functions of modern democracy deserve preservation in intent, if not in form, offers the opportunity to appreciate the rich complexity of democratic self-governance and its astonishingly diverse modes of participation and action. By attending to what made modern democracy successful we might learn a few lessons; extract some insights from the old model; and identify a few pitfalls we ought to avoid, even as we cheerfully acknowledge the inevitability of creating a new set of pitfalls.

I draw on personal experience in arriving at this conclusion. Working in the United States on democratic reforms (including campaign financing) for many years, I came to appreciate the difference between "reform" and "redesign." Although the former may occur more often in some limited way, the promise of the latter drives truly significant change. As Buckminster Fuller said: "You never change things by fighting against the existing reality. To change something, build a new model that makes the old model obsolete."[78]

But it is also true that there is nothing new under the sun. As JS Bruner points out, we humans tend to respond with "effective surprise" to

---

[78] Fuller, R. Buckminster (St. Martin's Griffin, 1982).

concepts and artifacts that take familiar things and rearrange them in new ways.[79] Those working with a chaordic model of change (in the zone where chaos and order overlap)[80] have found that the most fertile territory for innovation is in the boundary zone, where unlike things co-mingle. The chaordic model of self-governance has been described as a mix of Lao Tse, Adam Smith, and Thomas Jefferson.[81]

It is not that we dismiss what exists out of hand and live in a normative fantasyland, but that we honor what has been created even as we disrupt the familiar. There is much energy for wholesale change, and rightly so. As the editors of this book noted in their précis: "[B]ottom-up governance...resists the past for the past's sake and reinvents society anew constantly. It is innovative, preserving and cannibalizing the past to create better solutions to social problems each day. It is many small changes that add up to profound solutions, an order that is intended to change, everything that has made democracy the most compelling form of governance on Earth."

Therefore we should neither praise nor to bury the present. In some cases, we will merely be trying to reclaim what once was — or at least what once was possible. Since every generation must reinvent the familiar in ways just unique enough to claim originality, some of what we call "emergent" might sound very familiar to a suffragette or an abolitionist. Paine, Publius, and all the pamphleteers and organizers of the American Revolution would feel at home, we suspect — and hope! — with much of what is described and proposed between these covers. In two senses, we are radicals (both "beginning at the roots" and "departing from the usual").

We can take some of our cues from the places modern democracy has succeeded and failed, and perhaps most interestingly from the places of greatest struggle. In addition to obvious challenges like inequality and tyranny (as if those weren't challenges enough), emergent democrats face the vexing problem of creating forms of participation that embrace

---

[79] J.S. Bruner, *On Knowing: Essays for the Left Hand* (Harvard University Press, 1979).

[80] See www.chaordic.org for more information.

[81] M. Mitchell Waldrop, "The Trillion-Dollar Vision of Dee Hock" (*Fast Company*, Oct./Nov. 1996).

a variety of people and cultures, yet are flexible and responsive enough to avoid the "structure trap."

As will be explored more fully, the "structure trap" is the tendency to believe that we know exactly what we want to accomplish; who will do the work; how the work will happen; and what outcomes will occur. Accordingly, we build out elaborate rules, regulations, procedures, structures, and personnel to match our assumptions. Although useful for engineering bridges, in other applications this "trap" drives our efforts toward a pre-determined goal, even if the circumstances change or the outcomes don't match the intentions. Once locked in to a particular plan, we follow it to its logical conclusion: planned obsolescence, bureaucratic sclerosis, rising frustration, and inevitable breakdown. Arguably, we are approaching or have reached the limits of modern democracy's "structure trap."

Having arrived at a possible ending, we might consider what led us to this new beginning, and how to begin well.

# The Weblog: An Extremely Democratic Form in Journalism
## by Jay Rosen

In this chapter for *Extreme Democracy*, I revisit my list, "ten things radical about the weblog form in journalism." (PressThink's most popular post.)

"Journalism," James W. Carey tells us, "takes its name from the French word for day. It is our day book, our collective diary, which records our common life."

To record the events of the day is equally the aim of the newsroom and the diary writer. Carey, a press scholar who teaches at Columbia University, finds a connection at the soul between journalism and the practice of journal keeping. Both are trying to prevent events from disappearing without reflection, narration, and the means to look back. "That which goes unrecorded goes unpreserved except in the vanishing moment of our individual lives," he writes.

When Carey speaks of journalism, he means the practice of it. "Not the media. Not the news business. Not the newspaper or the magazine or the television station but the practice of journalism," which exists independent of any media platform. He goes on:

There are media everywhere. Every despot creates his own system of media. There is a news business everywhere; there just isn't all that much journalism, for there can be no journalism without the aspiration for or institutions of democratic life....

Just as medicine, for example, can be practiced in enormous clinics organized like corporations or in one-person offices, journalism can be practiced in multinational conglomerates or by isolated freelancers. Just as medicine can be practiced with technologies as advanced as magnetic image resonating machines or as primitive as an ear that hears complaints and an eye that observes symptoms, so journalism can be practiced with satellites or script. The practice does not depend on the technology or bureaucracy. It depends on the practitioner mastering a body of skill and exercising it to some worthwhile purpose.

And what is worthwhile about it? Carey puts it this way: "For journalism and for us, that purpose is the development and enhancement of public life, a common life which we can all share as citizens." The title of his talk where he says all this is, "The struggle against forgetting."

Journalism is a part of that struggle, the simplest act of which is recording the events of the day. So a journal writer has origins in common with a journal-ist. They are members of the same communication family. And this is one reason that weblogs, which the press calls "online journals," are an *event* within journalism — the practice of it, as well as our ideas about it.

Believing so, in October, 2003 I posted an item listing "ten things radical about the weblog form in journalism." In the rapid way these things happen online, the list became PressThink's most popular and linked-to feature, which means it embedded itself further into the Web than any other entry before or since. It was half the length of a newspaper op-ed. In it I was trying to find points where the weblog "reversed" things about journalism, or shifted a big pattern that had held for a long time. Thus:

1.) The weblog comes out of the gift economy, whereas most (not all) of today's journalism comes out of the market economy.

2.) Journalism had become the domain of professionals, and amateurs were sometimes welcomed into it — as with the op-ed page. Whereas the weblog is the domain of amateurs and professionals are the ones being welcomed to it.

3.) In journalism since the mid-nineteenth century, barriers to entry have been high. With the weblog, barriers to entry are low: a computer, a Net connection, and a software program like Blogger or Movable Type gets you there. Most of the capital costs required for the weblog to "work" have been sunk into the Internet itself, the largest machine in the world (with the possible exception of the international phone system.)

4.) In the weblog world every reader is actually a writer, and you write not so much for "the reader" but for other writers. So every reader is a writer, yes, but every writer is also a reader of other weblog writers — or better be.

5.) Whereas an item of news in a newspaper or broadcast seeks to add itself to the public record, an entry posted in a weblog engages the public record, because it pulls bits and pieces from it through the device of linking. In journalism the regular way, we imagine the public record accumulating with each day's news — becoming longer. In journalism the weblog way, we imagine the public record "tightening," its web becoming stronger, as links promotes linking, which produces more links.

6.) A weblog can "work" journalistically — it can be sustainable, enjoyable, meaningful, valuable, worth doing, and worth it to other people — if it reaches 50 or 100 souls who like it, use it, and communicate through it. Whereas in journalism the traditional way, such a small response would be seen as a failure, in journalism the weblog way the intensity of a small response can spell success.

7.) A weblog is like a column in a newspaper or magazine, sort of, but whereas a column written by twelve people makes little sense and wouldn't work, a weblog written by twelve people makes perfect sense and does work.

8.) In journalism prior to the weblog, the journalist had an editor and the editor represented the reader. In journalism after the weblog, the journalists has (writerly) readers, and the readers represent an editor.

9.) In journalism classically understood, information flows from the press to the public. In the weblog world as it is coming to be understood, information flows from the public to the press.

10.) Journalism traditionally assumes that democracy is what we have, information is what we seek. Whereas in the weblog world, information is what we have — it's all around us — and democracy is what we seek.

What is a weblog? A personal web page, or online journal, updated easily by an author, that links outward to other material on the Web, and presents original content — typically, links and commentary — in a rolling, day-by-day fashion, with the latest entries on top.

But also:

- Some weblogs have comment sections after every item, so in a sense every item is an item submitted for public comment.

- Some weblogs have a long list of other blogs they name, highlight and link to, (a blogroll, in the vernacular). This an author uses to define a conversational field, as if to say: "listen to me as I talk to them."

- Weblogs don't have to be, but they often are designed with a given look and feel, which is to say they define a particular kind of place. To Joi Ito, a weblog is primarily that, a place its users enjoy. He says that reading his weblog is something like visiting his house. If so, it's a talking house.

- Jeff Jarvis, author of Buzzmachine, a popular and newsy weblog, says: "know my blog, know me." According to Dave Winer, one of the pioneers of the form, a weblog is the "voice of a person."

All weblogs offer text, increasingly they have photographs, some include audio, some now present video (and some have ads.) The weblog incorporates these earlier media forms, turning them into tools of expression almost anyone can learn to use. The software behind the form allows for production values high enough that individual authors on the Web suffer no immediate disadvantage in comparison to very large commercial providers. There's something extremely democratic about that.

Remember the rationale for public access television? It was supposed to give individual television makers a place on the cable dial. Weblogs are a more effective public access point. Because they are "live" on the Web, and the Web is World Wide, the millions of weblogs already out there have some ability to compete in the same public space as hugely capitalized media companies.

Although it is still a tiny universe, and not a real threat to the established media or the professionals who operate it, the sphere of weblogs is capable of something bigger inventions have not achieved. As Jarvis says, the weblog gives people in the audience a printing press, and thus access to their own audience. There's something extremely democratic about that development, too.

And even though we know that only a small, unrepresentative fraction of a percent will start that press up, the fact that it can be done has a radiating effect. Andrew Sullivan got more readers for himself, through his weblog, than he ever had as editor and columnist of the New Republic magazine. Granted that he began with every advantage as a journalist and writer with a track record in public controversy; still, with andrewsullivan.com he showed that an individual provider could compete with long-established journals of opinion. "If the goal of opinion journalism is not ultimately money but influence and readers," Sullivan wrote, "the blogs are already breathing down the old media's neck."

Chris Allbritton, a former reporter for the Associated Press, took this empowerment further. From contributions solicited at his weblog, (back-to-iraq.com) he raised over $14,000 to report on the war in Iraq as an independent correspondent, answerable only to his readers and his conscience. Armed with a satellite phone, a global positioning unit, a laptop, and his reporting skills, Allbritton flew to Turkey, snuck over the border into Northern Iraq, made his way to Baghdad, and started posting live reports to his weblog, which had 23,000 users and supporters during the peak of his reporting (March 27, 2003.) That was an act of journalism--the social practice Jim Carey talked about--that cut out "the media" entirely, proving that one does not depend on the other. (See this about Allbritton's breakthrough.)

That is why I call the weblog the last mile in self-publishing. In cable television, the last mile, stretching from the system to the private home, is the most expensive and politically charged portion of the network. It's where greater media capacity comes down from the skies to plug into people's lives; and it is also the point where public regulation, the economics of television, the politics of municipalities, viewer choice, and a dozen other factors converge. The last mile brought us "public access," but it was under-funded and meant to lose out to the commercial channels people would pay for.

If cable television is the heavy industry of the media age, the weblog is of much lighter invention. In fact, it was hardly noticed at first, beyond a few visionaries who invented the form, and started fooling around with it. Anil Dash is a vice president for Six Apart, a company that makes the popular Movable Type program for webloggers. In a talk he gave at New York University's Law School, (February 20, 2004) Dash said that the weblog was a "boring" development to techies, who took one look and saw nothing original in the code or functioning.

Yet the genius of the weblog was not in any technological leap, but in completing the last mile in the two-way highway the Web has become. The form favors individual voices and self-publishers, most of whom will have no media institution behind them, and no hope of profit. What they are after is free speech and the enhancement of public life. Or as Tim Dunlop puts it, "an environment where ordinary people can use argument to increase their knowledge."

Institutions, too, will speak through weblogs (CEO's for example) as will professional journalists. For now, at least, amateurs, "isolated free-lancers" and random citizens speak in the same public space as these other voices. The equalizing effect can be extreme. Atrios, pen name for the one of the most successful political webloggers, had no background in either journalism or politics when he began. Now his blog claims more than 65,000 visits a day. (For more on Atrios, see this case study about blogs and the fate of Trent Lott from the Kennedy School at Harvard.)

On top of the Net was built the Web. On top of the Web sits the weblog and its mini public-sphere, (which Atrios and others call Blogistan) connected by links, public comment sections, search engines, online syndication (RSS), free and paid hosting hosting services, and indexes of popularity-- all the tools of the last mile. Now that it's up and running, the people formerly known as the audience, those we have long considered the consumers of media—the readers, viewers, listeners—can get up from their chairs, "flip" things around, grab the equipment, and become speakers and broadcasters in the public square.

It's pirate radio, legalized; it's public access coming closer to life. Inside the borders of Blogistan (a real place with all the problems of a real place) we're closer to a vision of "producer democracy" than we are to any of the consumerist views that long ago took hold in the mass media, including much of the journalism presented on that platform. We won't know what a producer public looks like from looking at the patterns of the media age, in which broadcasting and its one-to-many economy prevailed.

Weblogs potentially explode the world of authorship far enough that we can at least imagine a sphere of debate with millions of productive speakers, where there was once an audience of millions listening to a few speakers dominate the debate. The existence of such a tool is an extreme change in prospect and pattern for citizens of the media age. When I wrote my list, "Ten Things Radical About the Weblog Form in Journalism" I was discussing only that, the shift in what's possible, or at least thinkable within the social practice of journalism, worldwide. What's *probable* in the world we inhabit today is a far different story.

From what we know so far, it is probable that most weblogs will be short lived, and wind up abandoned, just as most conversations are abandoned. It is probable that a few popular blogs will have huge user base and the vast majority will be invisible most of the time, a pattern that reminds some of the "old" mass media. Since the software and interface are highly flexible, and the uses of an easily updated, good-looking page are endless, weblogs will be commonly used in closed systems—private and company networks—as much as the open waters of the Web.

Most, in fact, will not attempt to reach a public, even if they are in theory reachable by all Net users. The great majority of weblogs will probably be for personal use; and the user base will be peer to peer, not author to public. Teenagers will be the biggest market for weblog software and hosting services. For the public display of private life no easier tool has ever been invented, and it should surprise no one that people use it to record their lives, even when the details are, to most others, insignificant.

Now if the insignificant events in the daily life of celebrity blonde Anna Nicole Smith are worth recording and distributing to the world by cable--and the E! Cable Network thinks they are—then the sight of blogger Jane Smith recording the ordinary facts of her life, and distributing them via the Web, should strike us, not as a strange development in the life of media forms, or one to laugh at, but a far more sensible notion all around. Anna's show is the bizarre form. Jane's journal is a more natural—and a more democratic--thing to do.

# Section Two:
# Science, Technology
# and Politics

# It's the Conversations, Stupid!
# The Link between Social Interaction and
# Political Choice
# by Valdis Krebs

What influences people to participate in the voting process? How do voters choose which candidates and issues to support? These questions have been on the minds of both political scientists and campaign organizers. Various models of human behavior have influenced the answers to these two important questions. These models of human behavior span the extremes from very simple, and easily influenced behavior to very complex, interdependent behavior where nothing is linear nor easily controllable. Where on the behavior spectrum does political behavior reside? Is it simple behavior driven by data and facts? Or is it emergent behavior driven by the interactions, opinions, passion and relationships?

The oldest model of political behavior is that of the *atomized voter* — a view that has dominated the study of voter choice. This view assumes that voters and choices are independent of one another, a necessity for statistical inference. The voting public is an aggregation of autonomous decision-makers, each making a decision based on personal rationale and/or emotion. Further, the voter is influenced only by information and opinion obtained directly via mass media. The atomized voter listens, decides, and votes. Although this model has provided our initial understanding of voters, it is an incomplete account of how decisions are made. In order to simplify the statistics, this model over-simplifies human behavior.

A more complex view of human behavior is the model of the *demographic voter*. Here the voter is not viewed as isolated and autonomous, but as a member of a demographic group which can influence or predict the voter's choices. This model assumes that those with similar attributes will vote in a similar pattern. This model takes the atomized voter, realizes there are others who are similar, and aggregates them into a demographic cluster. Early models of this approach lumped people into very general categories by gender, ethnicity, education and income level. Current models are more sophisticated with categories such as soccer moms, NASCAR dads, and underemployed knowledge workers. Now political messages are targeted at specific clusters. These messages are delivered by better focused media. The analysis is more sophisticated, the view of human behavior is enriched, yet the complexities of voter influence and action are still under-represented.

A third model of the voter has emerged. Political scientists studying the voting behavior and outcomes of the presidential elections of 1988 through 2000 are seeing a more complex model. This is the *social voter* — modern citizens do not make decisions in a social vacuum. *Who we know* influences *what we know* and *how we feel* about it. After controlling for personal attitudes and demographic membership, researchers found social networks, that voters are embedded in, exert powerful influences on their voting behavior.

Very few people are social isolates that would fit the simple model of the atomized or demographic voter whose only interaction is with mass media. Most voters have interactions with a diverse set of others including family, friends, neighbors, co-workers, members of their place of worship, and acquaintances. We do not merely act on information we receive directly from the media. We get new information, interpretation, re-interpretation and influence via our social networks. It's the connections, stupid!

**Voter Participation**

Voter participation has been a concern in American politics. The United States is fifteenth amongst major countries in the percentage of voting-eligible citizens who actually vote. Often, those eligible to vote, do not register, or are registered and choose not to vote. A common excuse given is that a single vote does not count for much. We saw in the 2000 presidential election how the tipping point of the whole national outcome was determined by a few hundred local votes. The power of a single vote has never been so obvious. Another common excuse heard by those who are eligible, yet choose not to vote, is that there is no obvious difference between the candidates — they are all the same. A candidate that appeared acceptable during the campaign may turn out quite different after being elected. Those who pay more attention to mass media may get a homogenized view of the candidates. A final reason for not voting is often the personal circumstances of individual voters. Those suffering financial or emotional hardship — those out of work for too many months — have increasing difficulty participating in social and civic activities including voting. Also, it has been shown that populations who are regularly discriminated against have a more difficult time organizing and getting their views heard.

Research on voter participation in elections has revealed the importance of social networks. Voter turnout is highly correlated among family, friends, and co-workers. If those in your social network vote, and make that known, then there is a much higher probability that you will vote also. We are all influenced by those who we view as similar to us. We may adopt the actions of a similar others either through conformity or competition. To fit in with a group, we conform to the actions of others. To keep up with those we view as competitors, we mimic their behavior so as not to be left behind.

Trends in groups often start with one or a few persons taking a stand. Expressing your intent on voting in your network is one way to get other network members to the voting booth. Imitating those we like and respect, and keeping up with others, are strong forces that ripple through social networks. If everyone in your network holds similar political views [not always the case], then expressing your intent to vote is a powerful lever for your favorite candidate or issue.

Recent research in social networks has shown that human networks tend to follow the small-world model. The way people connect results in clusters according to common interests, views, goals, or affiliations — small worlds of people with similar sentiments. Yet, clusters are not isolated from each one another. They are connected to each other by bridging ties — Person X in Group A works with Person Y in Group B. Some of these bridges are cross-cutting ties, or shortcuts, that minimize the distance between all clusters. Shortcuts between otherwise distant clusters are what make the world seem small — strangers in the mirror are closer then they appear to be.

Using the small-world model, researchers investigated the effect of a single person's decision to vote. The person's influence spread throughout their local cluster. People were 15 percent more likely to vote if one of their political discussants made clear their intentions to vote. Within the research population a citizen would positively affect the turnout decision of up to four other people. The researchers called this a "turnout cascade". In addition, the increased turnout was found to favor the candidate of the initiator. Human clusters tend to contain similar preferences for candidates and issues, thus an increase in participation was equivalent to an increase in between two and three votes for the candidate. Denser clusters tended to show higher rates of voter participation.

In clusters where similar views were not predominant, the turnout cascades had neutral or negative effects for the cascade initiator's preferred candidate. Cascades could also influence abstention from voting. The researchers found that either voting behavior, participate or abstain, had similar imitation rates.

Turnout cascades were not just local phenomenon. Under the right conditions, they extended to indirect links also. Not only were the political discussants of the cascade initiator affected, but so where the discussant's discussants. Clusters with ties to other clumps in the network, where similar opinions may predominate, will find their influence ripple to those clusters.

# Figure 1 - Voter Participation

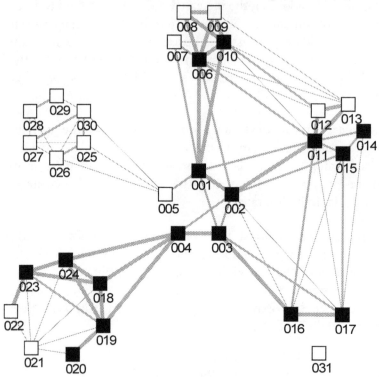

Figure 1 shows a small network focused around a political discussions taking place at work. The cluster in the middle [nodes 001-005] are the co-workers. They are connected by a grey link if they discuss political issues and candidates – a thicker line indicates more frequent interaction. The clusters around this work group are friends and family[F&F] of each employee who also have political discussions. Some of the F&F on the right side of the chart know each other [i.e. employee 002's F&F interact with the F&F of employees 001 and 003].

A node is shaded if the person has made public their intention to vote in the upcoming election. A node without shading has made no public declaration of participating in the upcoming election.

Figure 1 shows a small-world network of voters. The cluster in the middle is a group colleagues who discuss politics at work. Around the edges are clusters of friends and family of each of the employees. Two persons/nodes are connected if they have discussed politics in the last month. A thicker link indicates more frequent discussions of politics. A node is colored black if the person has announced the intent to vote, a node is colored white if the person has shown apathy or announced the intent to abstain from this year's election. A node is grey if no public decision has been made. Those clusters where the majority indicate their intent to vote will likely have all members in voting booths on election day.

Groups influence the behavior of their members. Key opinion leaders, and experts, also hold the power to persuade. Often we may know experts who have spent considerable time gathering and analyzing information on a particular topic or person. We use these persons as shortcuts and filters for our own decision-making. The implicit payment for the expert's political knowledge is pressure to participate in the voting process. Research has shown that those who regularly talk to political experts are more likely to participate in campaigns and to vote. Those with links to the experts may be key conduits of privileged information back to their own social network , thus making them a local expert and passing the influence on locally. The diffusion of influence is more likely if the group holds both the original and local expert in high regard.

### Voter Choice

We all belong to multiple networks. Some by choice — family and friends, and others by circumstance — work and neighborhood. This results in interesting connections across clusters. Not only do we receive information from those in our network, but we are more likely to use it. Each of these networks influence our thinking, opinions and choices. Common wisdom expects all people in a single network, or cluster to vote for the same candidate. Evaluation of voter selections in the 2000 presidential election found that not to be true. Researchers estimated that only one-third of the voters who chose George W. Bush or Al Gore were in homogeneous networks where all members made the same choice. The remainder of the voters for each candidate were in mixed networks where political disagreement was present and obvious. These clusters showed various combinations of support for the candidates. They provided opportunity for influence, change, and defection. Many voters changed their choice via discussions in the network. Initial support for a candidate did not last — even back and forth choices were documented.

Do all networks we are members of influence us equally? The research varies in this regard. There is no simple answer or common thread across all circumstances. It is expected that stronger ties would create stronger influence. Indeed the strongest influence occurs within family boundaries. Social influence among married pairs is very high. Our expectation is that influence along strong ties continues to friendships also. Here the data is mixed. Some research confirms the expectation that friends influence friends in political choices. Other research shows that political disagreement can be found amongst friends — all friends don't agree on political matters. The unexpected finding is explained via the different dynamics at play in friendships and political influence. We choose friends on many different criteria, including their opinions. We like our friends despite their political knowledge or opinions. Other research confirms the expected result that close friends influence each other on many choices including political candidates and issues. This affect appears to intensify in closed networks that have few connections to other clusters with different opinions and information.

A somewhat surprising finding is the strong affect that neighbors and other casual acquaintances can have on political choice. These connections can bring the voter information that is not available in their denser and more homogeneous family and friends networks. Neighborhoods, especially suburban bedroom communities, can be a meeting place of many diverse networks and information flows. We choose our neighborhoods for the school system, transportation efficiency, attributes of a particular house, and general cues such as a "neighborhood with school age kids". We do not interview all of the neighbors before making the down payment on our new house or signing a lease on an apartment. Therefore we often move into a neighborhood of others who are strangers to us. They are connected to networks of families, friends, and co-workers different than ours. In addition we bring in even more new connections to the neighborhood milieu. Neighborhoods are places where people will hear information and opinions that are likely to be different than those they hear at family occasions, at work, and at their place of worship. But, does this new information influence choices and opinions?

Not all neighbors become involved in the neighborhood. Some individuals and families in neighborhoods maintain very weak ties with their neighbors. They greet them on the street, or at the mailbox, may discuss the weather, but otherwise spend time with their original networks of family, friends, and co-workers outside of the neighborhood. Other individuals and families become more involved in the neighborhood. They help their neighbors, visit with them in their homes, have children that play together, or otherwise include the neighbors in their extended social network. These relationships were found to influence political choices. Especially if the neighbor had provided useful non-political information in the past.

The research into neighborhood affects of political influence reveal a dynamic that also shows up elsewhere. People with strong experience or expertise in political matters do not seek opinions nor are they strongly influence by the ones they hear. It appears that we are influenced by our social networks in various choices, but that influence is mitigated by individual thresholds of knowledge and experience. Your neighbor may be open to a lawn fertilizer recommendation because this is their first home with a lawn. But this same neighbor may ignore all political advice because of their past experience on political campaigns or seeking political office. One threshold for new information is low, while the threshold for other information is very high.

Not only do individuals have thresholds, but communities and networks also have thresholds. These are barriers to minor opinions taking hold. Opinions and information that run counter to the dominant view within the network are usually dismissed. Yet, in a network that contains many undecided voters and where the dominant view is held by much less than 50 percent of the total population can still be turned to support the previously minority view.

What happens to those who hold minority views in a cluster or community? Are they eventually converted to the majority opinion? Not if they have a high threshold for their opinion. Regardless of threshold, whether high or low, they will likely maintain that minority view if they have support for that view elsewhere in the cluster or outside of it. Research shows that support for a holder of a minority view does not need to be massive. Often just one link to someone who agrees, who says "It's OK" is all that is necessary to maintain minority views even in the face of majority efforts to convert. This support is especially necessary for a person to follow through on their views — to actually vote. An unsupported person may maintain their views, but is less likely to act on them. If a minority opinion holder can find just one person in their social network that echoes their stand they are much more likely to follow through, take action and vote on their beliefs. It appears that voters supporting third-party candidates especially need this support to overcome the uncommon behavior of voting outside of the two parties and of the prospect of wasting their vote. Almost 50 percent of those who supported the third party candidate in the 1992 presidential election did not actually vote for him. They either voted for a major party candidate or chose not to vote at all. Why? They had no one in their political discussion networks that supported their view. Social isolation, or the appearance of it, is a strong force, especially where personal thresholds are not high. Failing to find social support in their immediate social network, supporters of third-party candidates may conclude that the third-party cause is hopeless.

A person grossly outnumbered at work, or in their neighborhood, will maintain their support for a candidate or issue, if friends or family support their views. Not only are strong ties viable support mechanisms, certain weak ties can also support deviant views. Weak ties are significant support links if we need support for views different from our family and friends. Weak ties are usually established with others in clusters different than our own. These weak ties bring us information and views that are likely to be much different than those in our local cluster. In addition to bringing diverse viewpoints, the weak ties support them also. Weak ties are con-nections to people we know but do not interact with frequently. They do not extend to those who are basically strangers to us. We may be aware of someone, or had a superficial interaction with them, but that does not mean we have a weak tie to them. No evidence was found that strangers, or those with very superficial ties can support others with minority views.

The voter research found no apparent influence by strangers on citizen choice in political matters, the only exception being those of obvious political expertise. Interaction with public figures influenced both voter choice and participation. Shaking the candidates hand and getting your personal question answered obviously influences voters. Interaction with other known political elites has a similar affect.

## Influencing Voters

How does a campaign use social networks to influence voters on choosing their candidate or issue and then following up the choice with action by participating in the election? The network in Figure 2 shows the small-world voter network but this time the voters/nodes are colored by their initial political choice. Those choosing the Republication candidate are red, those choosing the Democrat are blue, those undecided are white and those leaning toward a third party candidate are grey.

# Figure 2 - Voters Initial Choices

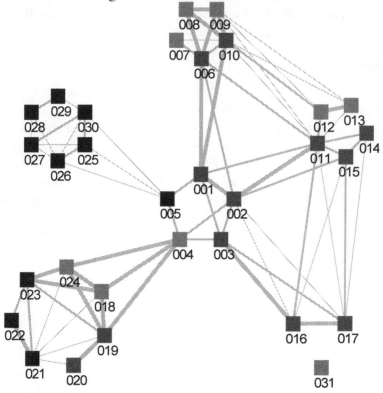

*Figure 2 shows the same network as Figure 1, but now the nodes are color coded by their current choice on who they will vote for President. Nodes in blue are choosing the Democrat, nodes in red are voting for the Republican, and the grey nodes are undecided or choosing an Independent candidate.*

We see many interactions amongst people with similar views. Yet, some who apparently disagree, are also interacting. Those who face disagreement at work, get support for their views from F&F.

Node 031 is an isolate in political conversations. Though 031 is a friend of 003, they talk about other matters, not politics – 031 has expressed a disdain for political discussions. Node 031 may be one of those rare individuals that get a majority of their political insights and opinions from mass media.

We will use five rules we learned from the recent research in presidential elections.

1.  One can increase voter participation by announcing plans to to vote. One must do this in a community that is predisposed to your candidate.

2.  Find communities that don't have a majority for the other candidate. Build connections to undecided voters and those who support your view. Aim for one or more ties to all supporting your candidate. These are the key battlegrounds in elections. See clusters in Figure 2 above.

3.  Scan communities that do have a majority for the other candidate for anyone supporting your candidate. Build at least one supporting tie to each person leaning toward your candidate

4.  If you are well integrated in your neighborhood, and are known for providing useful advice to neighbors then consider talking to them about your candidate. Also put out a yard sign supporting your candidate, and suggest others do so.

5.  Unless they are public figures, strangers do not influence. Instead of having strangers call voters, or knock on doors, the campaign should find well-connected supporters and have them go out into their clusters [workplaces, places of worship, neighborhoods, sports leagues, etc.] building support for the candidate. Bringing in masses of campaign workers, who are strangers, to contact local voters may cause more harm than good. This may have been part of the cause in the collapse of the 2004 Dean campaign in Iowa. The Dean campaign had a strategy called the Dean Storm — they would fly in people from across the country who they had recruited on the Internet. These outsiders would then go out into the public to persuade caucus participants. The Kerry campaign had a more successful strategy, and an apparently better understanding of social networks. The Kerry campaign connected to local politicians who had already build local influence networks over the years.

The Kerry people had friends, neighbors, and co-workers influencing each other, and a surprising victory.

Figure 3 - Clusters of Voters

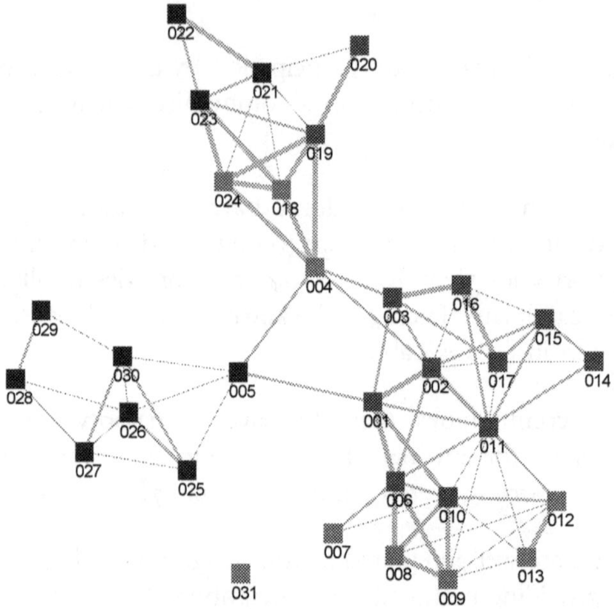

Figure 3 shows the same network as Figure 2 – all of the same people are connected to the same others. Now the nodes are arranged according to the emergent structure of the network – into clusters based on connections. The network topology is determined by who is connected to whom, both directly and indirectly. This shows a more accurate picture of the group structure. Notice the more obvious clustering of like nodes.

This emergent structure also gives us a better read on the voters 'in play' – the grey nodes. In addition to isolate 031, we see two clusters of grey nodes:

004, 018, 024

Which are the nodes the Blues should each focus on? Which are the nodes the Blues should each focus on? Is there one group that both would go after? Is it worth pursuing the isolate? Where is the most likely location for a cascade?

Obviously the social network approach to voter influence is not something that can be centrally planned like a big media campaign. The social network strategy is a local phenomenon. It is a face-to-face strategy supported by phone and internet. It is one-to-one, not one-to-many as big media efforts are. A campaign can give advice, outline the strategy, and provide talking points but it must be executed by individuals working locally for the candidate or issue. The social network strategy allows citizens to get involved in campaigns around issues and candidates they support. Citizens get involved on a level where they can influence others in their various social clusters.

How do you build networks of engagement? Beginning to build the network during the campaign may be a poor strategy. Just like the newly unemployed executive 'networking' for a new job comes across awkward and is often unsuccessful. So is the political campaign making big last minute moves. Networks are better formed when they are not immediately necessary. Networks take time to build and ties are easier to form when there isn't an obvious transaction immediately behind them.

The network strategy does not require a large war chest of political contributions. It does require time and energy and understanding of the social dynamics described above. The individual voter or political activist who builds a strong political network finds that this network is useful outside of campaigns. In fact a network that accomplishes many goals for its members may be ideal for political persuasion because the trust and affinity levels are high in such networks. Such networks are not viewed with suspicion — "Oh oh it's an election year and here comes my every two year friend with a big smile."

All politics are local. Citizens interact with those they know best, and have the most influence over. We make sense of the world and all of the information and data we receive through conversations with trusted others. Only the simplest decisions are made on information and logic alone — this toothpaste is 50¢ cheaper, I will buy it. Most important decisions are not made in a social vacuum. Who we vote for, what neighborhood we live in, what car we drive, which doctor/lawyer/plumber we use, how we see world events are decisions that are adjusted and refined through our social networks. We make sense of the world through conversations that mix various viewpoints, information sources and feedback. The election is a conversation, not a data flow.

# The Calculus of Political Power
# Mitch Ratcliffe

Networks and their effects on human relationships have been the subject of intense study for only a few years, but theorists propose a wide range of rules that describe the behavior of connected people, networked groups and organizations. These laws are double-edged blades for the aspiring social theorist since a "law" in the scientific sense when applied to groups of people is an appeal to reason in nature that may not exist in the population one is describing, because people can act irrationally or inconsistently in similar circumstances. The laws discussed in this essay are valuable because they are descriptive and can be used in retrospect to understand human events, but should not be understood as proscriptive of human behavior. Albert Camus wrote that when Lucretius first suggested that atoms clump to together randomly to form matter "the great problem of modern times arises: the discovery that to rescue man from destiny is to deliver him to chance." If the laws discussed here are to become useful in the socio-political arena, they need to be refined into a tool for increasing the probability that, given a knowledge of one's, or a collective group's, resources, informed decisions about how to accomplish a social goal can be based on the analysis of the social networks in which that person or group exists.

It is early and reductive to suggest that any of the rules suggested by network researchers guide our behavior to a significant degree, yet that is the tendency among many of the more influential contributors to this discussion. Despite the fact that the mathematics of networks are generally couched in value-neutrality, the absence of influence and the notion of frictionless transaction, they are projected onto a value-filled social networks of influence characterized by many forms of friction. What we shall see, however, is that network theory is useful, because it highlights the singular importance of influence and leadership within social and political networks.

Let us begin with the idea of scale[82], which in mathematics describes the place of any numerical expression relative to a chosen base. For example, a base ten system, the scale describing any value is demarcated by 10s; think of a topological map, on which a mountain range's height can be determined by counting the number of lines from the base elevation and multiplying the steps by the number of feet they represent. In social situations, we can think of scale as the number of steps it takes to accomplish a goal, how many people in city hall do you have to talk to in order to get your sidewalk repaired? How many people can fit into the local Starbucks before you have to build another one? Scaling issues are very important to any investment of social, political or economic capital, because if an additional step forward takes more effort than each additional step saves, society or your investments starting two steps back for each step forward. The critical mistake for many investors and managers working at Internet companies during the bubble years was assuming that any investment would pay itself back in multiples, when, in fact, many of the steps companies took led to low-revenue customers who weren't willing to pay a premium for the convenience of, for example, buying dog food on the Web.

In political networks, we are familiar with and react against the notion of power as exercised by individuals for their own benefit. Everyone has a story of a politician who, seeing only their own wellbeing, sacrificed the common good to maintain their power and privilege. Everyone knows someone who has monopolized connections for their benefit at the expense of others. Everyone knows any number of abuses. But experience does prove that people tend to remember the affronts to good behavior more often than good behavior when they have little at stake. On the contrary, when there is something at stake, such as in a lottery or at the craps table, people focus on the few moments of good luck. You've seen people win in Las Vegas, right? You remember those moments more than the losses, because we want to win or see people win; we want the best for others or we might envy their success. Casinos, like the mediascape, are designed to enhance the impression of success. When a player at the craps table is handed the dice, the chances are only 2.675 percent that they will be able to set a point on the first

[82] Barabási, Albert-László, Linked, How Everything Is Connected to Everything Else and What It means for Business, Science, and Everyday Life, Plume Penguin, 2003. P. 70.

role and throw a seven to win on the subsequent roll.[83] Awful chances, but the room is open and carries sound well in order to broadcast the sound of success from one of the hundred tables in the casino, along with the ringing bells of slot machines, all to reinforce the sense that everyone wins at least some of the time. This reduces the sense that the odds are against you, just as intense media coverage of unusual stories of bad works, good works, luck and profit (especially the state lottery, which features a winner on the weekly drawing, but ignores the millions of losers).

Yet good people do step up regularly and volunteer for the good of others. Cincinnatus, a patrician farmer, was called to be dictator of Rome and set the example for the office, which held total power, by finishing the task of defending Rome and foregoing power to return to his farm. Livy relates this act thousands of years later and it seems extraordinary, but people make these kinds of selfless sacrifices in many ways all the time. Total power is in our hands on many occasions, over life and death, promotion and being stuck in a dead-end job, and the ability to make life better or worse for others while our privileged situation is unaffected. Perception has everything to do with the use to which we put our networks, and that is what is missing from the analysis by most network theories.

There is an important distinction between the notion of a mass media and an egalitarian press controlled by many different contributors. The mass media, which Clay Shirky described as "media we've gotten used to,"[84] is much more than the information and entertainment sources with which we are familiar and comfortable. It is an institutional

---

[83] Krigman, Alan, Why It's Easy to Believe Rare Events Happen All the Time, Casino City Times, July 8, 2003: "The likelihood that a shooter will establish a point and throw a seven on the subsequent roll is 24/36 multiplied by 6/36. This equals 11.11 percent. In round numbers, it's 11 chances out of 100 for any shooter. And the probability it'll take place several times in a row is 12 out of 1,000 for two, 14 out of 10,000 for three, and 15 out of 100,000 for four. Chances are lower of Come bettors getting up on three numbers in consecutive rolls, then striking out on the fourth. Probability is 2.675 percent. This is roughly 27 chances out of 1,000 for any shooter, 7 out of 10,000 for two in a row, and 2 out of 100,000 for a terrible trifecta."

[84] Shirky, Clay, Power Laws, Weblogs, and Inequality, http://shirky.com/writings/powerlaw-weblog.html, February 10, 2003

structure owned by relatively few people who exercise a heavy hand on the tone and scope of coverage. It is a significant locus of power and funding for the research that produces excellent journalism — the owner of a major media empire can cut budgets for programming with which it disagrees. These owners are often a single family or a tightly knit group of investors, because the press and broadcasting businesses have their genesis in a kind of cottage industry in which small players accumulated distribution points. In broadcasting, one or more of the limited number of spectrum licenses available in a region or in print, one of the few viable economic niches in a market for expensive general coverage publications. The Cumulus Media decision to remove the band The Dixie Chicks from airplay after the singers criticized American foreign policy on stage was issued by the executives of the company ostensibly because of consumer demand. But, under examination by Senator John McCain of Arizona, Lewis W. Dickey Jr., chairman of Cumulus Media, admitted that if the decision had been handled democratically, local station managers would have been free to make the call themselves; meanwhile, the Dixie Chicks album sales skyrocketed, demonstrating there was no general consumer consensus about the band.

It is accurate to describe the mass media as autocratic. Clay Shirky suggests that some webloggers, writers of easy-to-update Web sites who tend to focus on narrow areas of interest, will "join the mainstream media.... as a blogger's audience grows large, more people read her work than she can possibly read, she can't link to everyone who wants attention, and she can't answer all her incoming mail or follow up to comments on her site." This presumes a very rigid definition of what "blogging is," which contradicts Shirky's other claim that "blogging will stop referring to any particularly coherent activity," while underscoring the salient characteristic of mainstream media: it is unresponsive or, more accurately, staff is not paid to be responsive and must concentrate on filling available page space or broadcast time rather than taking time to reflect and debate with the audience. This has been the rule in commercial media except at a few extraordinary moments in history, such as the heyday of CBS News or the Washington Post's risk-taking on the coverage of Watergate under Katherine Graham's stewardship of the paper. What is known as "enterprise reporting" these days, which is just old-fashioned research, which takes time and money, is a rare beast in the media menagerie.

A network's power and efficacy, then, is in large part the result of leadership and economic backing for particular ideas or, switching to the mechanics of connectivity, creation of important hubs that can influence the availability of resources needed to collect information. Most network theorists start from the suggestion that the capability of a node in a network is essentially equal and that is true if one ignores how a node can be augmented to increase its influence in the network.

According to physicist and network researcher Albert-László Barabási:

> "In a random network the peak of distribution implies that the vast majority of nodes have the same number of links and that nodes deviating from the average are extremely rare. Therefore, a random network has a characteristic scale in its node connectivity, embodied by the average node and fixed peak of the degree distribution. In contrast the average nod and fixed by the peak of the degree distribution implies that in a real network there is no such thing as a characteristic node. We see a continuous hierarchy of nodes, spanning the rare hubs to the numerous tiny nodes. The largest hub is closely followed by two or three somewhat smaller hubs, followed by dozens that are even smaller, and so on, eventually arriving at the numerous small nodes."

This paragraph from Barabási's book, *Linked*, describes the full range of phenomena at the center of network research today. Many network theorists argue scale is eliminated in dynamic networks, that these systems are "scale-free" and can add new nodes without incurring any additional inefficiency or cost in terms of the complexity users of the network must undertake to use the network.

Key to Barabási's argument is that because of power laws, the predictable pattern of connections within a network that ensure some nodes will rise to the top, visits to the most-trafficked node will exceed the traffic of the next by an order of magnitude and the rest trailing off rapidly into a large population of nodes with relatively few connections and very little traffic. In a graph, it looks like this:

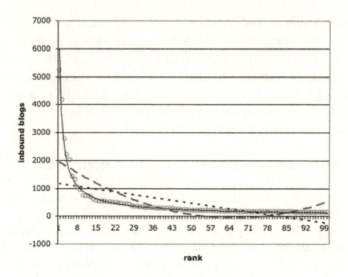

Figure 1: Technorati link
distribution. Source: Jason Kottke,
Kottke.org

Barabási and Clay Shirky[85] argue that this distribution is inevitable and it is if you consider only the connections and not the context of the connections within a network. The assumption is that any new player in a network will benefit from emerging early and enduring, wracking up additional connections and influence through a dogged determination to succeed or deep pockets — an echo of the Internet bubble era idea that if you build an audience it will eventually become profitable. The power law is a phenomenon of the whole, but not the specific way that

---

[85] Shirky, Clay, Power Laws, Weblogs, and Inequality,
http://shirky.com/writings/powerlaw-weblog.html, February 10, 2003:
"Inequality occurs in large and unconstrained social systems for the same reasons stop-and-go traffic occurs on busy roads, not because anyone's goal, but because it is a reliable property that emerges from the normal functioning of the system." What this fails to acknowledge metaphorically is that no one moves fast in a traffic jam, except those who have prepared to do so, by taking a rider along if a carpool lane is available; otherwise, everyone sits in traffic. It is simplistic to reduce the argument to this kind of metaphor and I acknowledge Clay Shirky's basic point that there are differences in the distribution of links within a network, but I do not agree they are permanent qualities of the early participants in a network that remain defiantly advantaged if they simply continue to play their role in the network.

people rely on networks for communication and information. The power law graph is discouraging to look at, because it implies an inequality that, once established, seems insurmountably permanent for newcomers to the network who might want to exercise influence and power. However, it is precisely the will to exercise influence and power that can set a "node," an individual in a densely connected society apart as a contender for leadership.

Why should the insurmountable curve of the power law be susceptible to conquest? The answer lies in the visualization and statistical limitations of a two-dimensional view of a network. When we draw a network, it invariable looks like a flatland with nodes distributed across its face (see Figure 2), when there is a third variable that adds a real-world dimension that makes the single peak of the power law an impossibility.

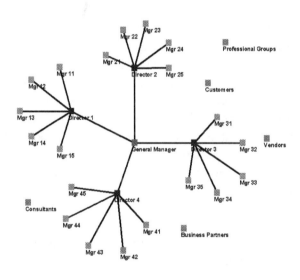

*Figure 2: Network Mapping*
*Source: Valdis Krebs, Orgnet.com[86]*

---

[86] http://www.orgnet.com/decisions.html

Two-dimensional analysis focuses attention on the connections without providing the flavor of those connections. By stripping the links of their meaning, the analysis of networks suggests that all links are equal. Barabási writes that modeling a growing network is a relatively straightforward exercise because "[a]t each moment all nodes have an equal chance to be linked to, resulting in a clear advantage for senior nodes."[87] This aptly describes what happens in the random networks, which Barabási says are not guaranteed to produce highly ordered networks, yet they often do. The reason is, he acknowledges, is that there is competition for links between nodes in a network. Competition is based on differentiation between what nodes have to offer, otherwise the choice between any two nodes in the network would be irrelevant and random because any choice would provide the same results.

Nevertheless, Barabási's early research focused solely on the number of links possessed by any node in the network. This leads to an oversimplification of network topologies, because, it seems to me, he wants to generalize about the applications of his research.[88] One of the most important ideas Barabási concentrates on is the notion of hubs that link nodes in a network. Google is his most prominent example of an Internet node and in the software business (and economics in general), he puts forth the idea that the rich-get-richer is an enduring law, using Microsoft as an example of a company that owns the entire market. Certainly, those with the capital to invest are better positioned to get richer, but the fact that markets are made up of people who lose the money others gain suggests that the rich who bet everything on one idea, one company or one node in a networked economy are more likely to get poorer — portfolio theory, which urges diversification on investors, proves this conclusively.

Network theory, however, concentrates on specific instances of connectivity rather than the general experience of living in a network; it

---

[87] Barabási, p. 83

[88] Barabási, p. 80: "If two networks as different as the Web and the Hollywood acting community both display power-law degree distribution, then some universal law or mechanism must be responsible. If such a law existed, it could potentially apply to all networks." For a field that is only about a half decade old, the establishment of a law that defines all networks is creating a kind of dogma that must be defended.

is quantum mechanics to the largely Newtonian world we exist in. This makes the reading of network theory a landmine for anyone inclined to apply analogy or metaphor promiscuously, because Barabási and others, in an attempt to generalize their laws, apply a shifting definition of "nodes" and "links" that conflate two very different types of networks. Though there are similarities between the ways networks grow, the way a physical network built on actual connections between points in space and time and the way that a network of relationships between people develops and endures are very, very different.

## Physical versus logical; growth versus evolution

Physical networks grow through interconnections that are largely scale-free for two reasons: there are always new nodes coming online and the geometric increase in the capacity of copper and fiber optic cables and switching semiconductor equipment erase the friction that would slow the delivery of data as the network grows. If the progress of Moore's Law, which describes the constant doubling of computer capacity and halving of pricing of components every 18 months, were not an integral part of the technology environment the Internet would never have been built; it would have been too expensive and too slow. Anyone who has used a personal computer for more than two years while continuing to upgrade the software that runs on the PC knows the slowing performance of aging information technology. The Internet was built on waves of innovation that, to many, appeared frivolously expensive, yet those sunk costs got us what we have today and it is a very good thing.

But what, exactly, is a "link" on the Internet? Is it a physical connection between two sites or the logical connection between information on two Web sites? It is both, actually. The example of Google as a hub of connections is misleading, because it is doing nothing more than examining the Web for the number of sites making logical links to particular sites in order to assemble a one-stop location for finding the information most often linked to by others. Remove Google and there is no severing of connections between the sites Google is pointing to, only the link from the Google search results to the target information is lost.

A physical connection, or more accurately several physical connections made this Web of logical links possible, but they exist at another lower level of connectivity that provides the foundation on which all the informational or "virtual" structures of the Internet are constructed.

Mapping the physical Internet and the logical Web produces an overlay that look largely similar, because Web sites and services that are most heavily trafficked tend to sit on or near the largest interconnections of physical networks. This ensures better performance, but it creates the misleading impression that the two kinds of links are the same thing. Physical networks, however, are expensive to build and maintain; they tend to stay largely intact and, while other links grow around existing physical links, the system has a sedimentary quality that gives it the permanence of an ancient seabed while logical networks flow like water above.

Why Google is successful tells us much more about the nature of the logical network. Google came into the market late and well behind the established players, Inktomi, which provided search results of Yahoo!, AltaVista and several other large search engines. Today, Google surpassed Inktomi in a few years and replaced it as Yahoo!'s search provider, only to see Yahoo! buy Inktomi when Google's business became a threat and restore Inktomi as its search engine. Barabási attributes Google's "new kid on the block" success to its "fitness," which he describes using the analogy of the social environment in which people who are more able to make friends produce larger social networks. Today, it is the most connected node of the network, because people point to a variety of types of Google search results.

"The fitness model predicts a very different behavior [than the scale-free network model]," Barabási writes. "It tells us that nodes still acquire links following a power law, $t^b$." That is, a node's connectivity increases as a function of time, though the pace of growth is a function of how early the node joined the network, according to the rich-get-richer model. But in the fitness model, "the dynamic exponent, b, which measures how fast a node grabs new links, is different for each node. It is proportional to the node's fitness, such that a node that is twice as fit as any other node will acquire links faster because its dynamic exponent is twice as large. Therefore, the speed at which nodes acquire links is no longer a matter of seniority."

What has happened to Barabási's formula is that everything has become dynamic. From an analytical perspective, it can describe anything, which isn't very useful, since the nature of fitness is vague. It has none of the virtue of Einstein's $E=mc2$ which very specifically describes the amount of energy in any body of matter (there is a whole lot more than anyone thought). The age of a node will differ and its fitness will differ, so that every node performs differently and, because the fitness of a node can be manipulated, the system will not behave predictably. If I invest in building my node of a social network based on these vague dynamic variables, I have no indication what I will get, because fitness, especially, can be augmented in a number of ways, from making one's node more prominent to those who might know about it (marketing) to publishing a seminal article that gets picked up and pointed to by many other sites (luck); both require an investment, but I cannot hope to know what the result will be, since so many undefined factors, such as the influence of other events of the day when I market or publish my paper could distract the world. Woe to the airline mileage program credit card that launched on September 11, 2001, for example.

What is useful to know based on Barabási's model is that no node is ensured success or doomed to obscurity in this model, which brings us unavoidably to the realm of the real world, where cunning, skill, brute force and all sorts of characteristics can change the outcome of a competition. From the perspective of the emergent polity or any other self-organizing entity, this is where the rubber meets the road and any predictions about what will come to pass in an evolving network are fruitless without God-like perfect knowledge.

We can learn from market-based solutions that the whole system does not matter, only the choices we make in specific circumstances. Lanchester's First Law, developed to guide combat planning at the dawn of the air age by British engineer Frederick Lanchester, is a pragmatic approach to choosing a path to success in a complex system, especially where there are stronger competitors. It doesn't guarantee success, but provides guidance.

Lanchester, who was trying to figure out how the British air force could win in a totally new battle environment narrowed the difference between two forces of equal size to the efficiency of their weapons. Winning depends on the fitness of the army's weapons for destroying their opponents, the reverse image of Barabási's fitness for making connections. Google's weapon, even though it was vastly outnumbered in terms of existing connections, was much more efficient than its competitors because of its constantly evolving search algorithms, which reduced the gaming of search results that other search engines suffered from since they focused on the content of sites rather than the links pointing at sites (in short, the utility identified by people who took the time to read pages and decide to link to them was scraped and aggregated by Google to provide more efficacious search results). Google compounded the efficiency of its search engine with a set of application programming interfaces that allowed programmers to use Google as a platform for adding Web search to their applications. The result was easily predictable based on Lanchester's First law. Therefore, Lanchester-based strategies, which have proved effective in warfare and marketing, are a more reliable approach than a dynamic variable that could describe any number of actual characteristics of a node on a network.

A second rule for planning combat based on Lanchester's theories, which has been applied by Japanese businesses in marketing with significant success, is the Law of Stochastic Warfare derived from scenarios in which weapons can fire randomly, allowing each member of a smaller force to kill more of the enemy in less time. In a nutshell, all the factors in the first law are squared, meaning that advantages in numbers, skill and weapons efficiency are amplified. But so are the costs of competing, since these weapons are more expensive. Google had solid venture capital backers who, seeing a powerful tool, gave Google the resources it needed to amplify the value of that tool in the marketplace, so that today Google is the most trafficked site on the Internet.

Finally, Lanchester's rules describe the scale problem that is inherent in any set of interactions. At a certain point, Lanchester equations suggest around 74 percent, it becomes more expensive to win new customers than those customers are worth. Competitors in niche markets pick off the customers who want, for example, better hardware designs (Apple) or more robust publishing tools (Adobe) and so on. Porsche, BMW and Lexus exist in similar niches of the automotive market. The evidence that Microsoft is well past that point with Windows is the low-cost licenses sold to PC manufacturers and the increasingly costly upgrades of those licenses made available to consumers. It is difficult to keep a Windows installation intact because the system is checking for changes to the hardware configuration to determine if it is running on the PC on which it was originally installed. This translates into a less pleasing experience for all Windows customers, meaning the company must pile additional features into its software to try to please everyone.

Here is where Barabási's conclusion about Microsoft, that "essentially Microsoft takes it all," is challenged. Networks seem to crave diversity or, at least, novelty, eating away at monopoly positions on small fronts rather than taking the whole monopoly position in one fell swoop. Microsoft knows that its position in the market is tenuous, because in order to take advantage of its 85 percent-plus market share it must hold the number-one position in each and every market it enters to justify the expense of its core monopoly. While the Windows operating system and Microsoft Office, the two dominant products Microsoft relies on to force its way into new markets, such as the Internet browser, email servers, Web servers, streaming media, and so forth, are robust and profitable, Microsoft loses money on virtually everything else it does. It must give away product to win market share, which it can do because it is a monopoly. Yet, as it gives away products it also lowers the price point it can charge for those products in the future once it has eliminated most competition. This has given rise to a low-cost approach to programming, open source software, that turns Microsoft's willingness to lower retail prices and raise future revenues from selling support, into a weapon that can be used against Microsoft in each of the markets it occupies. With open source software, users can download and modify application code to create robust alternatives to Microsoft products, often at no charge. The makers of open source software, usually distributed teams collaborating via the Net to assemble code much more rapidly than Microsoft ever could, is indicative of the small front challenges that can eat away at a dominant hub in the market.

Barabási and his colleagues searched high and low for formulas that could account for what he describes as the winner-take-all network and settled on the rather dense concept of the Bose-Einstein condensate, a physical phenomenon that was not observed until 1995 and yielded the observers a Nobel prize. A Bose-Einstein condensate occurs when you lower the temperature of matter very close to absolute zero and all particles condense at the lowest energy level, they become still and pile up at the center of a field like a mountain in the midst of a convoluted topographical region (Figure 3).

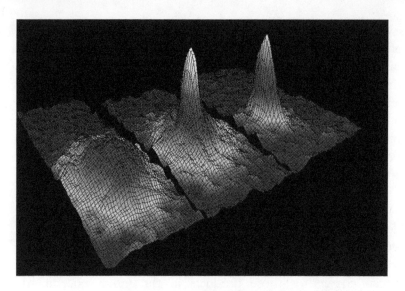

*Figure 3: Bose-Einstein condensate.*
*The white center, which rises as the*
*temperature is lowered from 400*
*billionths of a degree Kelvin (left)*
*to 200 billionths of degree (center)*
*and, ultimately to 50 billionths of a*
*degree above absolute zero, is the*
*densest concentration of particles.*
*Source: University of Colorado*
*Atomic Lab,*
*http://www.colorado.edu/physics*
*/2000/bec/three_peaks.html*

"...[S]ome networks can undergo Bose-Einstein condensation. The consequence of this prediction can be understood without knowing anything about quantum mechanics: It is, simply, that in some networks the winner can take it all. Just as in a Bose-Einstein condensate all particles crowd into the lowest energy level, leaving the rest of the energy levels unpopulated, in some networks the fittest node could theoretically grab all the links, leaving none for the rest of the nodes. The winner takes all.... Bianconi's calculation indicated that in terms of topology all networks fall into one of only two possible categories. In most networks the competition does not have an easily noticeable impact on the networks topology. In some networks, however, the winner takes all the links, a clear signature of Bose-Einstein condensation"[89]

This is a powerful analogy, but hardly descriptive of the roiling character of the exchange of information on the Internet. A network that became as still as the gases cooled to near absolute zero to create a Bose-Einstein condensate would be useless in a world where both people and physical connections are constantly changing, because it is the proverbial sure thing in which one node wins and always wins. The activity of adding new nodes on a network would never allow a network to approach the stasis that would erect a massive power law in the center of the network. Rather, it would tend toward dynamism that distributed the topology of connections and power more evenly. And it is this third dimension that provides a rich topology of peaks and valleys under normal circumstances that best describes why power laws are of limited importance to the functional destiny of any node on a network.

## Powerless law

Let us reexamine the notion of the power law in light of the third dimension and the way logical links are used by people on the Internet. A power law describes the blunt edge of the question of connectivity, measuring the number of links pointing to a site or the number of visits to a site. As Clay Shirky points out, any review of a the log files for a site will show that a few pages attract most of the traffic; this is partly an artifact of the design decisions made when the site was built, since the home or index page may be the first place people visit in order to orient themselves and find what new content they are looking for. Likewise, some pages will attract more links simply because they are more popular. In any case, the distribution will look the graph in Figure 1, above.

Imagine that we are looking now for another variable, this representing the ideological character of weblogs, which we will distribute across the base vector from left to right according to a simple assignment of sites to "left" or "right" categories. Some of each of the sites will be more popular and most less so, the result looking more like a normal bell curve (Figure 4). However, it is actually two power laws, one describing the popularity of left-leaning and the other of right-leaning weblogs,

---

[89] Barabási, p. 103-104

placed in opposition; in other words, power laws describe any one-dimensional distribution of network connectivity and the addition of another variable, ideology, produces a normal distribution of sites by popularity and ideology. In Figure 4, you will note that right-leaning sites have a few more sites that are popular than the left-leaning sites. This reflects the finding by Kevin A. Hill and John E. Hughes that although people who use the Internet for political activity tend to be more liberal, the right tends to produce more content.[90]

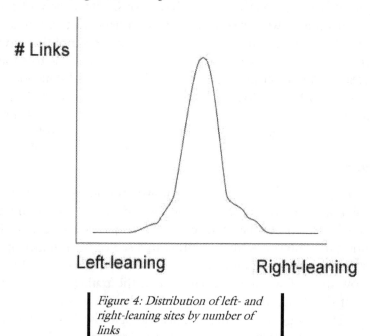

*Figure 4: Distribution of left- and right-leaning sites by number of links*

Of course, we know that there are far more grades of ideology than right- and left-leaningness, so being to think in three dimensions and the convoluted topology of the real Web begins to emerge from the details. Figure 5 (below) shows the distribution of ideology with a second ideological vector, describing sites as being left-libertarian or left-authoritarian and right-libertarian or right-authoritarian. This graph still does not show the traffic relating to different topics, only the

[90] Hill, Kevin A., and Hughes, John E., Cyberpolitics: Citizen Activism in the Age of the Internet, Rowan & Littlefield Publishers, Lanham, Maryland, 1998. P. 4.

distribution of traffic by two factors which could be applied to any topic, including abortion, the application of government power to redistributing wealth and teaching the Ten Commandments in school. We are still topic-neutral, although the values-related characteristics are beginning to pile up.

The sites described in figure five may represent any amount of traffic and could be blogs, portals or publications (hence the differently shaped dots), since the graph no longer accounts for the number of links these sites attract. It is as though one is looking down on a crowd of people who have separated themselves into quadrants based on their basic political orientation relative to the power of centralized government to enact social policy. Some of these sites may have hundreds of links that allow them to influence many people and others may be virtual hermits, albeit with strong opinions, isolated from virtually any interaction with other sites on the Web.

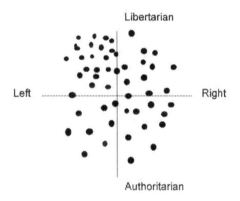

Figure 5: Distribution of ideology and views of the exercise of government power

It turns out that some of these sites are very strong connectors between their ideological neighbors and, in a few cases, bridging the boundaries between ideological groupings. These sites are the hubs, the "connectors" in the Malcolm Gladwell's terms,[91] that provide the glue that

---

[91] Gladwell, Malcolm, The Tipping Point, Little Brown & Co., Boston, 2002. Gladwell's description of how social trends are catalyzed relies on three key types of people, connectors, mavens and persuaders. Putting these three

holds society together and knits it anew each time the site ventures into a new topical area. (See Figure 6). These links, indicated in blue, are the conduits of public debate about the direction of society that can cause whole nations to slide in one political direction or another. They are as rare as a candidates' debate in terms of their statistical frequency and sit atop the power law graph in terms of their connectivity — they are everyone's source of information or friend, whether close or casual acquaintance, that they turn to for an introduction. Much of the actual discussion of social and political options happens in isolation from the hubs and is connected to opportunistically by hubs in order to wield influence. Hubs are in the position to lead in society, but don't necessarily do so, as we shall see later. They may have many connections or a few key links that allow them to bridge an existing barrier; this view is contrary to general view of hubs in network research, where it is assumed that a hub must have many connections. I argue that, especially in political situations, the ability to make a key connection is more important than having many connections, albeit having many available certainly gives the connector a larger inventory of options.

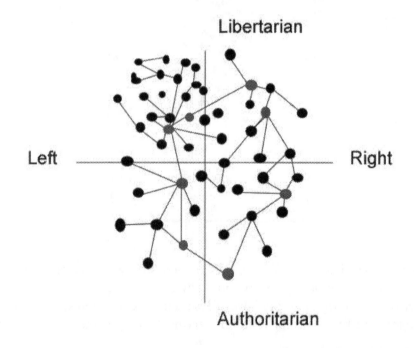

qualities together to raise the profile of a single Web site, brand or trend has powerful results.

Now, let's account for traffic. In Figure 7, red circles indicate the clusters of sites in the ideological scatter graph that represent the most traffic. These circles include several sites that are unconnected to other participants in the network webs described in Figure 6. Here is where we can begin to see the complexity of topic-based discussions, as there may be very popular ideological sites that fall into a particular range on this scatter graph but do not deal with an issue that is being discussed by many other sites. For example, the right-libertarian site that sits unconnected to any other node on the graph might be dedicated to fiscal responsibility and would not link to sites that are primarily concerned with social issues, such as abortion. Nevertheless, they represent important peaks in the distribution of traffic.

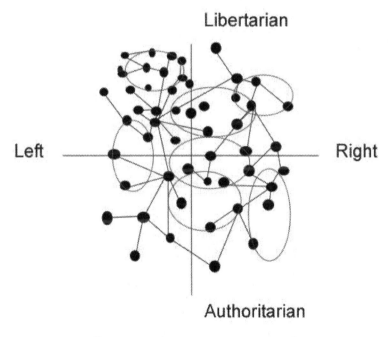

*Figure 7: Traffic concentrations among Left-Right, Libertarian-Authoritarian sites*

For ease of understanding, Figure 8 removes the network of sites and presents just the traffic concentrations on the two-ideology graph. You can see that there are two "twin peaks representing high-traffic sectors of the ideological spectrum indicated by the letters "A" and "B," and a two valleys indicated by the letters "C" and "D." Now, if you will look back at the rich topology of the Bose-Einstein condensate chart, particularly in the left, warmer field, you will see the origin of the many small peaks and valleys is quite clearly the multiplicity of issues and ideologies discussed on the Web. There may be sites about every conceivable variation of every topic, many of which sit at the bottom of valleys in the patterns of traffic, but there are also many peaks of popularity.

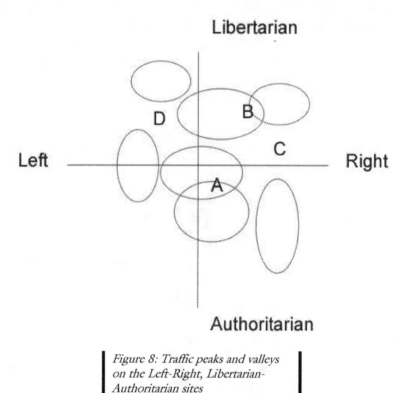

Figure 8: Traffic peaks and valleys
on the Left-Right, Libertarian-
Authoritarian sites

Compared to the mass media, which concentrate output and traffic in a few nodes, the many-dimension view of the densely networked environment of the Web presents many more opportunities for "local dominance" in traffic and influence regarding specific issues.

## Beyond statistics: The transformative value of human action

Here, let us return to some of the conclusions already being proposed by network theorists and reconsider them in the light of the many-dimensions view. I do not wish to suggest that there is something supernatural in networks which allows them to transcend physical laws, for I believe we are discovering many physical bases for human behavior. However, I do agree with philosopher Daniel Dennett and sociobiologist E.O. Wilson that human behavior is a dynamic combination of nature and nurture that produces extraordinary results within the confines of a largely deterministic world. We benefit from the fact that gravity exists and that networks tend to produce hubs that reduce the number of steps between any two points on the Web. It is very early, though, in our quest to understand networks and certain conclusions are premature.

Clay Shirky wrote "Inequality occurs in large and unconstrained social systems for the same reasons stop-and-go traffic occurs on busy roads, not because it's anyone's goal, but because it is a reliable property that emerges from the normal functioning of the system. The relatively egalitarian distribution of readers in the early years (of weblogging or, for that matter, the Web itself) had nothing to do with the nature of weblogs or webloggers. There just weren't enough blogs to have really unequal distribution." This comment was very controversial among webloggers, who understandably feel strongly about what they do. Shirky is right about one dimension of the problem, there is naturally going to be inequality in readership and traffic. He is wrong, however, about the nature of that inequality for three reasons:

1. Inequality in results in very different than inequality of opportunity. The nature of the Web, which facilitates easy and cheap logical connections between a wide variety of sites ensures that the difference in accessibility between any two sites is an order of magnitude smaller than the difference in reach between two mass media outlets. One need not gain distribution, as is the case in print and broadcast, to be heard; a single link can start a cascade of connections that elevate a particular author or just one article to the heights of popularity.

2. The fact that some Web upstarts will become employees of consumer media companies and, consequently, will adopt

different ethics, goals and styles that conform to their employer's priorities does not reflect on the nature of the network that elevated them to the attention of mass media. This is a process of cooptation of culture that is ongoing and, ultimately, is the result of individual decisions to conform. Just as there are popular writers and filmmakers who exist outside the mainstream media, there will be many Web content creators who content themselves with the longer, tougher road of building an large audience on their own terms.

3.  Individual sites do not scale to become general interest services without substantial investment. This has been true in mass media and, based on the evidence of eroding network viewership in broadcast and cable as audiences flee to niche channels or the Web, the increasingly specialized media will create an opportunity for the enmeshing of different audiences for specific topics to create meta-audiences that could, among other things, be a powerful political force, if mobilized to those ends.

Albert-László Barabási makes a number of statements that I agree with and several that do not make practical sense, I believe, because they are based on mathematics that relate to real life in the strange way quantum physics does. The plain fact that the spin of a particular particle can be affected by observing it does not translate to substantial changes in the gross phenomena in the world we live in and so it goes with network theory. Barabási makes a profoundly counter-intuitive leap from real life to the mathematics of connectivity when he writes:

> "The most intriguing result of our Web-mapping project was the *complete* [italics in orginal] absence of democracy, fairness, and egalitarian values on the Web. We learned that the topology of the Web prevents us from seeing anything but a mere handful of the billion documents out there.

> "When it comes to the Web, the key question is no longer whether your views can be published. They can. Once published, they will be instantaneously available to anyone around the world with an Internet connection. Rather, faced with a jungle of a billion documents, the question is, if you post information on the Web, well anybody notice it?"

He has obviously published, but Barabási has apparently never been a publisher. In mass media, specialized media or the Web, it is hard to get attention. As hard as writing, frankly, though I never gave my first publishers credit for what they could accomplish with my work. Then, I took on the job of publisher and learned that, while it is hard to gain attention, it is a skill that can be learned and applied, just like grammar and research skills, whether literary or scientific. In larger organization, particularly in general interest publishing or broadcasting companies, there is such a broad range of choices about what to publish or put on the air that most contributors compete for what space or time they get. This surplus of content acts to create sufficient impetus to keep audiences coming back, even if the offering of writers/contributors may be changing daily.

Clay Shirky's comment that beloved webloggers' sites would disappear if the bloggers stopped writing, meaning that no one would come to read them anymore, is dead-on. Building an audience outside of the mainstream press, where someone is always available to fill in if you can't work or if you are pursuing research that prevents you from writing, keeps people coming to the publication/network/site you work for, preserving your audience. It is not so when working alone in a niche category, nor can computer programmers rest on their laurels for even a minute if they don't have a massive organization pushing out other improvements while they take a sabbatical. Publisher Tim O'Reilly underscored this idea in his keynote at the Open Source Conference in Portland, Oregon in July 2003, when he said that in the current model of software development, there are people inside the software we use, who, if they stopped working to tune and update that software each day, would rapidly lose customers.[92]

The question, then, is not whether, having published, you'll be noticed, but how one organizes to be noticed and the tools at their disposal to keep the attention coming once it is turned, even momentarily toward a particular site or issue. Howard Dean's presidential campaign, for example, has used the Web with success to attract contributors and keep them both coming back and giving more as well as reaching out to others who might contribute even more. Dean is just one of the dozen or so "major" candidates and several hundred minor candidates

---

[92] Ratcliffe, Mitch, Report from the Open Source Conference, Correspondences.org, July 9, 2003:
http://www.correspondences.org/archives/000151

jockeying for contributions for a 2004 presidential run, but his organization has dedicated tremendous resources to creating an engaging experience for visitors to his site. Yet it is also feeling the strain of providing visitors and would-be supporters more than an initial rush of anti-George W. Bush rhetoric. It remains to be seen, at this writing, whether Dean will catalyze a movement or simply ignite a sense of rebelliousness. Google preserves its traffic and extends it by adding new features to its search constantly. Microsoft piles features into its gigabytes of application and operating system software, hoping to be all things to all people. Heft is an advantage and those with the wealth to buy attention do stand a better chance of getting richer, but they don't any type of guarantee in the sense that the network is suddenly going to cool down into a Bose-Einstein condensate of perpetual traffic and revenue streams.

The upstart needs to learn to see beyond the power laws to the simple insight mass media already possesses: Just get something up on the site according to a schedule your audience wants and make sure it is good, in the sense that you define good. An entertaining column by Dave Barry becomes a regular destination in the newspaper or on the Web, just as the comments of a Glenn Reynolds (InstaPundit and now an MSNBC columnist/blogger) have become for Web surfers. If Dave Barry stops, he might make a comeback some years later with the help of his syndicator and by reigniting the interest of old fans who will pass the word around that Dave is back, but if Glenn Reynolds stops writing today, he will be hard-pressed to comeback without a long track record and deep fan base. This goes to the issue of fitness, in the sense that Barry has earned respect and become reliable to his readers, like an old, familiar sports star who gets cheers just for stepping onto the playing field at an old-timers game. Reynolds is still the young phenom who, if he blows a few games, will be forgotten because he hasn't become reliable.

All this sounds terribly unmathematical, but it leads to the last step in this analysis, the idea of social networks and capital, particular as embodied in the idea of six degrees of separation.

Stanley Milgram's famous, though not most infamous, experiment on social ties, in which he asked people to try to get a letter to one of several targets by going through a network of acquaintances to find a personal connection to the target, provided the well-worn concept of "six degrees of separation." This is the idea that, on average, each person is approximately six social steps away from anyone else in the world. By asking a friend if they know a friend of someone we'd like to meet, according to this idea, we would find that the target was between four and eleven introductions away, with the average being six steps, or degrees. Milgram's 1967 experiment, which identified the "small world problem" (after the "It's a small world" uttered by people who learn they have an acquaintance in common) as a field ripe for investigation, was the basis of another breakthrough piece of research by Mark Grannovetter, who established that "weak ties," which are not central to the function of groups but happen to link clusters of people, are the primary vectors of the experience of small worlds. As described in Figure 6, above, it is the person who is able to leap barriers between two groups who is critical to the success of a six-degrees chain.

Of the 96 message chains that Milgram initiated, 18 were completed by the delivery of a letter to the intended target, an impressive 18 percent of the total sample. A recent email version of the study, conducted by Duncan Watts, Peter Sheridan Dodds and Roby Muhammad, tried to replicate Milgram's findings by targeting 18 people in 13 countries through more than 24,000 message chains.[93] One of the key findings, from the perspective of the email research team, is that because professional and academic ties tended to account for most of the successful chains, there may be fewer hubs in social networks than Barabási's research suggested: "We conclude that social search appears to be largely an egalitarian exercise, not one whose success depends on a small minority of exceptional individuals."

Mark Granovetter, commenting on the email study, suggested that people simply don't understand the importance of social networks or how to navigate them.[94] He isolated the question of the number of hubs in the social network as particularly troublesome issue, since other factors, such as a shared occupation or geographic proximity, were identified as important by participants when choosing the next links in

---

[93] Dodds, Peter Sheridan; Muhammad, Roby; Watts, Duncan J., Science Magazine, 2003 301: 827-829,
http://www.sciencemag.org/cgi/content/short/301/5634/827

[94] Granovetter, Mark, Science Magazine, 2003 301: 773,
http://www.sciencemag.org/cgi/content/full/301/5634/773

their chains. What is clear, it seems to me, is that there are a number of characteristics that make a person a potential hub. If this is the case, the influence of leadership, marketing and other fitness factors can reshape a social network dramatically. An efficiency variable like the one used in Lanchester theory may available for measuring the potential inputs and outputs, based on specific analysis of a network task, such as organizing a statewide political campaign, in light of the number of available first-degree connections one has the quality of those people's political networks.

The results of the email study, while the successful chains did average 4.05 steps, also raise a very serious question about what incentives are needed to activate social networks for political purposes, because it demonstrates that getting a social chain going is not easy. Compared to the 18 percent success rate Milgram had with paper mail, Watts, et al, had only 324 successful chains out of 24,163 that were initiated — a 1.6 percent success rate. One can speculate that Milgram had a higher success rate because a letter, especially a letter in the 1960s compared to today, when junk mail is much more prevalent, carried a greater moral obligation for interim recipients, so that they tended to carry out the requested act of forwarding the message. The email researchers suggested several reasons that chains might have broken, but concluded that "actual success depends sensitively on individual incentives."[95]

Incentives are not subject to mathematical certainty, they vary for every person and change in different situations. At this juncture, we've arrived at the political, again, and can relate network theory to the process of developing an emergent society built on a plurality of polities organized to address individual tasks. We know that social networks can be activated and, in a short series of connections, link people from different backgrounds and geographies. The question is, what keeps these links open and communication flowing once they are established. It is easy, relatively speaking, to tap a social network once and then move on.

Like a single-purpose social network chain, an emergent polity is only one expression of a person's interests. An emergent polity has the virtue of carrying substantial incentives for establishing and maintaining communication and collaboration between people. Bridging individuals,

---

[95] Dodds; Muhammad; Watts, ibid.

hubs or connectors in network theory terms, can be predicted to identify and initiate links around areas of potential overlapping concern between polities. If a polity is successfully addressing an issue that members of another polity recognize as a pressing need, the incentives for establishing a connection are self-evident. If, for example, I am a member of an emergent polity that provides supplemental retirement income derived from revenues generated by a group investment in local streets for which local businesses pay (e.g., for premium parking spaces near their storefront or for signage on the street) and I meet someone who is a member of a polity that has invested in long-term healthcare facilities, perhaps I can forge an alliance between the two to swap benefits while increasing funds for local road repairs. This is the essence of politics and the foundation of markets.

The interconnectedness of regions due to inexpensive travel, too, creates new opportunities for catalyzing emergent polities through existing social networks by meeting periodically to discuss social issues. Mark Buchanan points out in his book Nexus that the personal space of the typical individual today is ten thousand times larger than it was in 1800, when people traveled about 50 meters a day.[96] These face-to-face encounters, when connectors are gathered, are where the political tradition of the past clearly informs an emergent society.

While I would not conclude that the accessibility of others through networks will lead to an emergent society, but the statistical evidence and practical experience suggests densely networked societies create more and egalitarian opportunities for self-organizing solutions to social problems.

---

[96] Buchanan, Mark, Nexus: Small Worlds and the Groundbreaking Theory Of Networks, W. W. Norton & Co., New York, 2002. P. 121.

# Social Network Dynamics and Participatory Politics
## by Ross Mayfield

A disruptive movement is underway with the Internet being used for social means. The creative destruction of the tech boom gave us a legacy of physical infrastructure largely meant for transactions and email communication to build upon. But a funny thing happened on the way to the forum, people connected and used the Internet as a social tool. As a critical mass of mature users gathered in simple ways and co-created social infrastructure, complex patterns emerged.

It began with innovators at the tip of the technology adoption lifecycle. Geeks and hackers used the Internet for more than a platform, but having conversations about it, themselves and what they were building it for. The commercialization of industry research, the constraints of propriety on invention, the moves of monopolists and open standards became rallying issues. The open source, or free (as in "freedom") software movement was born.

Open source didn't just open a Pandora's Box for the software industry it was the emergence of an entirely new method of production based upon social interaction and low transaction costs. In *Coase's Penguin, or Linux and the Nature of the Firm* New York University Law Professor Jochai Benkler described this 15-year-old phenomenon as "commons-based peer production" in contrast to the property and contract-based models of markets and hierarchies described by Economists Ronald Coase and Oliver Williamson. Social signals, rather than price or managerial demands, drive contributions and coordination. [97] Benkler identified the systemic efficiencies of a model based on self-organization for resource allocation. A model of disruptive efficiency — driven by social network dynamics.

---

[97] http://www.benkler.org/CoasesPenguin.html

During the boom we thought frictionless communication of price would revolutionize industry after industry. But price alone favors incumbents. Indeed, the commoditization of everything is underway, but competing in commodity industries initially favors the economies of scale and speed that larger vertically integrated firms are positioned to realize. Assets of scaled production can be leverage to compete on volume. The disruption of business-to-consumer and business-to-business e-commerce and other alphabet economies was only televised.

Somewhere along the way we forgot that underpinning each transaction was a relationship. At scale this means financial credit. But there is value in the small. The smaller transactions that are underpinned by social capital yield emergent patterns that are perhaps more disruptive.

The technology adoption lifecycle rolls on towards later adoption – software, media, politics and other sectors are being disrupted by social infrastructure by order of their reliance on information goods.

## Ecosystem of Networks

Perhaps the most visible of the disruptive technologies that make up the social software ecosystem is Weblogs. Commonly understood as personal publishing tools, they have indeed made publishing accessible because of their simplicity in form and low cost (free in many cases). But the value of a weblog is greater than giving an individual a voice and power of blogs is much greater than the sum of its parts.

In "Power-laws, Weblogs and Inequality,"[98] Clay Shirky highlighted that the structure of blogspace is a Power law. When you sort blogs by the number of links to them, the value of the Nth position is $1/N$ (the second in rank has 1one-half the links of the first, the third in rank has one-third the rank of the first and so on). This paints a picture of blogs as publishing, where the most connected nodes hold the most value.

What's notable about a power law distribution (a scale-free network) is that it is an efficient structure at scale. Particularly in distribution of memes, following Sarnoff's Law where the value of the network is the number of nodes it broadcasts to, a cluster of highly connected nodes can indeed transmit information throughout the network.

---

[98] http://www.shirky.com/writings/powerlaw_weblog.html

Shirky's paper caused a stir in blogspace because it was interpreted to mean that the "A-list" bloggers at the top of the power law ranking held all the power. This is contrary to the experience of your average blogger and the ideals that a fit meme from a less popular blog could reach all of blogspace through social filtering.

How the A-list got to prominence and retains it is "preferential attachment,"[99] the desire for a new node to connect to the most connected nodes. Shirky did point out that besides blogs as publishing there were other modalities, blogging classic and blogs as dinner conversation. He saw the activity of blogging for your average person as something closer to a dinner conversation, read and converse with a small group of friends. He saw a scale above that as how blogging was at its inception, a knowable social network. It just so happened that that early knowable network became the top of a very big and growing pyramid that was adding to its base at a rate of 10,000 blogs per day.

Similar to how different physics at the nanometer scale allow the creation of new technologies, when you look closer at the power-law you find different patterns. Duncan Watts observed, "when you rachet up the requirements for what is a connection, connections diminish." [100]

Fundamentally, not all links are created equal. If you link to Joi Ito's blog, does that mean you are friends? If he links back? What the heck does "friend" mean anyway? You see, while Joi may have access to the best technologies, he is still constrained by time and neurological capabilities for maintaining relationships. The only category you can put all links to joi.ito.com is that they are representative affiliations, indicating that someone identified with him enough to link to him.

The problem is conversational relationships are not scale-free. Its impossible to have running conversations with thousands of people, recall who they are and maintain social context.

---

[99]http://www.amazon.com/exec/obidos/tg/detail/-/0452284392/ref=pd_sim_books_1/002-5054519-2389639?v=glance&s=books

[100] http://www.amazon.com/exec/obidos/tg/detail/-/0393041425?v=glance

Robin Dunbar postulated that group size is constrained by the size of the neocortical physiology[101]. The ratio of the size of the neocortex to total brain mass can project the maximum expected group size for a species. His work suggests that a person can only track the social relationships of a group of 150 people at any given time.

Its conversations that let us keep a mental network map of our social groups. Informal inter-personal communication, such as gossip or idle chit-chat, helps us understand who is relating to who in our little circles. We happen upon new ties or invoke latent ones from the past, but still, our buffer maxes out at 150.

Scaling group size beyond 150 requires hierarchy and formalized communication. While this helps organizations realize economies of scale and speed, it comes at a cost of social capital and intellectual capital that realize economies of span and scope. In other words, once formalized as process, its difficult to change. Recognizing this theoretical constraint is important for software and organizational design, but it's more important to recognize it is an existing structure in blogspace, with most blogs receiving approximately 150 links.

There is an even deeper level of relationships than informal ties. People we love, work with closely. Malcolm Gladwell, the author of *The Tipping Point*, who discusses Robin Dunbar's work also postulates another group size based upon intimacy. When most people are asked to list persons that would be deeply affected if they die, a measure of strong relationships; the average list is of 12 people. Not so coincidentally, workgroups start to burst into flames at this scale, with the optimal organizational form for everyday work being closer to eight.

Taking into consideration that groups behave differently at different scales, each demanding different modalities for interaction and the natural constraints for each scale, we can postulate a framework for thinking about the ecosystem of networks.

| Network Layer | Scale | Distribution of Links | Social Capital | Weblog Modality |
|---|---|---|---|---|
|  |  |  |  |  |

[101] Robin Dunbar, Co-evolution of neocortex size, group size and language in humans, Behavioral and Brain Sciences 16 (1993), pp. 681-735.

| Political Network | 1000s | Power-law (Scale-free) | Sarnoff's Law, N | Publishing |
|---|---|---|---|---|
| Social Network | 150 | Random (Bell Curve) | Metcalfe's Law, $N^2$ | Communication |
| Creative Network | 12 | Event (Flat) | Reed's Law, $2^N$ | Collaboration |

People use weblogs in different modes: Publishing; Communication and; Collaboration. Because of dramatically lowering the cost for these modes of communcation on the public Internet people are rapidly increasing the value of social capital through the act of communicating. Each mode provides different valuation methods:

- **Publishing:** Sarnoff's Law says the value of a network is proportionate to the number of subscribers.

- **Communication:** Metcalfe's Law says the value of a network is proportionate to the number of links.

- **Collaboration:** Reed's Law says the value of a network is proportionate to the number of groups.

This model radically changes the power-law equation and equality. While the nodes at the peak of the power-law have the most "power" to disseminate their views, the network as a whole gains greater value from smaller scales.

Blogspace is a large complex adaptive system with emergent properties. Creative networks deliberate and construct memes. Social networks, uh, socialize them. When a meme reaches the right node in a political network it can reach escape velocity. All these networks overlap (the A-list socializes too) and are different from each node's perspective. But the resulting heterarchy provides a path for memes to emerge from creative to social to political layers, undergoing a phase transition at each step – allowing the best content and expertise to rise to the top naturally. This is in stark contrast to hierarchical structures which are designed for control down and information flow up, but routinely impede information flow because of control as a check and the absence of lateral flow as a balance. Bloggers provide intelligence for what is of value with each link they vote with.

## Talking about social software

Clay Shirky defines "social software" as software that "treats groups as first class objects in the system. In other words, it treats triads differently than pairs. What's important about this distinction is that social systems can be broken down into triads, and no further; and when A connects to B and B to C, then a transitive relationship between A and C is possible."[102] Even more abstractly, I define Social Software as software that adapts to its environment rather than requiring the environment to adapt to it. Reason being, software is rarely executed without a social context.

Traditional enterprise software, for example, has focused on automating business processes. It institutes structure, business rules and rigid ontologies to realize efficiencies for transactions and reporting. This approach has three notable drawbacks. Much of knowledge work is unstructured, the domain of business practice, not process. Second, most business processes become out of date when they are created because of new environmental information. Third, it is designed by experts instead of users; and attempts to take change out of how the system is used. As a result, users default to email and attachments for most of their work.

This isn't to say that traditional systems and processes are not of value. IT provides productivity gains from automation and when processes provide social agreement for how to work together, according to Erik Brynjolfsson.[103] It's primarily that social systems are just beginning to accommodate the unstructured nature of knowledge work that is business practice (or, ad hoc processes), which accommodates informal social networks[104]. Creating such social software means giving greater

---

[102] http://www.blackbeltjones.com/work/mt/archives/000472.html>

[103] http://ebusiness.mit.edu/erik/JEP%20Beyond%20Computation %20BrynjolfssonHitt%207-121.pdf

[104] The Social Life of Information, by John Seely Brown, Paul Duguid. Harvard Business School Press, February 2000.

control to users to shape their own networks and information architecture in a dynamic environment.

## What's So Different about Social Software?

Groups have been forming for longer than the Internet. Online communities are not new, so what's new here? What may be different is greater understanding of the role social networks play in forming communities. Howard Reinghold, in *Smart Mobs*, highlighted the difference between networks and groups:

> Every time you interact with another person you potentially exchange information about and from people you each know. The structure of everyone's links to everyone else is a network that acts as a channel through which news, job tips, possible romantic partners and contagious diseases travel. Social networks can be measured and interconnections can be charted, from relationships between interlocking boards of directors of major corporations to terrorist networks. One of Wellman's claims is that "we find community in networks, not groups." He explained that "a group is a special type of network: densely-knit (most people are directly connected), tightly-bounded (most ties stay within the densely-knit cluster) and multistranded (most ties contain many role relationships)"[105] and challenged conventional thinking about how people cluster socially:

> "Although people often view the world in terms of groups, they function in networks. In networked societies: boundaries are permeable, interactions are with diverse others, connections switch between multiple networks, and hierarchies can be flatter and recursive. The change from groups to networks can be seen at many levels. Trading and political blocs have lost their monolithic character in the world system. Organizations form complex networks of alliance and exchange rather than cartels, and workers report to multiple peers and superiors. Management by multiply-connected network is replacing management by hierarchal tree and management by two-dimensional matrix. Communities are far-flung, loosely-bounded, sparsely-knit, and fragmentary. Most people operate in multiple, thinly-connected, partial communities as they deal with networks of kin, neighbours, friends, workmates and organizational ties. Rather

---

[105] Barry Wellman, "Physical Place and Cyberplace: The Rise of Personalized Networking," in International Journal of Urban and Regional Research25 (2001), Special Issue on "Networks, Class and Place," edited by Talja Blokland and Mike Savage.

than fitting into the same group as those around them, each person has his/her own "personal community."[106]

Here's a perhaps too simplistic framework to further draw out differences between the ideas of online community and social software that supports new group-forming activity:

## Online Communities

- Top-down
- Place-centric
- Moderated
- Topic-driven
- Centralized
- Architected

## Social Software

- Bottom-up

- People-centric

- User-controlled

- Context-driven

- Decentralized

- Self-organizing

To illustrate this, lets take an example from social networking and another from social software.

For example, consider Match.com as an online community vs. Friendster as a social networking service. Both serve the same market for online dating, but in vastly different ways. Match.com was architected by experts in how to match people. At a central site users fill out profiles,

---

[106] Ibid. Wellman, 2001.

search profiles, are provided suggested connections according to a secret-sauce algorithm and then initiate contact. This is driven by profiles as topics. Moderators actually play a smaller role than other communities such as discussion lists, but do constantly tweak the algorithm as they are accountable for the quality of the service. Search benefits from the structure of profiles, which consequentially takes change out of the system.

By contrast, Friendster provides a social substrate. Profiles are put in social context (explicit representation of friends, interaction on discussion boards), which drives activity. Because of social context, actions risk social capital, providing a basis of trust. An iterative implicit reputation system governs from the edge, with the centralized authority playing only a nominal role. Instead of an advanced algorithm, users provide the intelligence for what matches should be made using implicit and tacit rationale. Search is constrained by a user's location within the social network graph and degrees of distance (network horizon).

At last count, there were over 100 social networking services created and much talk of a "bubblet" because of venture capital speculation. One framework for understanding these models is to categorize them by the markets they seek to cannibalize, such as dating, classified ads, recruiting and associations. But it is also helpful to segment them by how people connect using the service:

| Social Networking Models | | |
|---|---|---|
| Network Type | Connection Method | Archetype |
| Explicit | Declarative | Friendster, Orkut, Tribe.net |
| Virtual | Avatar | EverQuest |
| Physical | In-person | Meetup |
| Conversational | Communication | Weblogs |
| Private | Referral | LinkedIn |

Of course, Friendster represents only a special brand of social context and serves certain facets of identity and makes explicit many things that should be implicit about relationships. With social networking, connection comes before content. With social software, content (actually, conversation) comes before connection. In the US in particular, there is a dearth of social capital. Say's Law says that the market flocks to abundance until it becomes scarce. The growth of social networking — Orkut became 500th most-trafficked site within two weeks of launch — can be partially attributable to the latent demand to connect.

Most notable exceptions to online communities as represented in the above framework actually suffer from openness. USENET, for example, was an online community that lacked centralized authority and design and remains open to participation. By consequence, spam degrades the health of the community, topic after topic.

The largest form of online community in use today is email discussion-lists. Moderators play a role in governing the community with issues such as spam. This maintains quality at a cost of openness. Quality itself is a moving target and maintaining scales participation creates significant administration costs and ambiguities.

By contrast, take Wikipedia.org, one of the largest social software communities. A wiki (Hawaiian for "quick") is a collaboratively editable website that doesn't require participants to learn HTML. The key feature is "Edit this Page" allowing anyone to edit anything at any time. Ward Cunningham invented the "Wiki Wiki Web" in 1995, spawning thousands of open source and commercial initiatives. Its counter-intuitive that giving up editing control to anyone that wants it actually works.

Wikipedia has demonstrated that collaborative editing can be constructive at scale and low cost – while maintaining quality. Andrea Ciffollili, in *Phantom authority, self-selective recruitment and retention of members in virtual communities: The Case of Wikipedia*[107] uses transaction cost analysis, team and club good theory to account for how wikis can deliver quality at a low cost and large scale of participation.

---

[107] http://firstmonday.org/issues/issue8_12/ciffolilli/

What's makes large scale wikis work includes:

- Low transaction costs for contribution and editing;

- A governance structure that hands over enforcement to users while allowing a core group to deal with major issues;

- Infinite storage capacity and logical space;

- De-emphasis of design to focus on content;

- De-emphasis of identity to focus on content;

- Fostering trust within participants by giving up control;

- Forking content creation from discussion about content.

An unknown number of anonymous contributors have helped build Wikipedia; 29,853 registered users of which 143 are administrators and seven out have developer rights. This plus one founder that plays the role of "benevolent dictator."

Unlike Slashdot, the prototypical example of an open self-organizing social software community with low administrative overhead, Wikipedia doesn't use an explicit reputation system. Instead, it functions at two levels. The first level, that of procedural authority, gives users the ability to contribute and edit at low transaction costs. The second level, institutional authority, is given to administrators.

About 150 administrators — there's that number again — a ceiling of cognizance for a social network. The eight people, a core group with developer's rights, is what some developers consider to be an optimal team size and within the boundaries of a creative network.

So behind the scenes of a successfully scaled community that empowers users is an active social network that relies on social practices that are not hard-coded or codified. The paper suggests that to scale further a reputation system may be required for this network, a major change to manage given the culture that reflects and drives its tools. Perhaps it should look for a set of new challenges to hand off to a new group of administrators to delay such a rash transition.

## Users as Developers

The very notion of a "consumer" is changing from someone that consumes to becoming a participant in the network of a vendor. Participants can rapidly spread favorable or damaging information about a product to their peers. Just as how the early days of the computing industry relied on user groups to provide support and learning, these groups now rapidly emerge to shape the experience of the service or product. Vendors that embrace this trend have to give up the pursuit of control and message to foster favorable network dynamics.

Jimmy Wales and Larry Sanger originally retained control when they were developing Nupedia, a free online encyclopedia that did rely on volunteer contributions but used a traditional editorial process for maintaining quality. A year into the project they let go of this authority that decision spawned Wikipedia, initially as a research project to serve their own needs and see if something so simple could work. Similarly, Evan Williams and Meg Hourihan created the Blogger weblog authoring tool for their own project communication while building a project management system. In both cases, the traditional project they were working on failed and the research project was put out into the world to become a phenomenal success.

Weblogs have since their inception been advanced in a decentralized fashion by users as developers, based on open standards and accessibility of contribution. Simple scripting languages and accessible developer communities lowered the barrier to contribution by code.

Wikis provide users the ability to participate in horizontal information assembly, just as developers participate in vertical information assembly. As a tool, it has the greatest promise to turn citizens into hackers, blur the line between users and developers and allow everyone to participate in the open source movement.

Similarly, low cost audio and video production tools like Apple's GarageBand and iMovie turn users into developers. In all sectors of information goods, this provides opportunities for organizations to re-align the value chain. Moveon.org's user contributed political ads, selected through an emergent process, is a perfect example of what's to come. Your users want to help you, help each other.

## Hypothetical Citizen Initative: Public Record

Public Record is a hypothetical independent self-organizing resource for voters that tracks the issues and influencers of the 2004 presidential campaign. Accountability and trust in the democratic process is at an all time low, which weakens our civil society and democratic institutions. An opportunity exists to provide a resource for citizens, by citizens to strengthen our civil institutions.

Primarily based upon wiki, Public Record allows any citizen to contribute to construction of a website at any time, a tool that fosters trust by giving up control. Augmenting the wiki with weblogs allows healthy debate on issues and content to occur without degrading the content itself — in a publish/subscribe format that does not overload participants. Wikis allow a larger portion of the citizenry to participate in the open source movement by allowing contributions through horizontal information assembly (in contrast to vertical information assembly only available to programmers).

Wikipedia has demonstrated that collaborative editing can be constructive at scale and low cost — pointing to a potential solution of developing a public record of accountability. An encyclopedia is a political artifact, as definition is fraught with controversy.

Public Record would be a collaboratively edited public record of accountability for the candidates and the media. Key elements include:

- Individual or organization Record Pages that build a record based on fact of what was said and done;

- Issue pages that cross-index Record Pages ;

- Blog discussion;

- Leverage link analysis of blog discussion to reveal what may be of more interest to readers and administrators;

- An administrators' edit-only homepage that provides key indexes and navigation;

- A core group of volunteers to maintain the wiki in its early days until users defend it themselves.

Unlike Wikipedia, which uses mailing lists and encourages discussion on separate wiki pages, a Socialtext approach would be to use its integrated weblog capability plus integration with existing blogspace primarily through Trackback for input, which lists other sites linking to a posting, and RSS, a syndication technology, for output to facilitate discussion about the content of the site. A single group blog aggregates all discussion — recent changes within blog posts — and blogs per content page.

**Hypothetical Government Initiative: Public Comment**

The government started listening back in 1997 when Kevin Werbach set up a an email inbox for public comment at the Federal Communications Commission[108]: "Right now commenting is a fairly arduous, archaic process," said Werbach, the FCC's counsel for new technology policy. "Remarks have to be submitted on paper, in multiple copies. So we're simplifying with a Web page form that will include a searchable database...It's a question of whether we have the manpower to deal with compiling and summarizing so many comments.

Therein lays the problem and the opportunity. On the one hand, every public comment needs to go on record and should be read. On the other, they are public comments, so the public can interact with them.

Public Comments could be submitted in weblog form, with each commenter getting their own blog which could be publicly anonymous or not. Comments may be direct comments or commenting upon comments by linking to them. Ideally, staffers themselves engage in external blogging to ask questions and highlight issues. A link rank measure of links within a span of time, points citizens making comments and staffers towards what may be of greater interest or value. For example, a group may post a deliberated comment and have supporters link to it in support, a form similar to a digital petition. Links themselves take advantage of the "Vote Links"[109] standard to allow people to provide comments and control how it effects the link rank. A Vote Link allows the blogger to tag if they agree, abstain or disagree with what they are linking to. Leveraging Vote Link metadata, those making

---

[108] http://www.wired.com/news/politics/0,1283,2956,00.html

[109] http://developers.technorati.com/wiki/VoteLinks

comments would be presented with blogs that have voted along side them as a cue for group formation.

Staffers do more than carry the burden of compiling and summarizing comments, they synthesize information to inform decisions. Similar to the Dean Campaign's use of Socialtext inside the organization described in [Chapter TK], staffers are encourage to track persistent issues in wiki and hold internal conversations by blog. A similar link rank is used, adjusted for scale of participation, and each wiki page represents the group voice of staffers within their social network.

### Emergent Pluralism

Joi Ito suggests there is a new pattern of emergent democracy being enabled through new tools such as weblogs. He suggests that as these tools evolve they could support a higher-level order through their emergent properties to result in a model closer to direct democracy.

To put it another way, these tools may support a new form of democratic pluralism. Pluralism is government carried out by a process of bargaining and compromise between a variety of competing leadership groups. There are two kinds of pluralism in American government today:

*Institutionalized pluralism* "depicts a society whose members are bound together by calculated fealty to a network of protocoalitions and a dense normative system for which bargaining is the prescribed behavior."

*Individualized pluralism* is a system "constituted of independent members who have few group or institutional loyalties and who are generally less interested in sacrificing short-run, private career goals for the longer-term benefits of bargaining."

In *Going Public*, Michael Gecan describes how until the 1980s the United States was governed through an institutional pluralism in which political parties were the dominant mechanism of influence. President Ronald Reagan subverted this pattern by going public with issues when negotiation between his Republican party and the Democrats failed. When he went public with an issue, lobbying organizations mobilized public to pressure congressmen with a deluge of calls, faxes and letters. [This is strategy that predates the Reagan Administration, going back at least to President Franklin Roosevelt's practice of appealing directly to the people for support through his "Fireside Chat" radio broadcasts. — *ed.]*

Today American politics has an unconstructive balance between institutional and individualized pluralism. Weakened parties reduce longer-term best interest decisions. Lobbying only is effective in highly organized groups on select issues that resonate for deep dedication and financial backing. And where lobbying groups do not achieve critical mass, decision makers rely short-term polling of sentiment. The majority of the U.S. doesn't participate in the party system nor special interest groups. This lack of participation results in a disenfranchised public and ineffective government of both long and short-term issues.

If simple tools could decrease the cost of organization as well as enable a transactional norm between organizations, a new form of pluralism could arise. Emergent pluralism depicts a society whose members who have institutional loyalties to easily formed issue groups that have direct interaction their elected representatives and the media.

While direct democracy is on the rise with increasing use of referendums and experiments at the local level, representative democracy is an institution worth defending. Without it, minority constituencies, complex issues and longer term considerations would not be represented. Its not that the masses are asses – responsible representation is effective when decisions are well informed, free of conflict of interest and held accountable.

Emergent pluralism is not direct democracy, it instead seeks to augment the capabilities of decision makers to serve their constituency. Just as representative democracy holds that representatives can carry the burden of governance so citizens can specialize in other fields, Emergent Pluralism needs to support this structure without creating undue burdens for decision makers. In other words, it is impossible for representatives to have direct interaction with every constituent.

The early days of interaction between citizen bloggers and the media have demonstrated the capability to enhance the capabilities of the media. Stories originated, sustained (e.g. the saga of Senator Trent Lott's comments about Senator Strom Thurmond, which led to his resignation as U.S. Senate Majority Leader), freshly sourced, framed beyond the episode or fact checked by blog result in better media coverage. This is done without creating undue burdens upon journalists to interact with readers. Part of this dynamic is complementary, part of it is competitive – but the two forms of journalism make each other better.

The experiences of the Dean Campaign and Moveon.org point to the promise and challenges for decision makers to gain new listening capabilities. The Dean Campaign took the revolutionary step of opening up comments for blog posts. This provided equal access for citizens to voice their views, some of which were brought to the campaign leadership's attention through the judgment of staffers. As comment volume increased, the lost their utility for reading and listening, requiring every contribution be read to determine its relevancy. Moveon.org used forums for feedback and instituted a rating system that Wes Boyd described as a key facet of how they listened to key constituents. The problem with rating systems is they loose potential participation and written context. A key design challenge remains — how to give everyone an equal voice to provide a sense of participation while filtering important contributions to decision makers? Perhaps the Clark Community Network established by the Wesley Clark 2004 presidential campaign, or the hypothetical civic projects described in this essay provide such a model that empowers people to create their own weblogs, encourages post-to-post conversation and leveraging of index tools like Technorati to reveal ideas that are gaining traction.

One thing the Dean Campaign demonstrated, without question, is the capability for flash fundraising when supported by the right conversational networks. The potential exists to couple this fundraising capability for new groups to gain representation through lobbying. Groups that leverage memetics, the study of how ideas spread and affect society, in blogspace for recruiting critical mass, connecting with other groups, deliberate positions and raise funds to engage decision makers will be most successful. In fact, this has already started to happen with lobbyists for hire organization such as Lobbysmith.com, although it has yet to be coupled with conversation networks. Emergent pluralism will only work when citizens learn to connect with decision makers.

## Social Networks and Influence

It is precisely the connection with the real world that calls into question our virtual advances. The Dean Campaign's rise and fall will be discussed at length but whether it was a victim of broadcast politics is beside the point. The reason the tech industry and Silicon Valley have been a success is because it developed a culture that rewarded and learned from failure. Blog Campaign version 1.0 will be very different when it appears as Version 2.0 in 2006 or 2008.

Speaking at the O'Reilly Digital Democracy Teach-in, former Dean campaign manager Joe Trippi highlighted the tension between the transparent nature of Internet campaigns and the traditional model of broadcast politics. He remarked that not only could competitors mimic tactics, but he lacked a backchannel to communicate with ardent supporters when it was a holy shit moment without alerting the media. This tension is similar to Individualized Pluralism and Institutionalized Pluralism. Aside from distributed organization, much of the campaign's communication and fundraising strategy was very similar to how special interest groups leverage individualized pluralism by going public with issues. It did so in a way that it lost the ability to privately coordinate and negotiate with decision makers (e.g. regional and local organizers). Further application of emergent social software as a private backchannel could have allowed Trippi to communicate as well as process feedback with the campaign as an institution.

The structure of a distributed campaign that fosters self-organization and social networking at the edge still holds promise. Not just because it cost-effectively engages activist support but because people make decisions in a social context. The work of Paul Beck shows that social networks played a critical role in encouraging political defection for the Perot Campaign in 1992[110]. Dina Mayzlin shows that targeting social networks can be an effective strategy of influence in product purchase decisions.[111] When both mass advertising and social networking is employed, social networks exhibit greater influence. However, broadcast is alone more effective when directly compared with a social networking strategy. Perhaps when the media turned against Dean, he lost the leverage of social networks, and competitive broadcast strategies won. But encouraging open deliberation and networking in physical and virtual Meetups will be a co-opted strategy for campaigns to come.

---

[110] http://psweb.sbs.ohio-state.edu/faculty/pbeck/encouragingdefection.pdf

[111] http://www.som.yale.edu/faculty/dm324/papers.asp

## Participatory Politics

Participatory politics is a disruptive movement. Leveraging social software and the role of social networking, it provides citizens a role more than every four years. The level of engagement it can provide with candidates, issues and institutions strikes at the heart of the sources of citizen disenfranchisement. Social capital, voter apathy and distrust in political institutions are all issues that connectedness can address. If you are reading this book, you have an interest in tools for change. Even if you are not making them, by using them in your own way your very actions have constructive consequence. Its time to put the demo back in democracy. One link at a time.

# Broadcasting and the Voter's Paradox
## by David Weinberger

Voting is gloriously paradoxical. Each person gets one and only one vote, equal to everyone else's. When we vote, we are mere faces in the crowd, yet we rejoice in our mere-ness. Yet with that one vote, we express what is unique about us. What other binary choice engenders such endless discussion? And am I the only person who has choked up in a voting booth from the weight of mere-ness expressing uniqueness?

Voting is paradoxical only because we normally resent being reduced to being members of a faceless crowd. "I am not a numbah!" as the hero of the cheesily existentialist UK show *The Prisoner* used to say. We especially resent it when the organization treating us as just another wallet pretends otherwise. "Your call is important to us": Then why don't you pick up the !@#$%-ing phone? "Dear YOUR NAME IN CAPS": Who do you think you're fooling?

Yet most of our interactions with large businesses suffer from the robotic-bonhomie of the junk mail salutation. What choice do they have? Employees at Prell shampoo can't hand-write letters to all 50 million users. Volkswagen can't tape a different commercial for each viewer. So, of course companies have to resort to marketing to demographic slices that reduce people to quantifiable properties they have in common: Urban church-going women age 18-24, male snow-boarding thumb-suckers age 45-54. Of course.

This type of mass communication is epitomized by broadcasting: a single message going out to a whole lot of people who are understood by what they have in common, not by what makes them unique and different. Not just TV and radio networks are broadcasters. By this definition, so are newspaper and magazine publishers.

And so are politicians.

That's where the Internet offers a difference. Perhaps masses of people can be reached without broadcasting. If so, then marketing and commerce will change. But so will politics and governance.

♋

When the Web started to become popular in the mid-90s, one of the first questions was: Would banner ads cut into TV advertising revenues? Would people switch from slick Hollywood products to homegrown programming? Would people stop watching TV and instead surf all the live long day? What would become of broadcasting?

Broadcasting has survived the Internet, even though the Internet seems to be partially responsible for reducing the viewership of network television. But this isn't merely about whether the attractions of the online world can peel back the number of people watching TV, for broadcasting isn't simply a technological solution to a communications problem. It's got economic, societal, political and governmental implications. Indeed, there's a sense in which broadcasting has given us a fundamental way of understanding how society operates. The biggest effect the Internet will have on broadcasting is on its dominance as a social metaphor.

Broadcasting is, in fact, a poor paradigm for communications. It allows only one person to speak at a time and, by itself, gives no way effective for the huddled masses to respond. If broadcasting didn't exist, and if money and technology were no obstacle, you might build a broadcast network, but you would reserve it for specialized uses; for example, it would make an excellent emergency notification system. Otherwise, you would probably not invest much in a national broadcast infrastructure like the one we have now, preferring something more regional, more interactive, and more open to the initiative of citizens. Unless your country were a monarchy, of course: Monarchies and broadcasting are a natural match.

We have a national broadcast system not because it's ideal but because it solved some problems of the day. Sending out electromagnetic waves was expensive, requiring a major investment of capital. So, companies were guaranteed a limit on competition in geographic regions, not only to prevent "interference" but also to entice them to risk their money building networks. Thus were channels born. But because it was such an expensive undertaking, the size of the audience had to be maximized. This meant that the field favored large companies. Hence the circumstances that made broadcasting appealing also tended to scale audiences up and scale the number of broadcasters down: if your program can reach more people, it is worth more to advertisers.

The economics were sound but the politics are dismal. Broadcasting works against the ideals of democracy.

Sure, having cheap or free access to news programming helps to keep a democratic citizenry informed. But we have seen a relentless degradation of news programming thanks to the economics of broadcasting: In their pursuit of ever larger audiences, broadcasters turn news into entertainment. This may not be inevitable, but it is what has happened.

Worse, the economic need to scale up a broadcast – to increase its viewership – has narrowed the range of acceptable opinion. There's a reason why extremist newsweeklies are handed out for free on a just a few street corners while you can hardly spin around without seeing a place to buy a copy of *USA Today*. Your broadcast business will do better if it upholds the values, ideas and opinions of the broadest swath of the market.

Of course, broadcast media, including newspapers, don't just reflect public mores. They also create them. Network television tells us what words are now acceptable: I know that "fart" and "suck" are ok because I hear them on sitcoms. Likewise, newspapers not only inform us about what's going on in the world, they also tell us what sorts of things our municipality finds interesting and acceptable. Reflecting and forming: That's the dialectic of broadcast media.

So, broadcasting is inherently anti-democratic not just because it gives special privilege to the ideas of a moneyed elite, but because its economics leads to a narrowing of opinion: there's only one socialist columnist in a major daily newspaper today because people don't want to read socialists, in part because the newspapers – anticipating and forming our tastes – don't run socialist columnists. (Sometimes the dialectic runs in a circle.)

But democracy was founded by enlightened rationalists who thought that truth emerges from vigorous debate. Limit that debate and not only might good ideas go unborn, but one's own ideas are weakened by the lack of challenge. If democracy was invented in order to resolve the problem that a nation comprehends a diversity of will, smoothing out that diversity weakens democracy. A nation with only one opinion doesn't really need democracy. Yet that is almost where we are today.

The presidential election of 2004, and particularly the Howard Dean campaign, taught us something important. Remember those 50 million Prell users? The CEO of Prell can't possibly have a real, human relationship with each of them. But now we can see how to scale individual relationships even with an organization dealing with millions of us. We can't all talk with the CEO of Prell, and we couldn't all have a real email correspondence with Howard Dean. But we could with one another. And that seems to count for a lot.

When people first started thinking about how the Internet could be used in national campaigns, a couple of ideas leapt out. You could use the Internet to do mass mailings, cutting down on postage. You could vote over the Internet, effectively enfranchising millions of people by taking laptops to them. You could post your policy statements online. You could maybe raise money through direct marketing over the Internet. Perhaps policy could be written by The People rather than by the candidate. At the very least, the candidate could listen to what her supporters were suggesting.

Most of these turned out to be bad ideas. Mass mailings are spam. Internet voting is insecure. Policy statements on line are as boring as policy statements on paper. Candidates come into campaigns with a set of beliefs, so they don't want to put them up for informal votes among supporters. And candidates really don't have time to read thousands of emails, even if some of them have great ideas.

Further, most of these ideas are continuations of the old broadcast model of politics in which the central figure beams her "message" to the faceless mass of supporters who, in return, chant, pump signs up and down, and send checks.

Campaigns have in fact become the most relentless of the broadcast marketers. Candidates are trained to do nothing but deliver their message over and over. If the message of the day was "Good paying jobs," then the candidate responds to a question about AIDS in Africa by saying: "Good question. We have to end AIDS in Africa while ensuring that every American has a good paying job." Tony the Tiger was no less predictable and formulaic.

No wonder the largest party in America has become the I Don't Vote Party.

The Dean campaign's initial insight, according to Joe Trippi, the campaign manager who oversaw the development of its remarkable Internet component, was that the Internet would be a great way to raise lots of money in small donations from lots of people. If two million people each gave $100, they would match George W. Bush's anticipated war chest from large donors. That's mass broadcast thinking.

But Trippi had the wisdom and the guts to let the Internet component develop its own role. In the Spring of 2003, the campaign began its own weblog. The handful of contributors signed their own name to everything they wrote, and readers came to know them and like them. Love them, even. That's one important way to get over the problem of mass communication: The CEO may not be able to correspond with each person individually, but there are some people in the organization who can speak in their own voice about what really matters to them. We hear those voices and respond in very personal ways. It's still a broadcast, but at least it's a person and not a marketing strategy that's talking to us. There had never been someone in the role of campaign blogger before – someone who speaks for the candidate but not as a direct representative like a press secretary, someone who speaks in her own voice. Remarkable.

At the same time, the campaign started using MeetUp.com, an online service that enables local groups to meet in the real world. And now the real solution to the mass broadcasting problem started to become clear: We can't all talk with Howard Dean or even with his campaign site's bloggers, but we sure as hell can talk with one another.

That doesn't reverse the flow of the broadcast – many talking to one. It blows apart the model. The many now form groups and talk amongst themselves.

In the months that followed, the Dean campaign tried to make it ever easier for groups to form. The campaign backed the development of open source software for groups that wanted to have virtual meeting places. It offered its own "social network" that encouraged people to find in cyberspace others nearby in real space so that they could organize local events. It even tried "point-to-point" communications by providing supporters with addresses of registered Democrats in states with early primaries so that the "Deaniacs" could write heartfelt letters explaining what they saw in the Doctor.

Blowing apart the broadcast model is no easy thing for a political campaign, for it means giving up at least some measure of control. But isn't the chief lesson of the success of the Internet that control is the enemy of scale? If you want something to grow big fast, you have to let it loose. For the Internet, that means the architecture has no central point of access and requires no permissions to join. For a campaign, it means that the candidate is no longer fully in charge of her or his message. The groups that formed using the Dean campaign Internet tools were free to create their own mission statement. The people writing letters to undecided voters in Iowa and New Hampshire were encouraged to come up with their own drafts. Even the make-your-own-sign facility on the Dean site had a blank where you could fill in your own message.

The result was some chaos around the message. And it meant that conversations among Dean supporters sometimes were about how strongly they disagreed with the candidate on this or that issue. Even so, the enthusiasm of the supporters – even with their variance from the official platform – has become legendary. Deaniacs, indeed.

Yet, all in all, what good did it do? Some have claimed that the architecture of the Dean campaign created "echo chambers" where people only listened to their own voices and shut out the voice of reality. I think that is a misreading of what happened. People did indeed use online Dean spaces to sing the praises of their candidate and his campaign, but these were like any other political gathering of supporters where one feels safe in one's enthusiasm and in which bonds of commitment are formed. If the Dean campaign was ever deluded into thinking it was doing better than it was, the high polling numbers, record crowds, and record-breaking fund raising were far more to blame than Internet enthusiasm could have been.

And others have complained that the Dean campaign didn't use this anti-broadcast infrastructure to bubble policy ideas up from the grassroots. Despite some fairly petty examples – campaign manager Joe Trippi got the idea to have the Governor brandish a symbolic red bat from one of the blog discussion boards – it is true that policy and strategy were set by the campaign management without much grassroots input. But that's inevitable for a political campaign centered on a candidate. The candidate has to come to the campaign with a set of ideas and policies; otherwise, she or he would be nothing but a blank slate, waiting to be inscribed by polling data. The problem with the grassroots writing policy is that it merely tries to reverse the flow of the broadcast, and that doesn't work very well – although it would have been fascinating if the Dean campaign had taken the opportunity to experiment with connecting all the policy conversations, from the candidate, through the campaign policy department, to the grassroots themselves.

Good came from the breaking of the broadcast metaphor. An obscure Vermont governor went from zero to a significant percentage of popular support. A way was discerned to raise money without having to pander to special interests. People felt themselves to be a part of the campaign that mattered. People opened their hearts to politics again, perhaps because politics was spoken not through ads and sound bytes, but through the voices of real people whom they knew or came to know. Democracy once again seemed to be something that we, the people, do, not something that every four years is done to us.

We don't yet know what the effect will be now that we have remembered that democracy is about connecting as much as about standing alone in a voting booth facing a lonely, existential decision. The Dean campaign may turn out to be an awakening of something we can't yet foresee, and if it does, it will be more because of our deep desire to connect – as individual voices paradoxically joined in a mass – than because of any of the stands taken by that particular candidate in that particular year.

# Sociable technology and democracy
## by danah boyd

In social networks literature, the term homophily refers to the idea that "birds of a feather stick together".[112] Usually, the most tightly knit groups share much in common - from philosophical beliefs to interests. Additionally, people who share a lot in common are more likely to get to know one another.[113] Although two close friends do not necessarily hold the same political views, the probability that they do is far greater than the probability that they do not.

Birds of a feather flock together because there is value in doing so. It is through this commonality that one can find security in one's views, feel validated and supported, and have the kind of environment that fosters motivation and joy. When communities reference the value of 'safe space,' they are referring to the homophilous environments in which people do not have to defend their minority status. Common ground is crucial to develop a safe environment in which to explore the personal and philosophical issues.

While homophily is personally valuable, its impact on emergent democracy can have dire consequences. Most noticeably:

1.  It is easy to overestimate the success of a movement;
2.  It is hard to rally diverse groups.

Homophily can often cloud an individual's perspective about the general trend. Living in San Francisco, I am constantly surprised to overhear people express genuine shock over every election and political decision. Who on earth voted for Schwarzenegger? What rational person is pro-life? Why is anyone upset that my gay neighbors can finally get married? Albeit, even as a diverse city, San Francisco is probably the largest political bubble in the United States, but this type of shock can be heard

---

[112] McPherson, Miller, Lynn Smith-Lovin, and James M. Cook. 2001. Birds of a Feather: Homophily in Social Networks. *Annual Review of Sociology*, 27, pp. 415-44.

[113] Feld, Scott. 1981. The Focused Organization of Social Ties. *American Journal of Sociology*, 86(5), March, 1015-1036.

elsewhere: on college campuses, in churches and throughout liberal and conservative, urban and rural communities. People within a community usually have the same views and they rarely know people with differing views. When reflecting on political events, people project their value system onto others and fail to comprehend how someone might possibly think differently.

Political views are not the only values that are densely clustered amidst people. (Sub)cultures consistently overestimate the popularity and spreadability of their perspective and values. For example, bloggers know other bloggers and tend to overestimate how much of the world blogs. More noticeably, bloggers value their activity and tend to think that everyone should or will blog without realizing that other people do not have the same value system that would make blogging appear appealing. Given the combination of limited lines of sight and applying one's values on others, it is not surprising that it is difficult for any individual to grasp the larger picture. Without broad awareness, people are likely to overestimate the success of their movement — it seems as though everyone agrees. Clay Shirky argues that this may be one of Dean's biggest problems when reflecting on how Howard Dean failed to capture the American voters amidst an apparent overwhelming support online and in the media.[114]

When considering the value of diversified networks, Granovetter argued that weak ties helped people find jobs because they allowed people to reach out to a more diverse audience with greater access to more diverse possibilities.[115] Strong ties are where the greatest overlap of commonality is found; weak ties open up difference. Thus, when thinking about how to reach out to people with diverse political views, it is crucial to think beyond the homophilous worlds in which we are most comfortable.

Technology connects people beyond the physical restrictions of place. While technology offers the potential to access more diverse audiences, it also allows people to extend their homophilous tendencies into the

---

[114] Shirky, Clay, *Exiting Deanspace*, February 3, 2004, http://www.corante.com/many/archives/2004/02/03/exiting_deanspace .php

[115] Granovetter, Mark. 1973. The strength of weak ties. *American Journal of Sociology*, 78, pp. 1360—1380.

digital realm rather than relying on physical proximity. As discussed below, technology tends to increase the connections of like-minded individuals more than increase the breadth of diversity. Although technology provides a public forum in which people can express different political views, this does not guarantee that those views are heard.

When Californians were up in arms about Proposition 54, which called for prohibitions in education and hiring based on classification by race, ethnicity, color, or national origin, Berkeley students covered the campus with anti-54 messages. Yet, unless one went to Berkeley, one was not likely to see these messages. Physical proximity was a barrier to spreading the physical messages. Online, many Friendster users converted their Profiles to express "no on 54" messages by changing their names, uploading pictures and talking about Proposition 54 in their Testimonials and Interests. Hundreds of anti-54 Profile connected to other anti-54 Profiles (or the anti-54 Fakester). Yet, when I spoke with Friendster users who purported to surf the network for hours daily looking for interesting Profiles, very few could recall seeing the anti-54 Profiles. They were not hidden, but they were clustered. Once one came across the cluster, one could see hundreds. Until then, they were invisible. Physical place was no longer the limiting factor - social space was. Collections of like-minded anti-54 activists connected throughout Friendster, but their message was barely heard by other participants.

## Social Technology and Homophily

Since its inception, the Internet has supported sociability. People flocked to BBSes and Usenet to find others like them and to engage in discussions about technology, politics, sexuality and a vast array of other topics of interest. Social support groups formed around common needs and issues.

While people were simultaneously exposed to like minds and diverse opinions, individuals chose communities based on their personal needs. For many, including myself, the Internet offered an idyllic space to find others of a similar ilk. This was particularly powerful for marginalized groups of people separated geographically who knew no one like them locally. Early social tools were fundamentally beneficial for all of the geeks, freaks and other social outcasts. Through online interactions, individuals could realize that there were others like them and find social support and validation in a way the helped people shape their views and identity.

Social technology support homophily in a new way. As people seek out groups, they searched for others like them. The technology does not prevent diverse groups from converging, but the needs and goals of the individuals determine the personal value of convergence. Of course, as groups formed around one type of similarity, other differences emerged. For example, the Usenet group *rec.motorcycles* attracted people interested in motorcycles, but they did not limit their discussions to the topic of the group. Regulars talked about their life and engaged in political debates. As I am writing this, there is a long thread on this group entitled "Riding Gear for the Homophobes of Reeky" where a discussing about a motorcycle issue spiraled into a political debate. While most would label this thread a flame war, it is precisely these types of conversations where differences can be seen amidst similarities.

While the public nature of Usenet allows people to cluster based on interests, the boundaries of unmoderated spaces have to be maintained socially instead of structurally. One cannot guarantee that all members agree on all issues. In a public environment, disagreements emerge and spiral into flames. There is little social pressure to stop. People express their frustration, but it only encourages the flames. Thus, people simply wait for flames to die or they leave in frustration. Flames almost always happen when individuals are attacked, usually because of something tangential to the topic at hand or because the core values of the group are attacked.

Consider the war between *alt.tasteless* and *rec.pets.cats*.[116] A community of cat lovers came together on the *rec.pets.cats* Usenet group to share stories and gain support. Usenet afforded this relatively non-controversial collection of people to converge to share stories and support one another with information about cats. Through regular posting, the subscribers to the cat group had evolved a set of norms that encouraged new posters to be active, positive and supportive participants. Yet, when regular posters at *alt.tasteless* decided to 'raid' the cat group, regular posters were horrified by the shift in social norms.

---

[116] Quittner, Josh. The War Between alt.tasteless and rec.pets.cats, *Wired*, Issue 2.05, May, 1994.

Postings about microwaving cats were not part of the community's values and the onslaught of tasteless and threatening messages created a mini-war between the two communities.

In the motorcycle newsgroup, it is not a heated discussion about motorcycle differences that created the flame; it is an argument about homosexuality. In the cats group, it is a difference about social norms. Disparate views can be very divisive to a public forum when there is no common ground. Usenet, like many other Internet tools, is technologically democratic: anyone is welcome to participate. Yet, embedded in the sites of interaction is a set of social norms assumed by the participants. Not all groups uphold the same norms and the convergence of disparate groups brings this issue to its head. As such, spaces that permit like minds to converge also supply fertile ground for disagreeing views to flourish.

The public nature of Usenet did not work for many people, particularly those wanting social support regarding controversial issues. Some of these groups evolved into protected mailing lists or otherwise hidden communities. Much of this can be attributed to the need for safe space. For heated discussions, people wanted communities with some baseline of commonality. As such, mailing lists and private forums emerged as a safe space for conversation.

For five years, I helped build and manage such a community. V-Day is a non-profit organization working to end violence against women and girls worldwide. Over 1,200 people organize productions of "The Vagina Monologues" each year to raise money, awareness and support. Through an internal site called the V-Spot, organizers and their colleagues can communicate with the vast array of activists working towards the same goal. Collective values around tolerance and support are articulated and maintained through the community. V-Day organizers are not a homophilous group — they do not share all of the same viewpoints, values or even language. Yet, in a constructed safe space, the organizers are able to put down their differences to communicate on common ground about ending violence against women. Muslims speak with sex workers; older women speak with teens. National and political boundaries are forgotten. At one point, a liberal college student voiced her outrage that Tampax was a sponsor. A woman from a conservative religious community wrote back to note that she was dismayed that Planned Parenthood was a sponsor; she said that she swallowed her disagreement and reminded herself that the goal was not to find differences, but to find similarities between the organizers, to remember that they were all working towards the same goal.

One of the ways in which V-Day has been valuable is by providing people with a mechanism to connect over commonalities amidst differences. Yet, it is not the online community that made V-Day effective. Technology operated as a glue between different active offline communities. Yet, by being a part of a larger community, V-Day organizers felt empowered and supported to fight to end violence against women locally as part of a global cause.

*Engaging People, Engendering Community*

Social tools offer a broader context in which people could ground their beliefs and actions. This is important because engaging people requires more than education; people feel empowered when they recognize that they can make systemic changes. In the Philippines, citizens rallied against their government using SMS to collectively gather and voice their opinion.[117] The power of collective action using technology was realized when they overthrew their President. This situation is particularly powerful because the motivating force was one's own social network, not an external source.

While media has a dramatic effect on our political knowledge, an individual's social network plays a much more critical role on affecting an individual's view. Parents help shape children's views as do other strong ties. While education, age and sexuality affect one's political viewpoint, religion, socio-economic class and cultural values ultimately have far more influence over our politics. Given that these are tightly coupled with one's family, it can often be hard to determine which factor is really key. In other words, an individual growing up in a rural conservative religious town with parents whose values match the social norms is most likely to have those same values.

It is important to consider the role of one's network when thinking about how technologies are used to engage people politically. In the United States, activists and technologists worked to harness collective

---

[117] Rheingold, Howard. *Smart Mobs*, Perseus, Cambridge, Mass. 2002

action via new tools like MoveOn.org and Meetup.com. Simultaneously, individuals used blogs and SMS to spread information and connect with like-minded people. Arguably, these technologies engaged a whole new cross-section of the population to participate politically. Yet, they are not being used to generate effective political coups.

In the Philippines, the people creatively used available technology to meet their needs. Conversely, American activists are building tools to encourage democratic participation and to empower people who are currently not engaged with the democratic process. It is important to recognize that these are two different uses of technology for emergent democracy. On one hand, people are using what is available to them; on the other, tools are being designed to meet specific people's needs. In considering how to evolve emergent democracy, it is important to consider the relevant social groups as well as traditional social theory concerning how and why people engage ingroup behaviors.

Democratic participation varies throughout the world. In some countries, such as Australia and Brazil, voting is compulsory. Failing to vote could result in fines, jail or other restrictions on one's rights such as the inability to travel. In other countries, such as the United States, voting is considered a privilege. Yet, in both compulsory and non-compulsory systems, there are always people who do not participate, either because they are ineligible or because they choose not to participate.

As groups fight to give rights to disenfranchised populations — such as those denied their vote through errors in the Florida balloting system that falsely accused them of being felons — there is another group of non-voters that must be considered: those who choose not to participate. A crucial assumption about these people is that they fail to grasp the importance and value of participating. This is particularly important when considered the declining American participation in democracy. Actions such as MTV's "Rock the Vote" and MoveOn.org are devised to engage people, to empower them through education. When interviewed, some people who are disengaged from the democratic process argue that they are wilfully, voluntarily disengaged.

This highlights a critical issue within democracy discussions. Compulsory systems solve this problem by mandating participation, resulting in far fewer by-choice non-participants. In other environments, efforts are made to educated, incent, or guilt people into participating. But citizens who opt out of civic participation often do so because they *already* feel disenfranchised, as when the lack of a palatable candidate creates an election with no desirable possible outcome.

When working to address by-choice non-participants, it is important to understand the factors of their non-participation. While education will address some concerns, systemic changes are necessary to address others. These are tightly intertwined problems. It is important to consider both how the collective can empower themselves and feel powerful enough to affect the systemic nature of their concerns.

In the Philippines, short messaging system (SMS) allowed tens of thousands of citizens to collect and voice their anger. SMS was not used to educate people; it relied on people's previous level of civic awareness. Furthermore, SMS was not developed to incite political revolutions; people used available technology to meet their needs.

In converse, consider the American Dean Campaign. Technology aided those behind Dean to form a strong collective voice; this allowed that group to educate others more effectively about why they believed in Dean. Yet, this technology did not offer the disengaged population a reason to get involved unless they saw their values represented by Dean.

Shirky argues that the digital fevor around Dean was a mirage — it reflected the ability for communities to form around a campaign and for money to be raised, but this did not necessarily translate into votes. The digital Dean Campaign represented an "affinity over geography" while voting is inherently "geography over affinity ." [118] Technology operationalized homophily and allowed like-minded souls to gather with ease. This is truly powerful, yet it is not necessarily the metric of success that participants imagined.

*Technological Considerations*

Given different approaches to emergent democracy, it is important to step back and consider how technology is involved. Current models

---

[118] Shirky, *ibid.*

seem to suggest at least three different uses of technology with respect to democracy:

1. People use available technologies in a creative way to communicate within their social network;
2. Technology is developed to connect physical communities for broader support;
3. Technology is developed to help educate and empower.

Each of these approaches has different strengths and weaknesses and appeals to different groups. Yet, there are two glaring differences embedded in these three examples. First, do people drive technological use or is technology created to incent people? Second, do people use technology to connect to people in their social network or to reach out and meet new people? If so, would they join a community or participate in connecting communities?

When considering this, it is important to realize that technology may not be able to change human goals. People either want to meet new people, or they do not, and if they do, they often want to meet people like them. Neither education nor the opportunity to create community will incent everyone to participate. The greatest incentive to participate is pressure from the everyday community in which the individual is already involved.

Herein lies the greatest challenge. If individuals determine the most effective ways to use technology, not the technology creators and activists, how can technology encourage repurposing for political action? This is a problematic statement. Meetup.com and MoveOn.org truly meet some people's needs — they are great technologies that have incented many new political participants. Yet, they are not for everyone. Some people have no interest in meeting new people while others are too overwhelmed by regular email about actions to do without incentive.

I would argue that the most clear predictor of someone's willingness to participate is probably that their friends are participating. When the United States started bombing Afghanistan, groups of friends gathered in San Francisco to collectively participate in MoveOn.org actions. It was precisely the combination of everyday community and actionable items that made this work for some new participants.

While new technologies cannot predict how they will be repurposed, they can be designed to help bridge the gap between people's everyday communities and the digital tools. Consider:

- How could local communities/friend groups be represented and collectively connect to new groups? It only takes one leader in a community to help build a larger network. In particular, how can disparate groups connect along an axis of commonality to be mutually beneficial in a way that will not spiral into a flame war?

- How could people see the impact of their local community/friend group on the whole? How would people feel if they could see how many of their friends voiced their opinion on an issue, participated in a poll or donated money? How could one use the power of distributed relationships to recognize one's significance in the process? If one person's public participation incents others to participate and this is made visible, perhaps people will realize that their vote is more than simply a vote, but an action that affects the whole chain of participation.

Embedded in this discussion are three important social certainties:

1. Not everyone wants to engage in online communities;
2. In building communities, people tend to seek out people with similar perspectives;
3. Community is valuable for support; outreach is limited by the diversity of a community's breadth.

Within democracy, effectiveness is measured in quantifiable terms: bigger is better — more money, more votes, etc. Communities should not be measured based on size — more does not mean better. Many Usenet groups and mailing lists die because too many people are involved. Furthermore, while poll numbers are valuable for candidates, those numbers become quickly meaningless for individuals on a personal, local level. Telling someone that 28 percent of the nation voted and that their vote was literally one in a million is quite different than telling someone that 28 percent of their friend group voted and that they were one of four that voted in their 15-person friend group. Localizing participation makes it feel far more visceral and important. On a technological level, scalability is crucial for creating a viable social environment.

As we consider how technology can be used to engage people in democracy, it is important to encourage diverse groups to connect and affect one another without overwhelming individuals. People must be able to find personal significance in the process. To be successful, technology must support people in negotiating their identity, relationships and community as part of the political process.

*Acknowledgements*

Thanks to Ronen Barzel, Jeff Boase, Cory Doctorow and Joi Ito for their constant critique and support. I would also like to express my eternal gratitude to V-Day for always reminding me that change can happen. Finally, "I love my country. By which I mean, I am indebted joyfully to all the people throughout its history who have fought the government to make right." - Ani DiFranco, *Grand Canyon*.

# eVoting
## by Phillip J. Windley, Ph.D.

If there's anything that the election of 2000 taught us, regardless of our feeling about the outcome, it was that elections are precarious things, run on unreliable systems using technologies and even procedures that left us all shaking our heads. I'd bet that there are very few computer geeks watching the fiasco unfold who weren't thinking: "give me a few weeks and I'd build something that worked." That's what we do: solve problems.

The lure of eVoting, or the application of digital technologies to voting systems, comes down to the simple idea that computers, and more recently, the Internet have have fundamentally changed other parts of our lives, so why not democracy as well. Since voting is one of the basic processes of democracy, it seems a natural candidate for electronic automation.

### How voting works

In the United States, voting is a local issue. The Federal government certainly has a lot of say about voting through the Federal Election Commission, but in the end, its state and local officials who administer elections. In most states, the secretary of state's office runs an elections office that sets rules and administers statewide elections.

The actual elections themselves are usually the purview of the county clerk. Moreover, counties and municipalities bear the majority of the cost of managing elections. In 2000, the total county election expenditures were estimated at over $1 billion, or about $10 per voter.

Voting is more complicated than simply tallying votes. In fact, most of the work in an election occurs long before the voter ever steps into the booth. Voter registration requires large databases of voters, their addresses and geographic calculation of precinct and district information. Ballot preparation is a long process that is complicated by myriad rules and regulations. The election itself must be administered, usually with the help of a large, volunteer workforce that gets to practice about once per year. All of these activities, in addition to vote tallying, are part of a voting system.

After the election of 2000, Congress passed the Help America Vote Act (HAVA). The act changes the voter registration system, requires that all punch card systems be replaced, and calls for electronic voting methods that will enable disabled citizens to vote without assistance. These mandates and some Federal money have resulted in a large-scale replacement of old voting systems. HAVA also increased the role that the Federal Elections Commission plays in state and county administered elections.

While the goals of HAVA are laudable, the move to new voting systems has created a hey-day for voting system vendors and caused a number of people to be alarmed over some very real security and integrity questions.

## Computerized systems have to work better, don't they?

Much as we'd like to believe that computerized systems work better than their non-computerized counterparts, that often isn't the case. The Caltech-MIT Voting Technology project found that of the five types of voting machines, hand-counted paper, mechanical lever machines, punch card ballots, optically scanned paper, and electronic voting machines, electronic machines have the second highest rate of unmarked, uncounted and spoiled ballots in presidential, Senate, and governor elections over the last 12 years. The only system that was worse was mechanical lever machines. Hand-counted and optically scanned paper have had the lowest rates over the same period.

So, while electronic systems may be more reliable than mechanical systems, and cheaper to administer than paper ballots, as electronic systems are currently deployed, they are not *better* in the sense that matters most: voting system integrity.

### eVoting integrity

Integrity is the central question in any election. For democracy to work, citizens must believe that their vote has been counted correctly and that the system can and will find and correct mistakes. The question of integrity is a critical one to opponents of current eVoting systems.

California Secretary of State Kevin Shelley in an address to the Voting Systems Panel said:

"The core of our American democracy, members, is the right to vote. And implicit in that right is the notion that that vote be private, that vote be secure, and that vote be counted as it was intended when it was cast by the voter. I think what we're encountering is a pivotal moment in our democracy where all that is being called into question — the privacy of the vote, the security of the vote, and the accuracy of the vote. It troubles me, and it should trouble you."[119]

These three issues: privacy, security, and accuracy are at the heart of the eVoting debate.

Questions surrounding eVoting hinge on the fact that software errors, hardware malfunctions, and even malicious tampering are unavoidable and as a consequence, systems that use software for preparing ballots, managing elections, and counting votes should be built to mitigate these errors and should include processes that create audit trails and cross-checks.

Software has caused many problems with elections. VerifiedVoter.org cites several examples from the November 2003 election:

> In Fairfax, Virginia, testing ordered by a judge revealed that several voting machines subtracted one in every hundred votes for the candidate who lost her seat on the School Board.

> In Boone County, Indiana, a software glitch caused 144,000 votes to be counted from a pool of 19,000 registered voters. Corrected accounting showed just 5,352 ballots cast.[120]

These problems, reported by the press for just a single election cycle, raise the specter of other, undiscovered problems. Would we know if there was a problem?

There are two approaches that have been suggested for mitigating the problems with electronic voting systems. Neither is sufficient on its own to solve the problem, but taken together, along with careful election practices, they provide significantly increased confidence in electronic voting systems.

---

[119] *Address to California Voting Systems Panel,* December 16, 2003, http://www.verifiedvoting.org/kevinshelley2003dec16.asp

[120] http://www.verifiedvoting.org/resources/hr2239_volunteers/Introduction -2-pages.htm

The first approach to the problem is called a "voter verifiable audit trail." The voter verified audit trail requires that electronic voting machines print out, before the voter's choices have been recorded, a tamper-proof paper ballot. The voter can verify that the choices on the paper ballot and the choices on the electronic screen are correct and then record the vote. The paper ballot is then deposited with elections officials and kept securely until after the electronic results have been certified. If there is a challenge to the election, or some other reason to suspect the results, the paper ballots would be available for inspection and could be recounted as an independent, second record.

The primary objections to the voter verified audit trail are twofold: cost and complexity. Neither are problems that can be ignored, but both are solvable. The cost issue is obvious and the solution requires that voting integrity be prioritized higher than other government functions. The complexity issue is more difficult to solve. Voting is already a process that is confusing to many voters. Further, voting is usually administered at the precinct level by volunteers with little training and experience. A complicated process requires increased poll worker training and better facilities for educating voters at the polls about the process.

The second approach is to open up electronic voting system software to inspection by anyone who is interested. A scenario where an insider maliciously alters the software in an electronic voting system to throw and election is not far-fetched. Such an alteration would be difficult to detect because US courts have ruled that the source code used to run electronic voting systems can be considered a 'trade secret' and not open to public scrutiny. Malicious alterations could be clearly visible in the source code, but difficult to detect in the compiled code running on the voting systems.

Furthermore, not only are the national standards for testing and certifying electronic voting systems weak, but enforcement is lax. Testing of electronic voting systems is done in secret by small groups and the results are not open to the public. The results of these certifications are overseen by elections officials who by and large know very little about computer security.

Recently, the source code for Diebold's electronic voting system was leaked to the Internet. The system in question has been used to run elections in Georgia and other jurisdictions. This leak gave computer security experts a unique opportunity to perform an independent, scientific analysis of the source code to a production-quality electronic voting system by a major manufacturer. Three scientists from John Hopkins University, Tadyoshi Kohno, Adam Stubblefield, and Aviel Rubin, and one from Rice University, Dan Wallach, issued a report that concluded:

> Our analysis shows that this voting system is far below even the most minimal security standards applicable in other contexts. We highlight several issues including unauthorized privilege escalation, incorrect use of cryptography, vulnerabilities to network threats, and poor software development processes. For example, common voters, without any insider privileges, can cast unlimited votes without being detected by any mechanisms within the voting terminal. Furthermore, we show that even the most serious of our outsider attacks could have been discovered without the source code. In the face of such attacks, the usual worries about insider threats are not the only concerns; outsiders can do the damage. That said, we demonstrate that the insider threat is also quite considerable. We conclude that, as a society, we must carefully consider the risks inherent in electronic voting, as it places our very democracy at risk.[121]

This example highlights an important point: if a single closed system has the number and severity of errors found in this report, what serious flaws might other, closed electronic voting systems contain? Unfortunately, it is impossible to know since we have only the assurances of the vendors and certification boards.

Manufacturer objections to open source are twofold. The first is a red herring that questions the open source development methodology as a reliable means for creating voting systems. This confuses a development methodology with a result. Opening the source code of electronic voting systems to inspection by the public at large does not require that the company adopt an open-source development methodology.

The second objection comes down to a business question. If electronic voting system vendors open up their source code for public inspection, how can they maintain a competitive advantage? There are many

---

[121] Analysis of an Electronic Voting System, Tadyoshi Kohno, Adam Stubblefield, Aviel D. Rubin, and Dan S. Wallach, IEEE Symposium on Security and Privacy 2004, *http://avirubin.com/vote.pdf*

companies who compete without keeping their source code a secret. MySQL and Redhat are examples. That said, as a society, we must ask ourselves whether maintaining the viability of a few corporations trumps our right to a voting system that we can trust. I'm confident that if elections officials required open source voting systems as a matter of gaining contracts, there would be companies who would find a way to do it and still prosper.

### Internet Voting

A subtopic in eVoting that deserves special attention is the subject of Internet voting. Often, voters do not, or cannot, vote because of the inconvenience of getting to a polling place. They may be home bound, traveling, or even living in a foreign country. Of course, absentee voting is an option in these cases, but comes with its own set of problems. First, you have to be able to predict, usually weeks in advance, that you will be "absent" and request a ballot be mailed to you. Furthermore, you usually have to fill out extra paperwork, and mail it in with your ballot. This is not only discouraging to many who might otherwise vote, but can also be a source of delay in election results.

The Internet has done so much to change how we interact with other segments of society, it seems a natural choice for solving some of the absentee voter problems. Indeed, the Pentagon nearly put an Internet voting system, called SERVE, into place for the 2004 election. The rollout was suspended, however, after a panel of experts issued a scathing report on the security problems inherent in the scheme.

The concerns can be summarized as follows:

> [B]ecause SERVE is an Internet- and PC-based system, it has numerous other fundamental security problems that leave it vulnerable to a variety of well-known cyber attacks (insider attacks, denial of service attacks, spoofing, automated vote buying, viral attacks on voter PCs, etc.), any one of which could be catastrophic.

> Such attacks could occur on a large-scale, and could be launched by anyone from a disaffected lone individual to a well-financed enemy agency outside the reach of U.S. law. These attacks could result in large-scale, selective voter disenfranchisement, and/or privacy violation, and/or vote buying and selling, and/or vote switching even to the extent of reversing the outcome of many elections at once, including the presidential election.

The vulnerabilities we describe cannot be fixed by design changes or bug fixes to SERVE. These vulnerabilities are fundamental in the architecture of the Internet and of the PC hardware and software that is ubiquitous today. They cannot all be eliminated for the foreseeable future without some unforeseen radical breakthrough.

We have examined numerous variations on SERVE in an attempt to recommend an alternative Internet-based voting system that might deliver somewhat less voter convenience in exchange for fewer or milder security vulnerabilities. However, all such variations suffer from the same kinds of fundamental vulnerabilities that SERVE does...

Because the danger of successful, large-scale attacks is so great, we reluctantly recommend shutting down the development of SERVE immediately and not attempting anything like it in the future until both the Internet and the world's home computer infrastructure have been fundamentally redesigned, or some other unforeseen security breakthroughs appear.

Ultimately, based largely on this report, that is what happened — the Pentagon decided to scrap the system, at least for the 2004 election. Its certain that various jurisdictions will continue to experiment with Internet voting because the benefits seem so great, but without significant, unforeseen technical advances, many of which are antithetical to the very design and operation of the Internet, voting over the Internet is likely to remain infeasible.

## A Call to Action

Voting systems are one of foundational technologies of our democracy, and make no mistake, whether digital or not, they are technologies. I think it's safe to assume that no matter how problematic the current systems and processes are, electronic voting systems are not going away. As a computer professional, you have a unique perspective on how digital technologies can affect voting systems and getting involved isn't that difficult.

Here are some ideas about how to get involved:

Start with your county clerk and find out what election system your county uses and how it is certified. What issues do they face? Is there a way you can help them?

Meet with someone in the state election's office. Ask them the same questions. What is the certification process is your State? State elections personnel have a difficult assignment, but they're approachable and willing to listen for the most part. Keep your tone helpful, rather than belligerent and you'll learn something and have a chance to educate them along the way.

Engage your legislators. Send them an email and ask to meet with them. Help them understand the issues surrounding eVoting so that they're educated. Most legislators I've dealt with want to understand the technology implications, particularly on issues as fundamental as voting. You may not get much traction when they're in session, but few states have full time legislatures. Contact them when they're out of session and you'll likely find that you're knowledge and willingness to help are welcome.

Finally, there a number of advocacy groups that are working with government to create trustworthy voting system. Advocacy groups can always use volunteer help and there's room to make your voice heard.

# Section Three
# Strategy and the Political Process

# Democracy for the rest of us: the minimal compact and open-source government by Adam Greenfield

In many ways, we human beings are cursed with a relatively short lifespan, not least because any one of us rarely lives long enough to perceive the longer waves unfolding through human history.

As a result, we tend to believe that the structures and agreements that obtain at the time of our first awareness of the world are somehow eternal. Even when, intellectually, we know better, emotionally it's frequently difficult to let go of the idea that (say) the nation state has both been here from the morning of the world, and is here to stay.

Countering this is a nascent recognition in some circles of my acquaintance that this form of sociopolitical organization while endemic to and characteristic of the twentieth century had historically arisen, and equally so, will one day subside. Some obvious questions then become *What comes afterward?* and, still more importantly, *What might come afterward if encouraged to do so?*

In other words: what kinds of constitutional structures are appropriate to an internetworked, interdependent age? What sorts of arrangements of power between humans can account for the deep variation in beliefs and assumptions among the six billion of us who share this planet, while still providing for a common jurisprudence? What measures can be taken that enhance the common security without unduly infringing on the sovereignty of the individual?

I believe that a useful model can be found in the open-source or "free" software movement. This mode (and ethos) of development provides several fertile metaphors, not least the basic, deeply appealing idea of a voluntary global community empowered and explicitly authorized to reverse-engineer, learn from, improve and use-validate its own tools and products.

Given the open-source software movement's self-evident success in spurring the spontaneous cooperation of a widely dispersed community, in an impressively short period of time, and without recourse to conventional incentives, it has to be taken seriously as a potential source of organizing principles for other realms of human endeavor. An added attraction is that open-source software is generally held to be superior in utility, adaptability and robustness to proprietary alternatives.

## What does "open-source" mean?

The open-source or "free" software movement is a rich nexus of ideas about the constitution of arbitrarily distal individuals into a community, as well as features of emergent cooperation and self-correction among the members of that community. Seeing how and why these innovations may be relevant to the political realm requires a more detailed analysis of the movement's innovations.

Ordinarily, when computer software is "compiled" for use in a given processor environment, its source code is obscured. Users can thereafter only see what the software does, not how its designers achieved those effects; without unusual (and illegal) exertion, they are forced into a consumer-product relationship with the software.

By contrast, some software is distributed along with its source code, ensuring that whatever methodological and structural innovations it presents are shared equally with all users. This is effectively a grant of intellectual property to the public domain, with certain licensure provisions designed to ensure that the insights literally thus encoded remain public and available for free use and reuse. Such software is known as "open source" or "free."[122]

Here is gnu.org's natural-language definition of "free" software:

Free software...refers to four kinds of freedom, for the users of the software:

- The freedom to run the program, for any purpose (freedom 0).

---

[122] Note: I have used the term "open-source" in preference to "free software" because, for better or worse, it has become the more prevalent of the two terms, and widely understand to mean the same thing despite meaningful distinctions between the two terms (and in the case of the latter term, the coiner's clear intentions).

- The freedom to study how the program works, and adapt it to your needs (freedom 1). Access to the source code is a precondition for this.

- The freedom to redistribute copies so you can help your neighbor (freedom 2).

- The freedom to improve the program, and release your improvements to the public, so that the whole community benefits (freedom 3). Access to the source code is a precondition for this.

A program is free software if users have all of these freedoms. Thus, you should be free to redistribute copies, either with or without modifications, either gratis or charging a fee for distribution, to anyone anywhere. Being free to do these things means (among other things) that you do not have to ask or pay for permission.

You should also have the freedom to make modifications and use them privately in your own work or play, without even mentioning that they exist. If you do publish your changes, you should not be required to notify anyone in particular, or in any particular way...

In order for these freedoms to be real, they must be irrevocable as long as you do nothing wrong. If the developer of the software has the power to revoke the license, without your doing anything to give cause, the software is not free.[123]

Key to this understanding is that users are free to make any desired modification to the code at all, *except those that restrict the freedoms enunciated in the license.* From version 2 of GNU General Public License, June 1991:

To protect your rights, we need to make restrictions that forbid anyone to deny you these rights or to ask you to surrender the rights. These restrictions translate to certain responsibilities for you if you distribute copies of the software, or if you modify it.

For example, if you distribute copies of such a program, whether free or for a fee, you must give the recipients all the rights that you have. You

---

[123] gnu.org, the Free Software Definition,
http://www.gnu.org/philosophy/free-sw.html

must make sure that they, too, receive or have easy access to the source code. And you must show them these terms so they know their rights...[124]

This guarantee of free self-replication in perpetuity gives open-source software several important advantages that packaged, proprietary software does not share. By lowering the barriers to entry associated with proprietary code notably, cost and technical controls on reproduction open-source code is "released into the wild," made available for use and testing by a highly-motivated international community of largely self-educated programmers, each pursuing their own end.

A free software advocate named Rob Bos put it this way, in February 1999:

Open source programs are tried and proven, they are constantly pressed from every direction to do specific tasks, and do them well; and for the simple reason that they are written to work, not simply to sell copies. Free software doesn't just work better, it works orders of magnitude better. Open sourcing an application gives the source code to a large number of developers, instead of a small, tight group. Free software projects have a pool of developers and an effective budget multiple times higher than an equivalent proprietary development project, and will, given all other equal things, advance at a rate many times faster because of their access to an much larger development team. Peer review of code isn't just a pipe dream, it is an essential means to writing superior applications, no matter where they are written.[125]

### Constitution as codebase and distribution

Of particular interest to our concerns is the concept of a "codebase," a core of universally-recognized and accepted instructions maintained on a public registry, and a "distribution[126]," which offers a praxis for

---

[124] Ibid., the GNU General Public License,
    http://www.gnu.org/copyleft/gpl.html

[125] From a no-longer extant *32bitsonline* article, quoted at
    http://academic.evergreen.edu/h/hardav14/section6.htm

[126] See, in this regard, http://www.orionlinux.com/distribution.html, "What is a distribution?"

supporting locally differing, self-contained (but essentially interoperable) variations on the single codebase.

Taking these as model, in February 2003 I published a paper called "The minimal compact: Preliminary notes on an 'open-source' constitution for post-national entities" (available at http://v-2.org/minimalcompact publicbeta1.pdf). The paper described the conceptual framework for a post-national, virtual mode of political organization: a hyperlocal polity whose constitution is conceived as codebase. Such a constitution would specify a minimum number of articles to which all signatories subscribe, allowing an instantiation of the compact to form anywhere and anywhen one or more signatories is present.

Compact communities, or "instantiations," would be free to supplement the core agreement with an arbitrary number of articles appropriate to local contexts and concerns. They would be further invited to submit such innovations to a central (but distributed) registry for prospective enactment by other signatory communities, and potentially even adoption into the core itself.

Provided thusly, the compact could manifest in and adapt to widely separated locations and contexts, much as anyone can produce, package and release distributions of "free" software, so long as the distribution itself offers in turn the same provisions for free licensure.

## Why minimal?

The core articles are envisioned as guaranteeing the individual signatory certain inalienable and unabridgeable rights, prescribing certain modes for resolution of the inevitable conflicts between signatories and no more. They would remain explicitly mute as to questions of a community's internal organization, ethical or moral norms, modes of resource allocation, ethnic or linguistic composition, and so on. They merely suffice to establish an arena for individuals and communities to pursue their ends in ways that are maximally mutually beneficial.

Implicit in the proposal was my belief that, in devising arrangements under which to live, human beings might (at least contingently) agree on the meaning and importance of concepts such as the basic security of the individual from coercion, but are likely to agree on little else.

I described the agreement under discussion as "minimal" simply because, as a practical matter, it is unlikely that effective percentages of the planetary citizenry could be persuaded to adopt any framework that spoke to anything other than an essential core of agreed principle. To be acceptable to meaningful numbers of potential signatories, it must limit itself to that which can be agreed on by all, at least provisionally. (As things stand, it is already easy to caricature any such project as guilelessly utopian.)

Provisions of the core agreement that seem crucial to its success as envisioned are those guaranteeing any given signatory individual freedom of movement, freedom of association, and freedom from coercion, as well as specifying that no human person may be kept from choosing to become a signatory.

## Why post-national?

I tend to think of nation states as essentially moribund, a recognition which stems from a variety of inputs, not least of which is personal experience. At the very least, it's inarguable that the nation state is the subject of increasing centrifugal tensions its power devolving both upward (toward hemispheric and global agreements), outward (toward transnational corporations, nongovernmental organizations, and media such as CNN) and downward (toward regional, local, metropolitan, watershed, ethnic and other constituencies, as well as various forms of "direct democracy").

This tension is expressed acutely in Niels Albertsen and Bülent Diken's paper "Mobility, Justification and the City." Albertsen and Diken[127] define power as inherently mobile "action at a distance," while understanding politics to hinge on a "hopelessly local" reliance on concentration, reflection and dialogue. Following this recognition, they diagnose an "increasing gap between power and politics": the inherent mobility of power in a networked age appears to be inimical to the civic and communal virtues that politics depends on vitally.

## The immanent polity: Portable citizenship for a mobile age

---

[127] Albertsen, N., and Diken, B, "Mobility, Justification and the City" http://www.comp.lancs.ac.uk/sociology/soc082bd.html

Partially, this is due to the survival of the historical identification of polity and territory into an age in which the binding makes little practical sense. The Marxist historian Eric Hobsbawm provides the best pithy definition of a nation state I've yet come across: "a bounded territory with its own autonomous institutions." The minimal compact, by contrast, imagines a situation that decouples allegiance from territoriality, finding physical location to be a remarkably poor predictor of a person's deepest beliefs and motivations.

Accordingly, the minimal compact is intended to allow for the formation of polities organized around whatever axis (or axes) of affinity the individual finds most definitive, rather than sintering people selected by a common accident of birth into a notional community. It is anticipated that the formation of such polities would go some way toward resolving the contradiction identified by Albertsen and Diken (following Virilio, Bauman and others), in that the compact's common framework for the resolution of political questions has been endowed with the same quality of escape enjoyed by power itself.

The rights and responsibilities of citizenship are thus made portable, set free to follow their holder wherever he or she may venture or settle in the physical world.

**Subsume, not supplant**

Realistically, any hope for usefully widespread adoption of these ideas resides in the ability of elites privileged by *status quo ante* arrangements to perceive an enlightened self-interest in a world governed by compact. Toward this end, a great deal of thought should be given to the problem of how to reformulate nation states as compact states, effectively translating them into a new idiom.

The present political situation offers at least some reassurance that this is realizable: despite the inevitable chafing, nationalists of various European origins have found themselves able to maintain their autonomous national and linguistic identity as citizens of a European Union. Similarly, adherents to one or another national identity would ideally come to realize that their essential Greekness or Americanness or Chineseness (or Basqueness, etc.) need not wither under the aegis of a minimal compact. Indeed, it is likely that many compact communities would accrete around just such notions of identity.

Given that some extant political entities (chiefly, the liberal democracies) would maintain far more of their character as instantiations of the compact than others, it is also worth noting that non-compact states could readily coexist with signatories. It is my hope that in the fullness of time, life in the latter would prove so overwhelmingly appealing that significant fractions of humanity would "vote with their feet."

## An open-source world?

What would an open-source logic look like, if extended to the documents that organize governance of human polities? Would conceiving of a given community's constitution as analogous to a distribution of software help resolve any of the issues that beset the nation state?

Some features of post-national states and other entities with "open-source" constitutions are foreseeable. Such an entity is

**Flexible, adaptive and extensible**: Given a relatively immutable core agreement of principles, a registrar to maintain and guarantee access to the current version of same, and a mechanism to supplement this body of understanding with locally-appropriate law, the instantiation is free to adapt to such circumstances as it may encounter. In areas where the compact is mute, there can be no puzzling over (nor recourse to) the "framers' intention."

By contrast, the minimal compact was designed to recognize what Toyota famously did, in applying the lessons of management consultant W. Edwards Deming: that very often it is the people "on the ground" that have the most intimate knowledge of, and creative solutions to, the problems that confront any human organization.

Such innovations as confer extraordinary advantages might be referred (by the originating instantiation or others) to the registrar for prospective adoption in future versions of the core agreement itself.

**Infinitely reproducible and nonlocal**: Much in the way "ad-hoc" wireless networks arise and subside as needed, a sovereign compact instantiation appears wherever and whenever one or more signatories appears. Law is thus freed from dependence on national or statutory borders; no longer does jurisdiction or venue override the rights afforded an individual.

**Interoperable and mutual**: Compact instantiations considered in the aggregate constitute a "metapolity," a hyperstate within which interaction is intended to be as nearly frictionless as possible. No matter what their other features, areas recognizing the compact by definition uphold the provisions specifying free flows of people, ideas and information.

In order to preserve the rights afforded compact members, as well as the economic advantages that flow as a consequence of membership in the ultimate free-trade zone (hopefully, sufficiently strong incentive), all signatories are enjoined to extend this full range of core freedoms to all other signatories.

**Highly robust:** As open-source software is constantly tested and validated by its community of users, and suboptimal code reformulated, so the compact is continually acid-tested by its signatories. By setting local communities free to innovate by the thousandfold; by providing for the incorporation of provisions that have been found to enhance the viability of signatory communities, promote wider-spread adoption, or otherwise further compact goals into the core agreement; and by similarly providing for the deletion of provisions that tend to work against such goals, this framework searches the space of possible constitutional forms more efficiently than comparable political arrangements.

Given the orientation of the core agreement toward personal freedom of choice, and the fact that there are arbitrarily many compact instantiations, running in parallel, those instantiations whose supplemental policies result in lowered quality of life for their membership would simply lose population to others not so burdened. Under such circumstances, any failure of policymaking would be local and self-limiting.

Interestingly, when taken together, all the above also implies that the compact metapolity is effectively indestructible, at least from without, at any level below that of extinction. With no national targets to strike at, no particular real estate or symbolic center, for strategic purposes the compact is a state with "no there there." As Deleuze and Guattari said of their figure of the rhizome:

You can never get rid of ants because they form an animal rhizome that can rebound time and again after most of it has been destroyed...may be broken, shattered at a given spot, but it will start again on one of its old lines, or on new lines.[128]

That the Internet also, at least notionally, "routes around failure" in just such a manner only buttresses the contention that communities self-consciously constituted in this way are harnessing usefully robust organizing principles.

## Conclusion: Democracy for the rest of us, redux

Ever since the emergence of the Internet as a force capable of transfiguring business conventions and social arrangements in the late 1990s, an interested subset of its participants have awaited signs of a parallel effect on politics that went beyond, e.g., the relatively banal application of mass email techniques to fundraising and canvassing.

The minimal compact described in the 2003 paper, and elaborated here, is to the best of my knowledge the first political program derived explicitly from the paradigm that has elsewhere been so transformative. While it is not an "Internet state" proper, it nevertheless has certain natural affinities with the "end-to-end" logic and original underlying ethos of the Internet, and would have been difficult if not impossible to imagine without its example of a shared community decoupled from physical space.

Whatever else it achieves, if anything, I hope you take from it the essential recognition it shares with open-source development: that we can teach ourselves what we need to learn, share whatever knowledge we glean, build on the insights of the others engaged in the same efforts. Just as the novice programmer is invited to learn from, understand, and improve upon to "hack" open-source software, the minimal compact invites us to demystify and reengineer government at the most intimate and immediate level.

*We can hack democracy.* You have all my faith.

---

[128] Deleuze, G., and Guattari, F., from "A Thousand Plateaus: Capitalism and Schizophrenia,"
http://www.gseis.ucla.edu/courses/ed253a/kellner/deleuze.html

Adam Greenfield
29 February 2004
New York City

# Making Room for the Third World in the Second Superpower
# by Ethan Zuckerman

In the rise to prominence of weblogs and other social software, Jim Moore and Joi Ito see a fundamental transformation in how people act, interact and make decisions. In essays first published in 2003 – Jim Moore's "The Second Superpower Rears Its Beautiful Head"[129] and Joi Ito's "Emergent Democracy"[130] – they paint hopeful, if sometimes vague, pictures of how Internet communities can show us techniques and tactics that could radically change real-world politics.

Where I'm uncomfortable with both essays is the fact that they extrapolate from the behavior of the people currently using the Internet to make generalizations about how a larger world might use these tools. My work for the past few years, helping spread information technology in developing nations, has convinced me that technology transfer is much more complicated than bringing tools to people who previously lacked them.

I think it's worth taking a close look at what happens when we try to include the developing world in the models Ito and Moore put forward - in other words, "Is there room for the third world in the second superpower?"

Moore's "Second Superpower" suggests that a group of people are changing democracy by using a three-part model for social engagement - collect information, comment and debate, then act. These three steps are all being transformed by new technologies. While we continue to be informed by mass media, we're also getting information from alternative media, published cheaply on the Net, and from personal accounts in weblogs. We're debating and commenting in entirely new ways, enabled by weblogs, discussion groups, instant messaging and mailing lists. And

---

[129] http://cyber.law.harvard.edu/people/jmoore/secondsuperpower.html, accessed 2/27/2004.

[130] http://joi.ito.com/static/emergentdemocracy.html, accessed 2/27/2004.

we're discovering that these tools also make some forms of action more efficient: fundraising, protesting, and organizing face to face "meetups".

Ito's "Emergent Democracy" focuses on the third, "action" phase, and suggests that forms of decision-making emerging from the world of weblogs might lead to a viable form of direct democracy. In the way that ideas percolate from personal networks, to social networks, to large, political networks, reinforced by positive feedback loops, Joi sees a possible path for decision-making to move from individual thinking to group action.

While Moore and Ito have justifiable enthusiasm about the phenomena we're seeing emerge from interconnected communities - the growth of weblogs as an alternative to "mainstream" media, the success of grassroots campaigning in the United States - this enthusiasm needs to be tempered by some skepticism about who is currently using social software, and who has potential to use it. While these tools, in theory, have the potential to increase citizen involvement in collection, debate and action, in practice, they're being used by a small, elite group.

Late in 2002, Nua Internet Surveys estimated there were 650 million Internet users worldwide, concentrated in North America, Western Europe and the wealthier nations of Asia[131]. This estimate suggests that fewer than one percent of Africa's 800 million people are Internet users, in contrast to nearly 50 percent of North Americans. The number of participants in the weblog community is likely to be a small fraction of those 650 million worldwide users. The Perseus Blog Survey estimated the existence of 4.12 million blogs, only 1.4 million of which were regularly maintained.[132] The NITLE weblog census, using a different methodology, estimates 1.7 million "likely" weblogs, 1.1 million of which are estimated to be active.[133] If we accept either set of numbers at face value, webloggers seem to represent a small fraction of Internet users, perhaps a quarter of a percent. The NITLE statistics go on to

---

[131] http://www.nua.ie/surveys/how_many_online/index.html, accessed 2/27/2004.

[132] http://www.perseus.com/blogsurvey/thebloggingiceberg.html, accessed 2/27/2004.

[133] http://www.blogcensus.net/, accessed 2/27/2004

suggest that 62 percent of weblogs are in English[134], implying that many of these weblogs are maintained by North Americans (with substantial blogging populations in Iran, Brazil and Poland.)

The small size of this community is not a reason to dismiss it. All new technologies get used first by a band of early adopters before reaching the mainstream. If these early adopters realize they're not representative of the wider world and work to bring others into the fray, there's a chance these technologies will evolve in a way that's inclusive. If that group forgets that they're outliers in terms of larger society and fails to include others in the shaping of these technologies, it's unlikely that these tools will be useful to the wider world and that the larger transformations Ito and Moore envision will take hold. Given Moore and Ito's prediction that these tools, and the patterns of behavior that accompany them, will change how we gather news and take political action, it seems critical to ensure these tools are as usable in the developing world as they are in the developed world.

Marketers refer to the challenge of selling products popular within a technical elite to the mainstream as "crossing the chasm", phrase coined by Geoffrey Moore in a book of the same name[135]. While marketers have a vested financial interest in ensuring that the mainstream uses products the technorati embrace, it's unclear whether webloggers have a similar incentive to open their community to the wider world. Indeed, the willingness of the first generation of tool builders and users to open their community may be the key determinant in deciding whether these transformations affect only the technical elite or the whole world.

It's my intent in this essay to explore the challenges we face in ensuring that the community growing around online newsgathering, deliberation and action includes the entire world, especially the developing world. I hope to flag situations where techniques and behaviors appropriate for the communities currently served by these tools will likely fail in developing nations. And I attempt to recognize efforts to ensure that these tools have as broad applicability as possible, as well as efforts in the developing world that parallel developments in the online community

---

[134] http://www.blogcensus.net/?page=lang, accessed 2/27/2004.

[135] Crossing the Chasm, Geoffrey Moore. HarperBusiness, 2002.

space. (The absurdity of a white male technologist from Massachusetts giving the "developing world perspective" on these issues is not lost on me – I think of my authorship of this essay as an object lesson in the need for more participants in the digital democracy movement from the developing world.)

As Ito notes in his essay, for a citizen to function in a democracy, a free, engaged and critical press is essential. From a developing world perspective, the mass media in the United States and Europe is badly broken. Corporate consolidation of media, the blurring of the line between media and entertainment and the unspoken bias towards U.S. government interests have combined to create a mass media that pays almost no attention to most of the developing world. My research on media attention and foreign news suggests that Africa, with almost a fifth of the world's population and more than a third of the world's active armed conflicts generally represents less than five percent of the foreign news stories reported by major media outlets.[136] Similar patterns are true for Central Asia, Eastern Europe and parts of Southeast Asia and Latin America. U.S. and European media sources systematically over-cover wealthy nations and under-cover poor ones.

Alternative media is of limited help in this situation. Weblogs have proven their value more as filters than as sources of original reporting. The career-destroying comment by Trent Lott regarding Strom Thurmond, repeated and amplified by Joshua Micah Marshall in his blog, Talking Points Memo, was originally reported by the *Washington Post*, buried deep within a news story.[137] Without a reporter at Thurmond's birthday party to document the comment, bloggers would have been unable to hold Lott accountable for his words. Until webloggers routinely receive journalist credentials and the access that goes with them, webloggers will be dependent on mainstream journalists for their information on many stories.

---

[136] http://h2odev.law.harvard.edu/ezuckerman/, published 8/26/2003.

[137] http://www.guardian.co.uk/usa/story/0,12271,864036,00.html. Dated 12/21/2002, accessed 2/27/2004.

When journalists don't cover parts of the globe, webloggers are like an amplifier without a guitar[138] – they have no signal to reinforce. There aren't enough bloggers in eastern Congo to give us a sense for what's really going on, nor will there be for many years to come. None but the largest news agencies are able to pay the travel costs and insurance for reporters to cover these stories. Most choose not to cover a conflict that's bloody, dangerous, difficult to summarize in a soundbite and unknown to most of their readers or viewers. The net result - we simply don't have information about many parts of the globe relevant to world debate.

Even when we do have some information about under-covered parts of the world, we have another problem, what Ito terms "the caring problem".[139] People pay attention to subjects they care about. They tend to ignore subjects they know little about. Media, trying to serve its customers in a free market, responds by giving them more information on subjects they've demonstrated an interest in and ignoring other subjects. As a result, consumers don't get interested in new topics, as they're not exposed to them. So even if people blog or report about situations in the Congo, readers don't pay attention to these reports and the noosphere, the realm of thought and culture, remains weak in those areas.

To make the data collection phase of Moore's model work for discussions of global issues, we need a media capable of covering the entire globe. That media will look a great deal different than CNN - it's going to be built of citizen reporters reporting local events and travelers with sharp eyes and interesting perspectives reporting on more closed societies.

Rebecca MacKinnon, a former bureau chief for CNN in Beijing, has recently launched a weblog titled NKZone[140] which attempts to cover

---

[138] This analogy shamelessly stolen from Joi Ito:
http://joi.ito.com/archives/2004/01/17/inequality_and_the_role_of_fitn ess_in_power_laws.html, accessed 2/27/2004.

139
http://joi.ito.com/archives/2004/02/15/communities_and_echo_chambe rs.html, accessed 2/27/2004.

[140] http://www.nkzone.org, accessed 2/27/2004.

North Korea from afar by asking journalists, businesspeople and tourists to write about current affairs in North Korea. Using her editorial skills and subject knowledge to filter the inputs of a diverse group of contributors, the site does something most mainstream news sources are incapable of – it provides complex, nuanced pictures of a country usually displayed in black and white.

The leaders in the field of citizen journalism are the reporters and editors at OhMynews[141], an influential South Korean daily Web news site and weekly paper magazine. The site mixes "straight" news with commentary, and editors filter incoming reports from over 25,000 "citizen reporters"[142]. Subang Jaya e-news in Malaysia has taken a similar approach, announcing on its homepage that it is "Not funded by government grants. Independent, Neutral, Responsible."[143] These new models are not limited to highly wired nations. Ghanaweb, founded by a Ghanaian living in Finland, aggregates headlines from the Ghanaian press (primarily for the benefit of Ghanaians living abroad) with lively opinion and commentary from people inside and outside the country[144].

To address Ito's caring problem– i.e., the difficulty of paying attention to news you have no personal connection to a citizen news network will need to go beyond reporting breaking news. It will also need give readers insights into the daily lives of people in other nations, much as blogger Salam Pax gave readers of his blog[145] an insight into Iraq preparing for, and under, attack. It's worth noting that Salam Pax was not an average Iraqi. Educated in Europe, a fan many of the same books and musicians as his readers, Salam was highly accessible to his American

---

[141] www.ohmynews.com, accessed 2/27/2004.

[142] Dan Gillmor, "A New Brand of Journalism is Taking Root in South Korea", http://www.siliconvalley.com/mld/siliconvalley/business/columnists/588 9390.htm, dated 5/18/2003, accessed 2/27/2004.

[143] http://www.usj.com.my/, accessed 2/27/2004.

[144] http://www.ghanaWeb.com/, accessed 2/27/2004.

[145] http://dear_raed.blogspot.com/, accessed 2/27/2004.

and European audience[146]. He was a 'bridge builder", a person with one foot in Iraq and another foot in the world inhabited by his weblog readers.

Solving the caring problem will require a focus on bridge builders: expatriates writing about their adopted nations for their countrymen at home; Peace Corps, Britain's Voluntary Service Organization and other volunteers blogging about their countries of service; exchange students; non-governmental organization workers. These people are well positioned to tell us about events in other nations in terms we can understand, or to tell their countrymen about Europe and the United States. One of the most productive steps the weblog community could take to ensure its inclusiveness is to arm people living outside their home country with weblog tools.

The emergence of an Iranian blogger community is an encouraging example of bridge building. Two years ago, Hossein Derakhshan (better known as "Hoder"[147]) posted a Web page with instructions on blogging in Farsi called "How to build a Persian weblog"[148]. NITLE now reports 62,901 Farsi weblogs[149], making Farsi the third most popular weblog language. As the Iranian blogger community grew, Hoder and others, including Pedram Moallemian of The Eyeranian[150] began blogging in Farsi and English, and encouraging others to do likewise, so that non –Farsi speakers could understand the current political and cultural situation in Iran[151]. Sites like IranFilter[152] now allow English speakers to understand the concerns of an Iranian community that's reaching out to the wider world.

---

[146] http://www.guardian.co.uk/Iraq/Story/0,2763,966819,00.html. Dated 3/30/2003, accessed 2/27/2004.

[147] http://www.hoder.com/weblog/, accessed 2/27/2004.

[148] http://mailpages.scripting.com/2002/05/21, accessed 2/27/2004.

[149] http://www.blogcensus.net/?page=lang, accessed 2/27/2004.

[150] http://www.eyeranian.net/, accesed 2/27/2004.

[151] From personal conversation with Pedram Moallemian, 2/10/2004.

[152] http://www.iranfilter.com/, accessed 2/27/2004.

BlogAfrica[153] is one of several projects underway designed to build bridges between bloggers in Africa and the rest of the world. The BlogAfrica site hosts a catalog of blogs written by Africans or Afrophiles and aggregates these blogs into an African blog RSS feed. Working with volunteers working in Africa with Peace Corps or Geekcorps and visitors traveling to Africa, BlogAfrica is running public workshops in Internet cafes and universities to introduce weblogging to a new population. In future trips, BlogAfrica plans to bring prominent webloggers to Africa to teach workshops, encourage local bloggers and share their perceptions of Africa with their blog readers. Early participants in the workshops include Adam Chambas, whose Accra Crisis blog[154] provides a first-person view of the 2004 Ghanaian presidential campaign.

While communities outside of the United States and Europe are beginning to use weblogs, it's unclear whether the conversations occurring in blogspace cut across communities or only involve the members of a single community. Moore and Ito both point out the value of IInternet-based community tools for enabling intelligent dialogue, even dialogue between people with radically opposing viewpoints. It's worth asking whom this dialogue is open to.

My sense is that these discussions are open only to people with the access to the Internet (which cuts out people in countries who censor, people in unsderserved rural areas, as well as people who don't have money to spend time online); primarily open to people who speak and write English well; primarily open to people who can afford to spend time online engaging in these dialogues (cutting out many people whose jobs don't afford them the luxury of working in front of a CRT.)

What happens to a blog discussion when the participants are interacting with the medium in radically different ways? When one has always-on broadband access and the ability to Google for arguments, while the other is writing entries offline and typing them in during a limited window at a cybercafe? When one is writing in English as a third or fourth language, debating a native speaker? Do the dynamics of weblogs favor better arguments, or just the more articulate speaker? Or perhaps

---

[153] http://www.blogafrica.com/index.html, accessed 2/27/2004.

[154] http://accracrisis.blogspot.com/, accessed 2/27/2004.

just the speaker who has more cultural commonality with his or her audience?

Clay Shirky observes that the popularity of weblogs follows a Pareto[155] or "power law" distribution[156]. This means that the most popular weblog is exponentially more popular, in terms of inbound links, than the 10th, the 10th an order of magnitude more popular than the 100th and so in. In other words, the vast majority of weblogs are read by only a few individuals, while a few are read by thousands of readers. These popular weblogs are "powerful", in the sense that they can direct a great deal of reader attention to a website or an issue. The authors of these weblogs – sometimes referred to as "the A-List"[157] – have, to some extent, the ability to set the agenda for the conversation that takes place in blogspace. If A-List authors link disproportionately to stories about emerging technology and American politics, dialogue will center around those topics to the exclusion of other topics.

Shirky argues that the power law is both inevitable and "fair", in the sense that it reflects the aggregation of choices freely made by individuals into a collective will. It is, he argues, a meritocracy, where bloggers are forced to maintain a high level of quality or risk losing their audience. All this is true, but it points to a fundamental constraint within the blog universe: for an idea to gain currency, it needs a pre-existing audience. Discussions regarding intellectual property, U.S. politics, social software or peer-to-peer filesharing all can take advantage of a large audience that (Ito theorizes) amplifies good ideas and filters poor ones – a meme will succeed in this space if it is on-topic, interesting and well articulated, i.e., if it crosses a quality barrier.

Ideas on topics not well understood by a large community of bloggers have two barriers to cross: the quality barrier and a second relevancy barrier. A brilliant commentary on Nigerian politics is unlikely to be amplified by bloggers with no understanding of or interest in the region.

---

[155] http://en.wikipedia.org/wiki/Pareto_distribution, accessed 2/27/2004.

[156] http://www.shirky.com/writings/powerlaw_weblog.html, dated 2/8/2003, accessed 2/27/2004.

[157] http://www.shirky.com/writings/powerlaw_weblog.html, accessed 2/27/2004. Shirky uses this term while denying existence of the A-List.

Without an understanding of the comment in context, it's difficult for a blogger to understand whether a comment is of high quality or not; if a blogger is not interested in the topic at hand, she is unlikely to encounter the comment in the first place, and would be hard pressed to link to the comment in a way that wasn't confusing to her readers, who expect her to write on American, not Nigerian, politics.

If the commentary is in Hausa[158], spoken as a primary language in Niger and Northern Nigeria, and as a second language throughout West Africa, it will be incomprehensible to the vast majority of the prominent bloggers. While companies like Systran provide online translation for 35 language pairs, available languages cover some of the Americas, Western Europe, Asia and the Arabic-speaking world, but not Africa, Central or South Asia. [159] Early experiments, based at Albion College, in machine translation of African languages cover Xhosa and Pulaar[160], but only provide simple sentence translation. Add to this the fact that Hausa requires special character sets for Unicode characters and either specialized keyboard software[161] or hand coding of Unicode decimal codes in HTML[162], and it's unlikely that Hausa bloggers will emerge without the help of a West African "Hoder".

Ultimately, the solution for a blogger who wants to share a new idea with a large population may be to build her own audience, as Iranian bloggers did. While this may increase the currency of an idea within that community, and improve its prominence in search engines, it does not ensure that the larger weblog community will adopt the idea. Instead, it's more likely that these communities are self-contained and insular.

For example: balmasque.blogspot.com, a Persian language blog, is the fourth most prominent blog tracked by Technorati, with 4,741 blogs

---

[158] Wikipedia reports that it is spoken by 25 million people as a primary language, and an additional 14 million as a secondary language (http://en.wikipedia.org/wiki/Hausa_language, accessed 2/27/2004).

[159] http://www.systransoft.com/LP.html, accessed 2/27/2004.

[160] http://mokennon2.albion.edu/language.htm, accessed 2/27/2004.

[161] http://www.quicktopic.com/8/H/JxKHyg9ccPUVB, accessed 2/27/2004.

[162] http://www.nationmaster.com/encyclopedia/Hausa, accessed 2/27/2004.

linking to it. Of the twenty most prominent blogs that link to Balmasque, seventeen are in Persian[163]. Of the three English language blogs in the top twenty, one is Technorati's top 100 list itself, and another is a commentary by Kevin Marks, where he notes his incomprehension of the site:

> ...*I look at blogs like this and feel like Ginger in Gary Larson's classic What Dogs Hear.* '*squiggle squiggle squiggle Blog squiggle squiggle squiggle Permalink* '[164]

Balmasque's popularity is not due to its adoption by the larger weblog community, but by a smaller subset of Persian-language bloggers. The problem persists when correcting for the language factor – only 2 of Technorati's top 100 bloggers (Dan Gillmor and Jeff Jarvis) link to IranFilter, the site explicitly created to share content from Iranian blogs in English.[165]

How do we ensure that the dialogues sparked on weblogs are open to all languages and cultures? Successful approaches need to address issues of translation and appropriate toolsets as well as cultural issues.

Blogalization is a new project that attempts to address the translation issue, by combining the efforts of multilingual bloggers into a single site. The logic behind the site: "if I have languages A and B and you have languages B and C, we can share memes across barriers of mutual incomprehension." [166] Blogalization participants index dozens of multilingual blog[167] and wiki[168] catalogs in the hopes of giving

---

[163] http://www.technorati.com/cosmos/search.html?rank=links&url=http percent3A percent2F percent2Fbalmasque.blogspot.com&start=, accessed 2/27/2004.

[164]

http://epeus.blogspot.com/2003_12_01_epeus_archive.html#1070272774 56428651, accessed 2/27/2004.

[165] http://www.technorati.com/cosmos/search.html?rank=links&url=http percent3A percent2F percent2Fwww.iranfilter.com&start=, accessed 2/27/2004.

[166] http://www.blogalization.info/reorganization/, accessed 2/27/2004.

[167] http://blogalization.org/conspiracy/NonEnglishOnlyBlogIndexes, accessed 2/27/2004.

contributors raw material for translating key posts for a global audience. They make a point of selecting posts with key ideas that they think have currency for their international audience, "memes" likely to be adopted and transmitted by their readership. Another site, Living on the Planet takes a similar tack, though unidirectionally, from various languages into English With sites focused on China, Latin America and India, bloggers summarize local media for an English-language audience. The project plans expansion into Europe, Central Asia and Africa, as well as an agency to represent the commercial interests of photographers, bloggers and writers, selling to U.S. and European markets.[169]

Open Knowledge Network (OKN) is less concerned with transmitting information about the developing world to the developed world, and more focused on getting people in developing nations to share knowledge with one another. It's stated focus is on "local content, local people, local languages"[170]. OKN tries to leverage existing content creators, and the network of cybercafes and community access centers emerging throughout the developing world. It tags content using the Extensible Markup Language for inclusion in international databases, which makes the data accessible to the widest variety of application software, and is developing open content licenses appropriate for indigenous knowledge. Importantly, OKN realizes that collection of knowledge in developing nations requires different tools than those designed for social interaction in developed nations – the network maintains offline-accessible "newssheets" at Internet access points, periodically updated when Net connectivity is available. They have also realized that computers far less common in developing nations than cellphones, and are piloting a set of short messaging system (SMS)-based services in Nairobi.

Bisharat.net, a project of African civil society portal Kabissa.org, gives an excellent overview of the challenges associated with making tools, including social software, accessible in local languages. Focused specifically on the challenge of the "africanization" (A12N) of software,

---

[168] http://www.blogalization.info/conspiracy/NonEnglishOnlyWikis, accessed 2/27/2004.

[169] http://www.livingontheplanet.com/about.html, accessed 2/27/2004.

[170] http://www.openknowledge.Net/, accessed 2/27/2004.

Bisharat maintains an extensive catalog[171] of links to Unicode-compliant fonts, keyboard layouts, machine translation services and other tools designed to make the Internet usable by speakers of African languages. Without these tools, languages that use characters outside of the Roman alphabet can't be accurately represented on webpages or in online discussions. Even with these tools, it's a challenge for African language users to publish online, as certain characters in the alphabet require multiple keystrokes, as they're not directly associated with keys on QWERTY keyboards.

What's clear from a cursory view of Bisharat is that it's a non-trivial task for speakers of African languages to create native-language Internet content. While some toolbuilders have gone to great lengths to make social software accessible to English speakers, few software creators have made such efforts to ensure that Africans can blog in Hausa or Xhosa Africans who want to participate in these communities have to take on the added load of ensuring that their content will be supported. People in developing nations – who already face a challenge in gaining affordable access to the Internet – face another set of technical hoops to jump through, an added barrier to their participation in online communities.

If the social software community cares about ensuring global use of their tools and global participation in discussions, we need to take a close look at the usability of our tools by people in other nations. For example, many popular blog hosting services are modestly priced, but require payment online via credit card. This creates an insurmountable barrier for the majority of people in developing nations, who while they may have the means to pay a $5 per month hosting fee (comparable to the costs associated with a few hours access to a cybercafe), but lack the method to make the payment, as credit cards are largely unavailable throughout Africa and much of Central and South Asia. Designers of social software who hope to have a global audience for their products need to start designing those products in conjunction with that global audience.

The most exciting implication of Ito and Moore's papers is the idea that social software may change the nature of political action. Moore

---

[171] http://www.bisharat.Net/A12N/, accessed 2/27/2004.

observes that this action is fundamentally different from political power as we know it – it's power from below, rather than from above:

*That is, it is the strength of the U.S. government that it can centrally collect taxes, and then spend, for example, $1.2 billion on 1,200 cruise missiles in the first day of the war against Iraq. By contrast, it is the strength of the second superpower that it could mobilize hundreds of small groups of activists to shut down city centers across the United States on that same first day of the war. And that millions of citizens worldwide would take to their streets to rally.[172]*

Recent political events in the United States have demonstrated the power of the grassroots. Despite Howard Dean's failure to become the Democratic presidential candidate, his campaign demonstrated that grassroots organizing over the Internet could organize massive, real-world rallies, raise huge amounts of money through small donations and raise a candidate seen originally as a fringe non-entity to the status of front-runner, at least temporarily. It seems likely that future political campaigns in the United States will attempt to use similar tools and strategies to motivate voters.

It's not obvious, however, that the form of grassroots organizing and action celebrated by Ito and Moore will gain traction in the developing world. In many developed nations, especially the United States, the greatest enemy of activism is apathy. Grassroots activism may turn out to be a powerful weapon to fight apathy and encourage engagement. One of the characteristics of the Dean campaign was an awareness of friends and acquaintances supporting the campaign. Through email lists, Linkster-like tools, and Meet Up invitations, Net users were constantly reminded how many of their friends were supporting the Dean campaign. The overwhelming cumulative message was, "It's important to be involved with this – your friends think it's important, and you should too." This social reinforcement encouraged many individuals who hadn't been previously politically active to overcome apathy, make a donation, go to a rally or otherwise get involved.

Apathy is *not* the primary problem in many other nations. In nations with a high degree of political repression, the enemy of activism may be

---

[172] Moore, cited above.

threats to personal safety. In these situations, transparent public debate leading to action is likely an unwise path to political change. Can we expect democracy to emerge from Internet communities in countries where political activity is constrained and the Internet is censored? Or are we assuming that these democratizing technologies are only applicable in places where democracy and accompanying rights of free expression are already well protected? While there is no guarantee that these tools will be used for democratization in closed societies, we have the power to ensure – technically – that they are unusable to help create more open societies.

One possibility is that the Internet will emerge as a tool to address political problems other than apathy. One obvious candidate is censorship. When The Daily News of Zimbabwe, the country's sole independent newspaper, was shut down by the Mugabe government in September 2003, it responded by moving some key staff to South Africa[173] and publishing in an online form.[174] It's worth noting that the Independent didn't consider this an adequate solution, and that the paper resumed publishing in print form within Zimbabwe as soon as it was able because so many more Zimbabweans are able to access the Daily News in paper form than on the Internet.[175]

Another possible application is the use of the Internet for anti-corruption activities. The Philippine Center for Investigative Journalism points to a number of Internet-based anti-corruption activities in Latin America[176], largely centered around the publication of the fiscal assets of elected officials. The most radical of the sites, the Dominican Alliance Against Corruption[177], has published bank account numbers, home

---

[173] "Daily News Reporters Disgruntled", The Herald, Harare, Zimbabwe, October 8, 2003. Downloaded from http://allafrica.com/stories/200310080262.html, accessed 2/27/2004. (Page is available to subscribers only.)

[174] http://www.daily-news.co.za/, accessed 2/27/2004.

[175] http://allafrica.com/stories/200402230001.html

[176] http://www.pcij.org/imag/latest/anti-corrupt2.html, accessed 2/27/2004.

[177] http://www.contracorrupcion.com/, the official Website for DAAC, is currently inaccessible. An archived version from May 16, 2001 is available through the Internet Archive at

addresses and national identity numbers of public officials to help citizens report corrupt behavior. One can imagine the value of a system that would allow citizens to report instances where they were asked for a bribe anonymously, using a cellphone, creating an online database that could be reviewed by the press, donor governments and other anti-corruption investigators.

Generally speaking, though, in most developing nations, the Net is not the obvious place to look for political change. So few citizens are online, and those who are generally are atypically wealthy and powerful that the Internet is a poor way to reach the grassroots. Instead, it's useful to think about what media are analogous to the Internet in developing nations. One likely parallel is talk radio.

The Internet is a fruitful space for political organizing in the U.S. and Europe because it is low cost, in comparison to buying radio or TV time, and is an open, bidirectional platform largely free of content controls. In nations like Ghana which have liberalized radio broadcast laws and allowed numerous private radio stations to open, talk radio fulfills some of the same functions. In a country where many voters have low levels of literacy and few have computers, calling into a radio program is a more realistic path for political expression than publishing a weblog.

Chris Lydon, a prominent U.S. talk radio host in the traveled to Ghana in March 2002 and spent two weeks running a nightly talk show on Choice FM, one of Accra's most popular political talk stations. He observes:

> It was talk radio, by some accounts, that crystallized Ghana's weariness with Jerry Rawlings and elected President John Kufour a little more than a year ago. It is a yeasty element in a reviving democracy.[178]

Talk radio was a key ingredient in one of the most interesting examples of technically-enabled democracy in Africa. During the 2000 Ghanaian presidential elections, citizen observers stationed themselves at polling

---

http://Web.archive.org/Web/20010516223127/http://www.contracorrupcion.com/.

[178] http://www.transom.org/guests/review/200204.review.lydon.html, accessed 2/27/2004.

places throughout the country. Armed with cellphones, they called talk radio stations when they saw evidence of vote fraud or obstruction occurring at polling places. Because these reports were broadcast over the radio to hundreds of thousands of listeners, the police were forced to deploy to polling sites and ensure open access to the ballot box.[179] A similar situation occurred in Senegal's 2000 presidential election. Perhaps not coincidentally, both elections brought opposition, reformist pol-iticians to power.

Given the challenges of involving the developing world in the world of online reporting, discussion and activism, it's worth asking whether it's reasonable to try to make room for the Third World in the second superpower. Are technologists in developed economies being absurdly arrogant in speculating that a set of tools and behaviors used by less than one percent of the world's population – a disproportionately wealthy and powerful group of people – can help change the political lives of people around the world?

My strong suspicion is that the answer to this question depends a great deal on the actions of the people using and developing these tools in the First World. In designing the tools to enable communities, are we thinking about the full spectrum of people we'd like to use these tools? Are we helping people join our dialogues, or are we content to keep them out? If we are committed to the long, hard project of ensuring that the whole world has a chance to participate in our conversation, there's a chance that emergent democracy can be a force in emerging democracies. If not, we help ensure that the community phenomena that have developed around social software won't extend to the people who could be most positively affected by this technology.

---

[179] From a personal conversation with Patrick Awuah, 1/14/2004. Confirmed by Gamal Nkrumah, "Overturning the idols of inertia", Al-Ahram, Cairo, 1/3/2001, accessed from http://weekly.ahram.org.eg/2000/514/fo2.htm on 2/27/2004.

# Exiting Deanspace
## by Clay Shirky

I wanted to wait 'til the February 3rd polls opened to post this, because I wanted it to be a post-mortem and not a vivisection. What follows is a long musing on the Dean campaign's use of internet tools, but it has a short thesis: the hard thing to explain is not how the Dean campaign blew such a huge lead, but rather why we ever thought that lead actually existed. Dean's campaign didn't just fail, it dissolved on contact with reality.

The answer, I think, is that we talked ourselves, but not the voters, into believing. And I think the way the campaign was organized helped inflate and sustain that bubble of belief, right up to the moment that the voters arrived.

Take this as an early entry in a conversation everyone who was watching Dean's use of the internet should contribute to: what went right? what went wrong? and what to do differently next time? We should do this now because 'next time' still includes a passel of primaries and then, most importantly, the general election. If we have the conversation now, we won't have to wait til the few uncontested House races of 2006 to see if we learned anything.

Two caveats at the beginning: first, the stupidest thing I've said on this issue was in "Dean: (Re)stating the Obvious":

"...the most salient characteristic [of the campaign] is the style of engagement, including the use of social software." Dumb.

The most salient fact of Dean's campaign was Dean himself. Whatever conversation we have about the use of internet tools, Dean himself was the most important factor in the losses.

The analysis here is not concerned with the candidate, however, but with the campaign. So with additional caveat that a political campaign strategy is so absurdly multi-variate that certainty is impossible, those of us who care about the use of the internet in politics need to talk about how to use those tools better than the Dean campaign did.

## Mental Models

Howard Dean had the best-funded, best-publicized bid to be the Democratic nominee; he was so widely understood to be in the lead that the inevitability of his victory was a broad topic of discussion. (Google "Howard Dean"+inevitable if you need independent confirmation.) Even the people disputing the posited inevitability burnished the idea; no one bother debunking the idea of, say, Kucinich's inevitability.

I've had a hard time processing his Iowa and New Hampshire losses because I'd spent months hearing about how well he was going to do. It has taken me two weeks to decide that my mental model — how could such a successful campaign suddenly do so badly? — was the problem.

Dean's campaign was never actually successful. It did many of the things successful campaigns do, of course — got press and raised money and excited people and even got potential voters to aver to campaign workers and pollsters that they would vote for him when the time came. When the time came, however, they didn't. The campaign never succeeded at making Howard Dean the first choice of any group of voters he faced, and it seems unlikely to do so today.

If this thesis — call it the 'mirage' thesis — is too strong for you, consider its cousin, where the campaign *was* doing well until the last few days. In this version, one New Hampshire voter in three dumped Dean after no event more momentous than a third-place showing in Iowa (rarely known to track to New Hampshire elections) and a little hootin' and hollerin' in the concession speech (to use Sharpton's memorable phrase). Not one Dean supporter in three, mind, one *voter* in three.

In this view, Dean's support was real, but so thin and vulnerable that a mere political pin-prick was enough to cause the whole thing to collapse. Call this the 'soap bubble' thesis; the only difference between it and the mirage thesis is that in some other version of the election, if Dean had done everything perfectly, he could have performed well. I leave the likelihood of a primary race going perfectly as an exercise for the reader, but neither model suggests a campaign prepared for the real world.

## Durham NH, December 9, 2003

We must take care not to re-write history so that we 'always knew' what was going to happen. I, like many, believed Dean would win the early primaries right up to the moment he cratered. To keep myself honest, I've spent some time reading Dean coverage pre-Iowa, and have come across an article that, if you want to understand the Dean campaign, should be required reading.

It is a Washington Post piece by Hanna Rosin called "People-Powered"[180] (free registration required) and sub-titled "In New Hampshire, Howard Dean's Campaign Has Energized Voters." It's about campaign volunteers canvassing for votes in New Hampshire in early December, and it's not particularly broad or critical — rather it is an unintentional preview of the subsequent failure in that state, by presenting the techniques of the campaign in terms of motivational culture.

The piece is long, and almost every paragraph has something interesting in it. I can't really do it justice here, but I'll quote a couple of passages so you can get a feel for it:

> But Moore [the Dean campaigner] has been trained to connect through the simple technique of telling a story. It's a story he's told dozens of times, not counting rehearsals. It's a story not about Howard Dean but about James Moore [...] It's the type of tightly constructed inspirational story that climaxes in a moment of hopeful decision
>
> [...]
>
> Soon some of the women are sharing their own stories. One, a retired psychotherapist, says she's "distraught at what's happening to this country. I actually lie awake at night with my eyes wide open." Another talks about a close relative who recently passed away and how it changed her. The women ask Moore questions about Dean's positions — on the war in Iraq, the Confederate flag, Medicare — but mostly they share their fears and worries. The atmosphere is less like a political meeting than a support group.

---

[180] Rosin, Hanna, "People Powered." http://www.washingtonpost.com/ac2/wp-dyn/A47440-2003Dec8?language=printer. Washington Post, December 9, 2003.

Yet from Moore's point of view the bottom line is achieved. Several who came just because they were curious now seem enthusiastic about Dean: "He sounds like a listener." "He's cute when he's angry." "He's cute, period." At least two have agreed to hold similar house parties so they, too, can spread the word about Dean.

The story goes on:

> There are many reasons why Dean has shot to a 30-point lead in New Hampshire [...] the house meetings and similar one-on-one sessions seem to be the heart of it. Not so much because of the aggregate numbers — although in a state the size of New Hampshire, personally pitching 15,000 voters can make a difference. But because it so perfectly connects to an America that buys millions of self-help books.
>
> [...]
>
> Jim Mitchell, an older man who showed up at a recent Meet-Up event in Derry: "I have the sense I'm being listened to. They're not so much about pushing Dean as they are about engaging people in conversation. It's — what's the word I'm looking for? — empowering."

These passages, I want to emphasize, are from a piece that presents Dean as an all but certain winner, and yet the description now sends another message entirely: *Less about Howard Dean than about James Moore, less like a political meeting than a support group, not so much about pushing Dean as they are about engaging people in conversation...*

Several times Rosin comes right to the edge of predicting the events two months hence: those women were happy to have that nice young man come and listen to their stories, but in the end they weren't going to vote for Howard Dean. She even provides a comparison to self-help books, and then finishes the sentence before she finishes the thought: self-help books sell well, but mostly don't work.

The exit polls from New Hampshire were quite instructive. Kerry beat Dean in every demographic and psychographic group, including "voters under 30", with but three exceptions: people for whom the Iraq war was the most important issue; people who labeled themselves not just liberal but very liberal; and people who'd made up their minds more than a month earlier.

So where did his 30 point lead go? Why would someone say they would vote for Dean if they weren't actually sure? I believe that last category contains a clue as to Dean's collapse in the polls – Dean lost among voters who waited til January to decide who to vote for, which is to say almost everybody.

Prior to January, "Howard Dean" was pronounced "Anybody but Bush." The thing Dean did spectacularly right was to pick a fight with the President, a hugely polarizing and therefore energizing figure, on the issue most Democrats wanted to keep quiet about. Even if you'd been only been following politics casually, you would have known that Dean was the person who had most directly challenged Bush. For any Democrat whose primary motivation was not a bundle of particular policy proposals but the chance to send the current President home, Dean was the man of the hour.

In this view, the change in the poll numbers in January reflected not a transfer of votes from Dean to Kerry but rather from the general to the specific. Voter's polled as to their choices last year were not bound by their answers, and nor had most of them bothered to sort out the candidates positions from one another. (My wife and I, both deeply interested in the primaries, couldn't always remember all of their *names*.) A couple of weeks before the primaries, though, voters in those states started to have to make some real decisions, transferring their sense of "Anybody but Bush" to a specific Democratic candidate. And sometimes that candidate was Howard Dean. But mostly not.

## How Did We Get Here? What Should We Do Next Time?

So how did this collective delusion of Dean's front-runner-hood happen? And what if anything did the use of the internet contribute to it?

Here are a number of effects that I think led us to the false conclusion that Dean was, if not inevitable, than at least tipped to do very well. The bad news is that these effects, taken together, swamped what might have been a better-run campaign. The good news is that most of the effects are easy to recognize in retrospect, and therefore may be easy to defend against in the future.

The first and most obvious effect was novelty. Although there are already people running around claiming that the Dean campaign wasn't really an internet campaign (on the grounds that such a campaign will, by definition, be successful), for those of us watching for the use of the net in politics, Dean was our guy, and we should remember that. He and Trippi and many of the Dean staff put the internet to the best, most vivid, and most imaginative use it has ever gotten in any national campaign.

That, of course, is a story in itself, and the press treated it as such. The NY Times, normally scrupulously balanced at election time (they gave front page coverage to a profile of Carol Mosely Braun) wrote article after article, including a cover story in the Sunday magazine, on how the Dean campaign had managed its "Come from nowhere" movement, the by now familiar story of MeetUp and MoveOn and internet donations and Dean weblogs.

The story took on the characteristics of a firestorm, where the original fire pulls more oxygen in, fueling the flames higher. The perception that Dean was first the strongest challenger, and then the frontrunner, was part cause and part effect for those stories.

We don't need to worry about this in the future, I think. The press has a way of running fast epidemics, where an idea virus runs its course quickly, leaving everyone inoculated in its wake. The problem we will now have to watch for is where a candidate that makes innovative use of the internet will be cautioned about what happened to Dean.

*Support isn't Votes*

Other than this one-off effect, though, there are a number of more serious issues to contend with. The first of them is the difference between signs and the thing they signify. (Steven Johnson wrote about this over the weekend as well.)

Getting people together in the real world is hard – the coordination cost of any gathering runs into the inertia of modern life at every turn. (Robert Putnam in one sentence.) For many of us, the first time Dean appeared on our radar was when 300 people showed up for a Howard

Dean MeetUp in New York City in early 2003. This was unprecedented, and Dean himself took note of it, coming down from Vermont to speak to his supporters.

We were right to be excited about this MeetUp, but wrong about the reason, because *MeetUp was founded to lower the coordination costs of real world gatherings.*

The size of the MeetUp in NYC was as much a testament to MeetUp as to Dean — it's a wonderful tool for turning interest into attendance, but it created a false sense of broad enthusiasm. Prior to MeetUp, getting 300 people to turn out would have meant a huge and latent population of Dean supporters, but because MeetUp makes it easier to gather the faithful, it confused us into thinking that we were seeing an increase in Dean support, rather than a decrease in the hassle of organizing groups.

We've seen this sort of effect before, as when written correspondence on letterhead stopped being a sign of a solvent company, thanks to the desktop publishing revolution, or with the way email to politicians matters less than telegrams, because email is cheaper and easier to send. As we get the tools to make such gatherings easy, we need to concentrate on the outcome of those gatherings, rather than assuming strength simply by looking at the number of attendees.

*Fervor Isn't Votes*

Margaret Mead once said "Never doubt that a small group of thoughtful, committed people can change the world. Indeed, it is the only thing that ever has." Generations of zealots have tacked these words up on various walls, never noticing that the two systems that run the modern world – markets and democracies — are working right precisely when they defeat these attempted hijackings by small groups.

Voting in particular is designed as a repudiation of Mead's notion. In the line at the polling booth, the guy with the non-ironic trucker hat and nothing other than an instinct for who he trusts cancels the vote of the politics junkie who can tell you the name of Joe Lieberman's Delaware field manager.

In Is Social Software Bad for the Dean Campaign?, I suggested that Dean had accidentally created a movement instead of a campaign. I still believe that, and this is one of the things I think falls out from that. It's hard to understand, when you sense yourself to be one of Mead's thoughtful and committed people, that someone who doesn't even understand the issues can amble on down to the local elementary school and wipe out your vote, and its even harder to understand that the system is designed to work that way.

You can ring doorbells and carry signs and donate and stay up til 4 in the morning talking with fellow believers about the sorry state of politics today, and you still only get one vote. If you want more votes than that, you have to do the hardest, most humbling thing in the world. You have to change someone else's mind.

Internet culture is talking culture, so we're not used to this. In our current conversational spaces, whether mailing lists or bulletin boards or weblogs, the people who speak the loudest and the most frequently dominate the discussion.

Imagine if a mailing list had to issue a formal opinion on the issues discussed, and lurkers got a vote. The high-flow posters would complain that the lurkers votes would not reflect the actual discussion that took place, merely the aggregate opinions of the group, and yet that is how the primaries work. Talking loudest or most or even best means nothing.

*Effort Isn't Votes*

Here's a catchy phrase: "Design, Create, Produce to Elect Governor Howard Dean for President." That's the slogan atop DeanMediaTeam.com; can you spot the error? (and we'll let the fact that Dean is not currently Governor slide.) Designers don't create votes, voters create votes, one per, and its votes, not stylesheets, that do the electing.

It is natural for a campaign, attracting so many eager young people, to oversell them on the effect they'll have, when the truth is so rough – you'll work 80 hour weeks while sleeping on someone's sofa, and in the end, your heroic contribution will be a drop in the bucket of what's needed.

So a little pep talk now and again can't hurt. However, you can go too far, and too far is when people begin selling one another on the idea that their work for the campaign has a direct effect on getting their candidate in. Someone at Dean HQ should have sent out a bulletin to the staff – all effects are indirect. Money, bell ringing, blogging, advertising, none of it will get Dean elected unless it convinces voters to elect him. If you can't point to ways your work is getting votes, you're not helping. In particular, if you are preaching to the converted (see "Fervor Isn't Votes", above), you're *really* not helping.

## Money Isn't Votes

This is the big one. Dean's internet strategy was a curiosity until there was money involved, and when it got involved, it got involved in a big way. We mustn't forget how enormous a change this was – an upstart politician blew past all the favorites and even exited the public funding system because he got enough money soliciting donations from the internet, a few bucks at a time.

If none of the rest of it, the MeetUps and weblogs, had ever happened, but Dean's campaign had still done this, its place in political history would be assured.

And yet money does not in fact buy votes. As candidates like Michael Huffington and Ron Lauder have shown, you can be very rich and still very lose. In Dean's case, though, the effect was compounded by two other effects from above. By moving campaign donations online, they made it much easier to donate, so much easier in fact that raising millions from individuals was never the sign of strength we thought it was. (Support isn't votes.) Like MeetUp, a lot of what the campaign achieved was by lowering the threshold to contributing, which helped create a false sense of strength.

The other effect was that last fall, when Dean announced his desire to top the fundraising list, a lot of us gave him money, self included, as a vote for that method of fund raising, without that meaning anything about whether we'd vote for him.

We were donating to the use of the internet as a tool, in other words – in the same way that the voters heard "Anybody But Bush" when Howard Dean was mentioned, a lot of us heard "Contribute to the use of the internet for politics" when the collection plate came around. (Novelty campaign.)

This won't happen again – there will never be a second candidate to use the internet first. However, as with other shows of seeming strength, we need to be careful not to equate the advantages of online fund raising with electoral success in the future. When you change the game, the old rules are useless for figuring out who's winning.

*Sometimes Votes Aren't Even Votes (Depending on Who's Counting)*

None of the above needed to be fatal. Having a high profile, even if not for your policies; eager supporters, even if a little too confident; and good fund raising, even if it didn't translate directly into votes, could have been a pretty good place to start, and after losing in Iowa and New Hampshire (which, let's remember, Clinton also did), it could have provided a cushion to catch the fall, and to help bounce back as a more appealing candidate.

The moment for me, and I think for many of us, when we realized that Dean was sunk was on Wednesday after New Hampshire, when the press reported that he'd spent most of his $45 million war chest already. The obvious question, "How did he think he could do the rest of the campaign on a few million dollars?" has an obvious answer: "He thought he'd raise more, when Iowa and New Hampshire anointed him frontrunner."

This was a fatal flaw in the campaign – they believed their own press. Dean was so out of touch that he had not prepared a concession speech in Iowa, a state where his third place finish was so bad that if he'd gotten every single Gephardt vote as well, he would still have been in third place, and would still have been double digits behind Kerry.

This is the question within the question. Out here, we had an excuse (albeit a flimsy one) for believing Dean was the frontrunner: it's what we read in the papers. But campaigns don't just use the pollsters, their field operations also keep their own numbers. And for Dean to blow all his cash and then not even prepare for anything other than victory means their internal numbers predicted certain victory as well.

Back to Hanna Rosin's story in the Post:

[The Dean worker] leaves knowing at least a handful can be logged into the central campaign database as No. 2s — leaning toward Dean — and even 1s — definite supporters — which means he's done his part to reach the campaign's total of 180 identified Dean voters in New Hampshire that day.

But how does he know that? He is, by his own admission, a newcomer to this game. How does he know that a middle-aged New Hampshire lady is a "definite supporter?"

Consider his incentives – he is out proselytizing for a guy he's dropped the rest of his life for, campaigning on stories that are more about him than Howard Dean, and getting a reaction from his listeners that is closer to revival tent than political kaffeeklatsch, and then there's that daily quota of 180 to fill. What's he gonna say? "None of them think Dean is any good"? "I tried my best, but I couldn't convince them"? "They said they were going to vote Dean, but I think they were just being polite"?

Amateurs and zealots both have strong incentives not merely to misrepresent reality, but to actually misunderstand it. If you're on a mission to change the world, you have an incentive to believe it's changing.

Furthermore, if this is your first campaign, and you are doing it not because you want to be in politics but because you want to make the world a better place, what happens if you mark a bunch of people as "definite supporters" who really aren't? Nothing, really. You have no professional reputation on the line – if you put your thumb on the scale, even if only unconsciously, no one will ever call you on it, because by the time the actual votes are in, no one will remember how many "definite supporters" you said you had.

For Dean to have spent everything on a momentum strategy so secure that he didn't bother contemplating even second place, he must have heard from his field operatives that things were just great, super, you wouldn't believe how many "definite supporters" we converted today.

It's not clear what to do about this – skepticism is a hard virtue to put into software. Maybe a reputation system, or a market for accuracy, will convince eager amateurs to be careful about the difference between politeness and voting intent. But this is the hardest problem, because many of the other forces listed here make it easier to recruit and use the efforts of amateurs. Unless they face pressures that dissuade them from happy talk and mutual affirmation, however, they will end up convincing their candidate to misallocate precious or even irreplaceable resources.

## Affinity Over Geography

A number of people, disputing the idea that the use of the internet had anything to do with the gap between Dean's predicted and actual support, have advanced the "internet minority" thesis, as in "The internet is used by a minority of citizens", or, in its more regionally biased version, "Who in Iowa has computers anyway?"

With national internet penetration at roughly two-thirds of households, it's long since time to retire this canard. More people use the internet than read a daily newspaper. More people use the internet than vote in general elections, much less primaries. Iowa and New Hampshire both have better than 50% penetration (as does most of the country except the antebellum south.) Furthermore, one of the commonest uses of the internet is getting daily news. The internet is now, and from now on, a political media channel.

That's a sideshow, however, compared to the internet as an organizational tool. The main effect of the internet on politics is as a lever, not a hammer.

Culture matters, and since the 1970's, anyone who has looked at the cultural effects of the internet has picked the same key element: the victory of affinity over geography. The like-minded can now gather from all corners, and bask in the warmth of knowing you are not alone.

And yet as wonderful as this effect can be, it carries pitfalls. Liberal judges become more liberal on panels of all Democrats, as do conservatives with Republicans. Support groups can become maintenance groups by accidentally reinforcing the normalcy of deviant behaviors. (One of my former students presided over the removal of YM magazine's "Health and Beauty Tips" BBS, because it had become a place for girls to swap tips on remaining anorexic by choice.)

Voting, though, is the victory of geography over affinity. Deaniacs in NYC could donate money and time, blogging like mad or tramping through the cold to talk to a handful of potential voters, but they couldn't actually vote anywhere but NYC. Iowa was left up to the Iowans.

The easy thing to explain is why Dean lost – the voters didn't like him. The hard thing to explain is why we (and why Dean himself) thought he'd win, and easily at that. The bubble of belief, which collapsed so quickly and so completely, was inflated by tools that made formerly hard things easy, tricking us into thinking that getting votes had become easy as well — we were all in Deanspace for a while there.

It was also inflated by our desire to see someone get it right, a fact that made us misunderstand the facts on the ground – we suffered the same temptations as the campaign workers to regard our fellow citizens as "definite supporters", even when we ourselves were supporting a movement rather than a campaign.

It's been a shock, but it doesn't have to be a fatal one. Lowering coordination costs and making it easier for citizens to create media and distributing fundraising to the masses are all good things. This year, however, to the surprise of many of us, pasting those things on to relatively traditional campaigns has worked better than the Dean campaign's organic strategy did. The biggest difficulty for whatever version of next time comes around will be remembering not to believe our own PR.

# 6.4 Billion Points of Light
## Lighting the Tapers of Democracy
## by Roger Wood

As humans we know from personal experience that very few situations are simple; that very few decisions are simply yes or no. We know that something as basic and consequence-free as picking ice cream is not just a "vanilla or chocolate?" decision; it is a series of choices of varying complexity – Cup or cone? One scoop or two? Three? Organic, regular, low-fat, extra-fat, lite or sugar-free? Chocolate, Vanilla, Chunky Monkey®, or some combination of dozens of others? Sprinkles? Nuts? It can take 10 minutes just to read the menu. With experience, we even know that no two chocolates are the same. Our personal experiences teach us that there is detail and nuance and complexity in our everyday decisions, and reason leads us to believe that the decisions made on our behalf by our government are no simpler. Good conscience demands that when decisions affect the lives of thousands or millions or even billions of people, they deserve a bit more than 10 minutes of consideration.

As citizens, we respond to events and circumstances. We watch, powerless, as terror, tyranny, scandal, destruction, death and suffering are brought into our homes through our radios, televisions and computers. We crave simpler times and simpler problems – simple enough to understand. It may take 10 minutes, but we can wrap our minds around an ice cream menu. These bigger, political decisions we don't understand. We don't understand the repercussions of withdrawing from a treaty, or the economic implications of different industrial emissions standards – even people who have spent their entire careers studying these things cannot provide a simple menu of options for us to understand. We rely on our governments to understand, to make decisions and to take action. We feel like spectators as the issues we consider important flash through the public conscious. If they never make the news cycle, we feel disenfranchised and irrelevant.

Politicians feed on these feelings by creating the impression that situations are black and white, decisions are yes or no, and answers, and more dramatically, questions, are obvious, clear and simple. They craft and test slogans and sound bites. They give us debates with 90-second answers and 30-second rebuttals. The media feeds this impression because it's easier and cheaper to work with a slogan than to explore an issue. The only issues worth exploring are the ones that can grab the attention of the mass market so that attention can be sold to advertisers. Both are betting that we can't understand. Both are counting on us to remain ignorant and uninterested so they can remain unaccountable.

It is the very definition of representative democracy that citizens place their trust and fate in the hands of their chosen leaders. Citizens must believe that their leaders act in their collective best interest; that they will do the right things. They must believe, even as they are increasingly uncomfortable with the results. Today, those results are brought to everyone instantly, from around the world, through a global real-time media network. Perhaps it is, in part, a loss of faith in these leaders and the social and political structures upon which they rely, which brings to our attention the questions Joichi Ito, Ross Mayfield, Jon Lebkowsky, Mitch Ratcliffe and others explore as we consider this concept of emergent democracy.

It is the nature of democracy that there is no final answer. Democracy is always unfinished, always adapting and always inadequate. Emergent democracy is a synthesis, bringing together several seemingly unrelated ideas. It is an attempt to address some of the problems of modern government. It is not a prescription, solution, or a formula for success. It is a model, and an incomplete one at that, but it is enough to begin the debate. Here, I hope to provide some perspective – to give you a few broad concepts to consider, from the most general (the problems of scale) to the most specific (individual legal precedents) as we begin to develop the tools of a new democratic form.

Please select your ice cream, citizen, and explain why your selection is better than any other. You have 90 seconds.

Let the debate begin.

### The Functions of Democratic Government

Broadly speaking, the functions of a democratic government are similar to those of any form of government; to do for its citizens what they cannot do as individuals. As expressed in the United States Constitution, to "establish justice, insure domestic tranquility, provide for the common defense, promote the general welfare."

The word democratic has been used to describe a vast array of institutions, ranging from utopian visions of enlightened self-government to the German Democratic Republic and its infamous *Ministerium für Staatssicherheit* (Stasi).

> Democracy is perhaps the most promiscuous word in the world of political affairs. She is everybody's mistress and yet somehow retains her magic even when a lover sees that her favours are being, in his light, shared by another[181]

Here, we use *democratic* to describe those governments that derive authority and power by the consent of the governed and include both free universal elections and guarantees of personal civil rights. These features impose additional challenges: to preserve liberty and freedom for the governed, to protect the minority from the majority, to bear the inefficiencies of the democratic process, and to maintain the trust of a distrusting electorate.

Democracy is neither simple nor efficient; it is deliberative and redundant. Democracy requires that the same questions constantly be asked. It requires that decisions be reviewed and considered before being put into action. It is ponderous and tedious and frustrating, but it is also resilient and strong.

> Many forms of Government have been tried, and will be tried in this world of sin and woe. No one pretends that democracy is perfect or all-wise. Indeed, it has been said that democracy is the worst form of government except all those other forms that have been tried from time to time.[182]

With effort, democracy might be more agile and responsive.

### Is the Democratic Republic Viable?

Democracy exists at many scales, and it is at the highest scale – the nations and the world – that democracy meets its greatest challenge. It is

---

[181]Crick, Bernard (1964) *In Defense of Politics.*

[182]Churchill, Sir Winston (1947, November 11), Hansard.

a bold thought to consider that ordinary persons have the wisdom to govern themselves at this scale. In the democracies of the world, we live a grand and amazing, but forever unfinished, experiment. Merely being democratic does not guarantee the long-term security, freedom and rights of the citizens – an incomplete gloss of history reveals that democracies are overthrown in military coups (Spain – 1923, Argentina – 1943, Ecuador – 1963, Pakistan – 1999). They self-destruct when opposition is outlawed (Italy – 1926, Germany - 1933). They collapse under the boots of invading armies (Belgium, Denmark, France, Netherlands, Norway – 1940). They suspend or revoke democratic institutions (Greece – 1936, Philippines – 1972, India – 1975, Zimbabwe – 1987). They even, occasionally, go to war with each other (American Civil War – 1861, Spanish-American War – 1898, Boer War – 1899, First World War – 1914, Croatian Revolution – 1991). Perhaps democracy doesn't work in the long term; perhaps there is something better. Establishing a democratic government is not the ultimate and permanent solution to the challenges of governing a nation, but democracy does have a fairly laudable track record.

From the ancient democracies of Greece and India to the birth of the American Republic and on to the crafting of the 2003 Afghan constitution, educated persons, having the luxury to ponder and write on the subject, have debated this question...

> The mere establishment of a democracy is not the only or principal business of the legislator, or of those who wish to create such a state, for any state, however badly constituted, may last one, two, or three days; a far greater difficulty is the preservation of it.[183]

> ...whether societies of men are really capable or not of establishing good government from reflection and choice, or whether they are forever destined to depend for their political constitutions on accident and force.[184]

> But a constitution is not a model for a new society. It is an agreement among the people of the existing society about how to live together in a better way. It has to embody the people's hopes for a better life, but

---

[183] Aristotle, (350 B.C.E.) Book 6 – Part V, *Politics*

[184] Hamilton, Alexander (1787, October) Federalist #1 – General Introduction, *The Independent Journal.*

if it cannot be implemented, it does not matter how good it sounds on paper.[185]

The question remains unanswered, and it is important to keep asking. It is the continuous debate of the governed that keeps democracy from degenerating into tyranny or crumbling in the hands of despots. Democracy distrusts institutional power. Democracy vests power in the individual and makes the bold assertion that we, as individuals, should not blindly trust our leaders. Rather, we should question, challenge and change them often.

A genius of the democratic republic is that it also recognizes the limits of human knowledge and experience. The founding documents of the United States, more than anything else, provide that they are incomplete, that they are flawed, and that they can, and indeed, should be changed as time and wisdom reveal their shortcomings.

## The Source of Power

No social or political structure is endowed with reasoning abilities or the power to cause action. It is not the society or the state or the corporation or the family that takes action. Individuals may act with consideration of their role in a larger structure, but it is always the individual that formulates a thought and chooses how, or whether, to act. The individual chooses the social structures in which they will participate. The individual chooses how much participation and attention they will devote to these structures. The individual balances the demands on their time and attention, and sets their own priorities. Individuals decide to engage or disengage each issue they face in their daily experience. All initiatives are born, all decisions are made and all actions are taken by individuals. The individual human, uniquely endowed with the capacity for thought and reasoning, is the source of all political action. Power, as the ability to cause action in society, comes only from people.

Respecting this, democratic institutions rely on and place the full burden of responsibility on the individual. Democracy relies on the the ability of individuals to transcend their personal priorities and act on behalf of the

---

[185]Rubin, Barnett R., (2003, June 5) Presentation to the Constitutional Commission of Afghanistan, Kabul

larger social unit – the town, the city, the state, the nation and even the world.

> ...all power is vested in, and consequently derived from, the people; that magistrates are their trustees and servants and at all times amenable to them.[186]

> And for the support of this Declaration, with a firm reliance on the protection of divine Providence, we mutually pledge to each other our Lives, our Fortunes and our sacred Honor.[187]

Individuals may act alone or in groups. It is the structure of these groups that determines the character of a society and the nature of the governing structures within that society. Individuals do not; however, act in isolation – they communicate within social groups, and both influence and are influenced by them. The social and political structures we create are the results of, not the source of, individual human interaction.

## Platforms and Privacy

Debate is a foundation of functional democracy, and free, open and spirited debate requires both a platform from which to speak, and the assurance of privacy to consider the material presented from the platform.

To preserve the substance of debate, those willing to speak – willing to share their thoughts – must be given a means to reach an audience. This platform must provide exposure to supporters, dissenters and the merely curious, and it must be available to even the most radical and threatening people.

> We must learn to welcome and not to fear the voices of dissent. We must dare to think about 'unthinkable things' because when things become unthinkable, thinking stops and action becomes mindless.[188]

---

[186]Mason, George (1776, June 12) The Virginia Declaration of Rights, adopted by the Virginia Constitutional Convention.

[187]The Unanimous Declaration of the Thirteen United States of America (1776, July 4) Signed by 56 representative individuals.

[188]Fulbright, James William.

Individuals must be free from threat or intimidation as they explore the materials provided in the public discourse. The ability to listen, reflect and respond to ideas, even controversial ideas, must be preserved.

> It does not require a majority to prevail, but rather an irate, tireless minority keen to set brush fires in people's minds...[189]

These principles are enshrined in the United States Constitution (First and Fourth amendments), the Universal Declaration of Human Rights (Articles 12, 18, 19, and 20), and the constitutional documents of most (if not all) modern democracies, including the new Afghan constitution (Chapter 2).

A healthy debate need not take place on a stage between people standing behind lecterns. Debate can occur in any forum, through any medium that provides communication among the people which have taken an interest in a given issue.

Facing what was, at the time, probably the most significant decision of their short life as a state, the people of New York struggled with the question of the form of government under which they would live. Perhaps it is a rare subject that merits such intense and serious debate, but the ratification of the United States Constitution gives us a window into an amazing deliberative process that took place in the state of New York beginning in the fall of 1787.

> After an unequivocal experience of the inefficiency of the subsisting federal government, you are called upon to deliberate on a new Constitution for the United States of America. The subject speaks its own importance; comprehending in its consequences nothing less than the existence of the Union, the safety and welfare of the parts of which it is composed, the fate of an empire in many respects the most interesting in the world.[190]

Thus began a series of papers written by three individuals (Alexander Hamilton, John Jay, and James Madison), and published anonymously in a number of newspapers, to make the case for the adoption of the recently-drafted United States Constitution. The 85 Federalist Papers

---

[189] Adams, Samuel

[190] Hamilton, Alexander (1787, October) Federalist #1 – General Introduction, *The Independent Journal.*

contain nearly 200,000 words. If they were read aloud at a comfortable 150 words per minute, the presentation would last more than 22 hours. This was just one side of the debate, and only one presentation of the federalist case. These papers prompted countless words (and no doubt, the occasional physical confrontation) among their readers. Unfortunately, no Neilsen ratings for the Federalist Miniseries are available.

Today, what passes for debate and discussion is still the final product of a long and deliberative preparation process, but the citizens are only invited to witness the final presentation. We citizens are only engaged once the ideas and statements have been clarified, simplified, and reduced to phrases that the professional issue-handlers believe we can understand. Our prospective leaders are presented to us with short, convenient lists of talking points, in short and over-simplified sound bites and campaign slogans, with very little substantive material. The issues are packaged together into party platforms and sold, in bulk, to the electorate based on one or a few issues that that polls show the likely voters (and not just citizens) feel strongly about.

This distrust of the electorate, the assumption that the citizens are incapable or unwilling to consider issues of substance sows the seeds of distrust of the elected. Worse, for discourse, the issues presented are often issues of principle and personal responsibility carefully selected to win or avoid losing votes, so the attention of the citizenry is consumed on subjects that have little bearing on the operation of government. Little time is left to discuss matters of state.

I believe this distrust is based on a flawed presumption. It is not that the citizens can't understand the issues that are important, it is that they don't have the time or disposition to understand *all* of the important issues. One insight of emergent democracy is that some people understand each issue, even if all don't understand all issues. The challenge (and opportunity) is to find a way to bring relevant material to interested citizens, and then give them both a platform for debate and the security to think and debate freely.

### Evolution of Media

Long ago, the herald and the handbill fell out of favor as means of reaching a significant audience and communicating an idea. Certainly, they are still used, but they have a limited reach, and often only reach the agreeable people that are nearby.

Now, the platform is the media, but media is a product of available technology, and change in technology is relentless. From vehicles that could move papers quickly over a large geographic area to radio and television that blanket entire metropolitan areas, to telecommunications networks that span the globe by bouncing messages off satellites and pushing them through glass under the oceans, technology provides the new platforms from which individuals make their cases today.

We have built these new, global platforms, and done so at great expense. Now we have to ask if we are using them effectively for debate. We have to ask if we are using them to further the democratic process or to stifle it.

We can delegate our opinions – we can certainly join organizations or groups and designate individuals to speak on our behalf on some issue – we can even pay them to do so. But political action is about focusing the attention of individuals, not accumulating or spending money, and there is a failure when the people in an organization divide their attention between between raising funds and addressing issues.

## The Burdens of the Past

In the experience of modern democracy, we live with a number of burdensome legacies. Transcending these may be the greatest challenge democracy faces in the modern world. I can't possibly address all the issues that face democracies, but I will attempt to explore several that have become quite prominent in the United States. Beginning with the most general, to some that are very specific, it is important to recognize that these are inter-related and not permanent conditions.

### The Burden of Scale

Having earlier identified the source of power and the foundation of all social endeavors, we find the first critical limitation of the democratic structure: No individual can possibly understand all the issues that a large social or political structure will face. No one person has the mental capacity or education to comprehend, consider and make informed, intelligent decisions on everything. If such a person did exist, they would function much more efficiently in a monarchy – they would not be burdened by the thoughtless, irrelevant and time-wasting concerns of their fellow citizens. Given a sound moral perspective, our leader would always make just and proper decisions.

> To balance a large state or society, whether monarchical or republican, on general laws, is a work of so great difficulty, that no human genius, however comprehensive, is able, by the mere dint of reason and reflection, to effect it. The judgments of many must unite in this work; experience must guide their labour; time must bring it to perfection; and the feeling of inconveniences must correct the mistakes, which they inevitably fall into in their first trials and experiments.[191]

Absent the omniscient (and moral) philosopher-king (and with appropriate apologies to Plato), we operate in an inefficient democratic framework. This framework expands to address the increasing complexity of modern society, with advisors brought in to address particular issues. Whole new organizations are created and staffed by thoughtful, motivated and generally noble (if underpaid and underappreciated) individuals that have decided to work on our behalf to provide some measure of understanding for our chosen leaders.

This evolution of support around our democratic institutions largely parallels the hierarchical structures of business and corporations. Departments, administrations, industry groups, lobbying committees and other organizations are created. Budgets are allocated, organizational charts created, procedures and policies are crafted and implemented. The structure expands as new needs or new issues are identified - a new group of people is brought in to study, understand and address each. People are hired to influence other people, to speak on behalf of people, to make a point or craft a position. Titles and duties of these individuals are adjusted as priorities change and philosophies conflict. This is the history of our democratic political organization, but as it happens, it means we citizens influence an ever-smaller subset of the government we elect to serve us. More and more of the decisions and action occur outside the elected leadership and inside the unaccountable support structures that grow up around them.

---

[191]Hume, David (1742) Of the Rise and Progress of the Arts and Sciences, *Essays, Moral and Political,* Volume 2.

This is an entirely reasonable response to the ever-expanding number of issues and decisions that face leaders in a complex society. There is no practical way we could hold enough elections to pick enough people to think about all the problems we face as a nation. Even several steps removed, electing people who elect people who think about issues and then elect people who make decisions, we simply cannot practically address everything that must be addressed. To even consider otherwise is simply unreasonable. Or is it?

## The Burden of Growing Demands on Our Individual Attention

In the course of human events, we are faced with an ever-expanding array of things demanding and competing for our attention. We have work, school, food, personal interactions, finances, entertainment, traffic, weather – and a thousand other things that we focus on to navigate through our daily lives. Scattered among most of these is a constant barrage of advertising for products, services, and, in the periodic election season, political issues. As these demands on our attention increase, the amount of time and energy each individual allocates to social or political issues they consider important is threatened. Every person is faced with decisions that seem overwhelming – do I stop for 10 minutes at a fast-food restaurant on the way home, or spend 45 minutes cooking after I get home? Few would question that a nice well-prepared meal at home is certainly the preferable option when it comes to quality and health, probably even personal enjoyment, but 35 minutes is 35 minutes, and we all have things to do.

In this environment, where the overall constraints are not subject to change (there are only 24 hours in a day), what becomes important is the effort to capture those fleeting moments of attention from a busy individual life. In politics, the response to this has traditionally been to isolate and simplify the content. Our prospective leaders approach us with statements that fit on bumper stickers, and repeat them until we offer them no more attention.

This is not a constructive engagement and does nothing to further the democratic process or the underlying critical debate. Given a global platform, and the multitude of messages that individuals feel are relevant, we face again a problem in the modern process of democracy: the limited attention span of the normal, busy, human.

The limits of language have been recognized at least since the story of the Tower of Babel. A more modern observation by George Bernard Shaw, that "England and America are two countries separated by a common language," only begins to illuminate the issue.

As we specialize more and more in modern, complex, technological societies, the participants in a given field develop a language particular to their works and interests. Within the field, this facilitates rapid, efficient communication, forming a shorthand and providing a set of common references and metaphors that allow the participants to make progress rather than constantly rehashing familiar territory. To the rest of us, it's jargon.

The problem of specialization and jargon becomes apparent when an issue rises to prominence in the general public debate. When the broader audience comes to the platform without the correct jargon, even when these newcomers ask important and relevant questions, they are often dismissed out-of-hand. Outsiders are ignored or actively shunned because their contribution to the discussion is not easy to integrate into the established language. When debate is approached with different languages, it becomes an exercise in talking past one another rather than actually engaging in matters of substance. Issue handlers define new less-precise but more palatable terms to simplify complicated issues and limit debate.

> But no language is so copious as to supply words and phrases for every complex idea, or so correct as not to include many equivocally denoting different ideas. Hence it must happen that however accurately objects may be discriminated in themselves, and however accurately the discrimination may be considered, the definition of them may be rendered inaccurate by the inaccuracy of the terms in which it is delivered. And this unavoidable inaccuracy must be greater or less, according to the complexity and novelty of the objects defined. When the Almighty himself condescends to address mankind in their own language, his meaning, luminous as it must be, is rendered dim

and doubtful by the cloudy medium through which it is communicated.[192]

Lacking a universal language, we are forced to spend time educating participants before the substance of a discussion can begin, or, perhaps more often, the would-be participants give up and move on to other things.

## The Burden of Increasing Regulation of Expression

The concept of intellectual property was created largely to provide economic incentives for people to think, invent and create new things – to contribute to and advance society. The first copyright law, the statute of Anne in 1710, is specifically crafted to encourage learning:

> An Act for the Encouragement of Learning, by Vesting the Copies of Printed Books in the Authors or Purchasers of such Copies, during the Times therein mentioned.[193]

In the United States, copyright is created by Constitution, also specifically to stimulate those fields of human endeavor that contribute to the social good:

> The Congress shall have Power... To promote the Progress of Science and useful Arts, by securing for limited Times to Authors and Inventors the exclusive Right to their respective Writings and Discoveries[194]

Today, with the expansion of intellectual property and the litigation that surrounds it, we find these original values compromised. Copyright, patent and trademark laws are increasingly used to stifle and limit thought and expression. No longer a tool to temporarily limit economic competition and provide an incentive to create, these laws are expanding in both letter and application to restrict commentary and criticism.

---

[192]Madison, James (1788, January 11), Federalist 37, *Concerning the Difficulties of the Convention in Devising a Proper Form of Government*, Daily Advertiser.

[193]Statute of Anne (1710).

[194]United States Constitution (1787), Article I, Section 8.

This discussion is important to the evolution of democracy for one simple reason: only within the sphere of unregulated thought and expression can multilateral open political debate exist.

If we restrict access to the debating platforms only to those people with substantial economic resources and powerful legal representation, we have effectively ended the debate. Intimidation by lawsuit is as deadly to democracy as a violent coup. Without a broad, available and accessible culture to draw upon, even those individuals with interest, the time to engage, the attention to understand, and a platform from which to speak on an issue have no way to express their thoughts.

The Burden of Expanding Corporate Power

While corporations have done amazing work in economic terms, they represent a gathering threat to democracy and its citizens.

In the past, the platforms for debate were generally public spaces – they were the street corners, the town halls, and the air that carries the sound of the voice. As public spaces, they were available to all, accessible to all, and provided no advantage to one voice over another in the democratic discourse. Only the power of an argument and the person delivering that argument mattered.

Today, this has changed significantly. While the electromagnetic spectrum is, in theory, a public space, it is licensed to corporations with few obligations. The satellites and glass fibers that carry the bulk of our communications in this modern world are privately owned. We've allowed this to happen, with the assumption that communications is good, and the corporations that can afford to provide the necessary infrastructure must be granted the ability to operate them in the free market and make a profit. There's nothing wrong with this approach, except that we have made no provision for the operation of our human society among the corporate players.

Corporations are generally chartered to make money. They are held to no standard other than return on investment and growth. As such, the horrible inefficiencies of the democratic process are in direct conflict with the fiduciary responsibilities of the corporate decision-makers. Nothing about discussing agricultural subsidy structures helps the bottom line at the satellite operations center, so someone must pay to have the issue placed on that platform. We have compromised the public good for the sake of the quarterly financials.

The town hall simply does not compete effectively with the geostationary satellite in the service of democratic debate, and the geostationary satellite is not available unless you can afford it.

## The Burden of Legal Precedents

Of particular interest in the discussion of democracy in general and emergent democracy in particular are two United States legal precedents that conspire to diminish the influence of people in their own democracy. These two precedents create the legal fiction that money is, in some matter, equivalent to speech and that corporations are, in some manner, equivalent to people.

*Buckley v. Valeo* (1976) gives us the theory that money is equivalent to speech. The issue is ripe for debate, if for no other reason than money is not equally available to all citizens in society, while we are all equally endowed with one mind. This, combined with the expansion of corporate control over the platforms of debate give some members of society a much different sort of voice than others. Many of us may be able to launch a free blog and share our opinions on an issue with everyone on the web, but only a few of us can afford to operate 24-hour media outlets or launch communications satellites to drive attention to our issues.

Money is not speech, it merely creates (or pays for) a platform for an individual to speak.

A corporation is a social construct. It has no mind, no reasoning, no thought and no action absent the people that operate on its behalf. Corporations are granted perpetual life (something that would be interesting for citizens) and, to varying degrees, are sheltered from liability (something that would also be very convenient for people). Over the past 100 or so years, corporations have accumulated many of the rights and protections guaranteed to persons by the Constitution, without also being subject to the burdens or responsibilities that are incumbent on persons.

A series of court cases have established 1st, 4th, 5th, 6th and 14th amendment protections (and surely, many others) for corporations. This trend apparently begins with *Santa Clara County v. Southern Pacific Railroad Company* (1886) which seems to have established that the corporation is a natural person, without actually ruling on the issue.

Corporations are not people, they are legal fictions we allow to operate because they provide economic efficiency that individuals cannot, on their own, achieve.

## Overcoming the Burdens

Progress is made at the expense of the past. This is not to say that there is no value in history. There is, and I've made an attempt to draw some relevant lessons from the past. The legacies of our democratic institutions are not the only possible answers to the problems they address. We often accept them without question, and this is counter to the critical debate necessary for a functional democracy.

*Scale*

Perhaps the most fundamental limit is that of scale. There are simply too many issues that are relevant to each individual. The scope of issues, from how often trash is collected in the neighborhood to multinational trade agreements is simply beyond the comprehension of any one person. To address scale, we can designate people we trust to act on our behalf on particular issues. This creates specialists (and more problems), but it works.

The United States Congress is filled with committees and subcommittees. They conduct their deliberations and go through their processes, and make recommendations to the whole of Congress on issues that merit a vote. Not every congressperson is fully engaged on every issue. We know this, we accept it, and generally it serves us well. Where it fails is that while our leaders acknowledge that they cannot comprehend the full scope of issues placed before them, they assume that their electorate cannot either. These structures operate behind closed doors, on appointment and with no substantial accountability to the public at large. The voice of the public is dismissed, because it takes a panel of experts to even begin to address the problem.

A response to scale may be focus, not dismissal. Those members of the electorate that are interested in an issue could engage that issue. They could then hold both the process and the participants accountable. By making the debate granular and specific, perhaps reasoned, intelligent conclusions can be reached.

## Attention Limits

As we engage the members of the electorate on specific issues to address the problems of scale, we can also begin to address the issues of attention limits. By providing access to smarter, focused debate, the tendency to oversimplify complex issues is reduced. By limiting the engagement to issues of concern to particular individuals, the total demand on their time can be reduced, and the demands that are placed on their time and attention are more welcome, because they are considered more relevant.

If the electorate is invited to participate in a comfortable manner, on issues they find worthy of attention, they are both more likely to contribute to the debate and the value of their contribution is likely to be higher. To do, citizens may be engaged on a continuous basis and only on those issues that they consider attention-worthy. Rather than devoting the majority of media resources to rehashing the same small set of divisive issues and packaging them to appeal to established constituents, people who have devoted their attention to more specific issues may be granted the platform from which to engage the debate.

Given the opportunity to make a substantial contribution to issues that concern each citizen, the perceived value of that contribution may lead to greater participation in general.

## Specialization and Communication Barriers

This is, again, related to the value of the minority opinions in the democratic process. Either specialists must adapt to a more general form of the language (less jargon) or they must be willing to take the time to educate their audience, or no effective communication can take place.

Here, the emergent democracy framework provides some potential, in that the debate can be continuous, documented and available to the public. Jargon can't be eliminated, but if specialists are encouraged to

257

engage the broader public on a more continuous basis, those citizens that do devote some of their attention to the field may be able to make substantial, relevant contributions.

## Regulation of Expression

A response to the increasing regulation of expression may simply be a return to unregulated, free speech. The people of the Creative Commons project are working to re-establish the public domain, and it is an important first step. Another step may be to challenge existing intellectual property regimes based on their actual effects, which seem largely to stifle and limit the progress of the sciences and useful arts.

By framing the question in terms of individual expression and the stated intent of intellectual property laws – to encourage progress, not discourage it – it may be possible to develop a new, democracy-friendly intellectual property regime.

## Expanding Corporate Power

To address the growing influence and power of corporations, we must decide if the social structures we create exist to serve the individual, or if the individual exists to serve the structures. We must continue to ask the question, and consider whether we are comfortable as a nation of employees and consumers, or a nation of citizens.

## Legal Precedents

The response to the legal precedents is generally new precedents. Cases must be brought to the courts that can challenge and eventually reverse the established legal constructs of both speech and corporations. These opinions were not reached without dissent.

> To ascribe to such entities an 'intellect' or 'mind' for freedom of conscience purposes is to confuse metaphor with reality.[195]

> The state need not allow its own creation to consume it[196]

---

[195]Dissent by Justices Rehnquist, Stevens and White, in *Pacific Gas & Electric Company v. Public Utilities Commission* (1986)

The blessings of perpetual life and limited liability... pose special dangers in the political sphere[197]

...it cannot be said to be deprived of the civil rights of freedom of speech and of assembly, for the liberty guaranteed by the due process clause is the liberty of natural, not artificial, persons[198]

The prevalence of the corporation in America has led men of this generation to act, at times, as if the privilege of doing business in corporate form were inherent in the citizen; and has led them to accept the evils attendant upon the free and unrestricted use of the corporate mechanism as if these eviles were the inescapable price of civilized life, and hence to be borne with resignation. Throughout the greater part of our history, a different view prevailed[199]

These comments form a basis for reviewing and perhaps changing the concepts that threaten the democratic process. I've highlighted two principles (accepting money as speech and corporations as persons), but there are many more dangerous precedents in our American legal history.

These burdens can't simply be whisked away with some carefully-crafted bits of technology. Technology provides tools that may, to some extent, mitigate these issues, but it is often a matter of how you use the tools that determines the outcome.

While the specific challenges I've described here are very much based on the American democratic experience and its long history, they are important to discuss in other contexts. Perhaps newer democratic structures can avoid some of these mistakes entirely. Perhaps others can avoid following the same path without asking critical questions.

---

[196]Dissent by Justices Brennan, Marshall and White in *First National Bank of Boston v. Bellotti* (1977)

[197]Dissent by Justices Rehnquist in *First National Bank of Boston v. Bellotti* (1977)

[198]Comments of Justice Stone in *Hague v. Committee for Industrial Organization* (1939)

[199]Dissent of Justice Brandeis in *Louis K. Liggett Company v. Lee* (1933)

## Restoring Trust

To operate in a democratic republic, we must trust the process, if not the people. Individual representatives may be untrustworthy, but we must believe that the system will identify them and correct their indiscretions. To secure and maintain the benefits of democracy, the electorate must maintain a healthy measure of distrust, but this distrust must manifest in a change of representatives, and not as resignation that all representatives are unfit and untrustworthy.

Trust is not a measure of agreement, but of expectation. It's possible to trust that some people will consistently do the wrong thing. You can trust that some people will make reasoned decisions. You can trust that some people will be late. You can trust that some people will take risks. It is subjective, personal, and non-transferable. It is fragile. And it has been compromised.

> The law giver, of all beings, most owes the law allegiance. He of all men should behave as though the law compelled him. But it is the universal weakness of mankind that what we are given to administer we presently imagine we own.[200]

Once the trust relationship is violated, it's much more difficult to restore. Today, our leaders attempt to restore trust when the lapses become so obvious that they cannot be ignored. Independent commissions, blue-ribbon panels and special prosecutors are drafted into service to lay bare before the people the facts of a situation. They expose the unseemly details that led to an unfortunate crisis or action. They are supposed to be above the process, so they can fairly and reasonably examine the process. These responses are reactionary, and it is increasingly obvious that we don't trust these independent institutions either.

A transparent process is the only way to establish and maintain the trust of the electorate. For any issue an individual considers important, the current decisions (and actions), as well as a record of the deliberative process through which those decisions were made should be readily available.

---

[200]Wells, Herbert George.

The evidently general assumption in much of modern politics is that the crucial decisions are already final. Minds are made up. Very little effort is spent on major issues anymore, and the individuals (citizens, voters) are a lost cause – they can't be educated, they can't be converted, they can only be polled and assembled into voting blocks. I think this assumption is simply false. I think that citizens are not convinced by politicians making political pitches because they don't trust that the politicians understand the problems they claim to address – they have no credibility as anything but politicians (and sometimes, not even as politicians).

We have not agreed to disagree on some issues. We do not hold our representatives accountable to all citizens. Our elected officials increasingly cater to the few, large issues that they managed to assemble as the focus of a successful campaign, and ignore or suppress the opposition.

> The best weapon of a dictatorship is secrecy, but the best weapon of a democracy should be the weapon of openness.[201]

The world is not a simple place – nuance is critical. As we explore technologies that allow people to participate in ongoing critical debate on subjects that concern them, so-called domain experts – the people who have spent their lives studying a given problem, may be faced down by people who have spent their lives experiencing the results of expert but remote decisions. Debates that have been largely theoretical, if only because the affected population has no means to respond, are given not just a voice, but a presence in the political process.

No longer can we go to war against a population and avoid broad exposure to the perspectives of people on the ground, under our assault. No longer can we espouse economic policies and avoid exposure to the realities of the people affected. No longer can we assert moral authority based on questionable intelligence information. The truth will come out, the perspectives of all the people affected by our decisions will be available. We can decide to embrace these perspectives and engage them, or we can wait for scandal and intrigue to further erode public confidence in our governments and their decision-making processes.

---

[201] Bohr, Niels

## Better Government Than We Deserve

Do we trust representatives to set aside personal gain for the larger social structure? Do we trust representatives to apply judgment and not bend to popular opinion? Do we trust representatives to act in our best interests, even when we disagree with those critical decisions? Do we trust the democratic process to self-correct when flaws are found? Increasingly, it seems that we don't. We seem to have adopted the position that our representatives should merely echo our own opinions on matters of state.

If this is the government we deserve, then our technologists can build secure polling systems that collect and present statistically valid majority opinions on every issue, and we can eliminate the representatives from our democratic republics. We have this technology. This is a simple problem.

> Democracy is a device that ensures we shall be governed no better than we deserve.[202]

On the other hand, if we demand restored trust in our representative processes, we have a much more difficult task before us. We have to be willing to accept mistakes and disagreement in a democratic society. We have to acknowledge that issues are complex, that decisions are made with incomplete information. Most importantly, we have to trust that the people making decisions on our behalf are, in fact, considering our best interests.

The framers of the United States Constitution hoped to provide the people with a "more perfect union." They aspired to address the weaknesses of forms of government that had come before, and to provide a foundation that would evolve and change with time and wisdom. To a large extent, it has been a successful experiment, but now, with more than 200 years of experience, and under the heavy burden of modern communication and commerce, flaws have been exposed. The solutions to these flaws are not quite as obvious.

---

[202]Shaw, George Bernard

We must continue to ask the questions. Should those that govern us be the ones that govern us? Have they demonstrated moral and proper action on our behalf? Have they earned our trust? Can we do better?

Government must also protect us from ourselves. No person can reasonably be expected to know, understand, consider, debate and act on every issue that impacts their lives in modern society. Today, it is certainly possible to equip the whole population of the world with a simple voting device and periodically ask them to vote on various issues. We can have a global, gadget-enabled direct democracy, but we need something better. We need to engage people who aren't merely voting their instincts or self-interest to make decisions on issues that we do not and will not understand. Mindless representation is the worst possible democratic circumstance.

"Certainly, gentlemen, it ought to be the happiness and glory of a representative to live in the strictest union, the closest correspondence, and the most unreserved communication with his constituents. Their wishes ought to have great weight with him; their opinion, high respect; their business, unremitted attention. It is his duty to sacrifice his repose, his pleasures, his satisfactions, to theirs; and above all, ever, and in all cases, to prefer their interest to his own. But his unbiased opinion, his mature judgment, his enlightened conscience, he ought not to sacrifice to you, to any man, or to any set of men living. These he does not derive from your pleasure; no, nor from the law and the constitution. They are a trust from Providence, for the abuse of which he is deeply answerable. Your representative owes you, not his industry only, but his judgment; and he betrays, instead of serving you, if he sacrifices it to your opinion."[203]

### Emergent Democracy?

When a great truth once gets abroad in the world, no power on Earth can imprison it, or prescribe its limits, or suppress it. It is bound to go on till it becomes the thought of the world[204]

---

[203]Burke, Edmund (1774, November 3) Speech to the Electors of Bristol.

[204]Douglass, Frederick.

Democracy has blossomed across the world in the past hundred years, surging after each of the two World Wars and again starting in the late 1970's. Today, just less than 60% of the world's population lives under a democratic government (with another 5% under a restricted democratic government)[205]. As more and more of the world's population embraces democratic values and begins to engage in the perpetual debate, more individual perspectives become available. Each mind engaged in the deliberative process casts some bit of light onto the issues that have gained the attention of that individual.

> Democracy is not utopia. It is an imperfect, incomplete and
> challenging form of government.

As telecommunications technology advances, allowing small groups of people with similar interests to cluster, engage and debate each other, the number of issues that become available to the debate increases.

Did you select the chocolate ice cream? You might be responsible for the destruction of rain forest that was cleared to make room for a plantation. You might be responsible for the exploitation of child laborers that harvest the plantation. You might be responsible for the job loss impact and agricultural waste product impact of sugar and dairy subsidies.

Then again, that wasn't on the menu, was it? By the time you make your selection, a whole web of previous decisions by other individuals, acting on behalf of social, corporate and political structures have already been made. You may not care so much about the rain forest, but do you trust the people that made the decision on your behalf? If you do care about the rain forest, are you confident that your opinion was heard when those decisions were made?

The challenge of emergent democracy is to describe a framework that avoids the impossible technological utopia, embraces the human component of debate and reason and does not presume to provide all the answers, but can be extended to address new challenges.

---

[205]Freedom House (1999, December), Democracy's Century: A Survey of Global Political Change in the 20th Century.

## Lighting the Tapers

> Our deepest fear is not that we are inadequate. Our deepest fear is that
> we are powerful beyond measure. It is our Light, not our Darkness,
> that most frightens us.[206]

There are some 6.4 billion individuals on this lonely planet Earth, and
each of them has a unique set of interests, experiences and values. Each
person brings some measure of attention to those questions or problems
that concern them individually. Prosperity allows some of us the luxury
to bring our attention to bear on problems esoteric and general – those
that do not have specific bearing on our own lives. Each of these issues
may ultimately affect us all.

Every individual has a contribution to make; the question is will they be
empowered to make it? Perhaps 6.4 billion points of light is enough to
illuminate our path into the future. Perhaps with each issue illuminated
by the thoughts and consideration of those that share concern, that
deem it worthy of their attention, some measure of understanding and
well-considered decision making is possible.

> He who receives an idea from me, receives instruction himself without
> lessening mine; as he who lights his taper at mine, receives light
> without darkening me. That ideas should freely spread from one to
> another over the globe, for the moral and mutual instruction of man,
> and improvement of his condition, seems to have been peculiarly and
> benevolently designed by nature, when she made them, like fire,
> expansible over all space, without lessening their density in any point,
> and like the air in which we breathe, move, and have our physical
> being, incapable of confinement or exclusive appropriation.[207]

We are meant to keep doing better. Perhaps we will.

---

[206]Williamson, Marianne (1992) A Return to Love: Reflections on the
Principles of A Course in Miracles.

[207]Jefferson, Thomas (1813, August 13) Letter to Isaac McPherson.

# Section Four:
# Activist Technology

# Virtual Bonfire: A Brief History of Activist Technology
## by Jon Lebkowsky

### Evolution: the Internet, social software and post-broadcast politics

It is not proper to think of networks as connecting computers. Rather, they connect people using computers to mediate. The great success of the internet is not technical, but in human impact. Electronic mail may not be a wonderful advance in Computer Science, but it is a whole new way for people to communicate. The continued growth of the Internet is a technical challenge to all of us, but we must never loose sight of where we came from, the great change we have worked on the larger computer community, and the great potential we have for future change.

– David Clark, Senior Research Scientist, MIT Laboratory for Computer Science, in "RFC 1336 - Who's Who in the Internet: Biographies of IAB, IESG and IRSG Members."[208]

When you understand that the Internet was always about connecting people, not just machines, you can begin to understand why the system has an inherent political value. Since the global network of networks formed and began to evolve in the 1980s and 90s, we've developed a better understanding of human social networks, as well, and we've begun to think about how groups and communities form and how technology can mediate group-forming with significant effect, as noted by David P. Reed in his paper "That Sneaky Exponential — Beyond Metcalfe's Law to the Power of Community Building."[209]:

In networks like the Internet, Group Forming Networks (GFNs) are an important additional kind of network capability. A GFN has functionality that directly enables and supports affiliations (such as interest groups, clubs, meetings, communities) among subsets of its customers. Group tools and technologies (also called community tools) such as user-defined mailing lists, chat rooms, discussion groups,

---

[208] RFC-1336, "Who's Who in the Internet," G. Malkin, May 1992, 15.

[209] Reed, David P., "That Sneaky Exponential—Beyond Metcalfe's Law to the Power of Community Building," http://www.reed.com/Papers/GFN/reedslaw.html.

buddy lists, team rooms, trading rooms, user groups, market makers, and auction hosts, all have a common theme — they allow small or large groups of network users to coalesce and to organize their communications around a common interest, issue, or goal. Sadly, the traditional telephone and broadcast/cable network frameworks provide no support for groups.

What I found that's surprising and important is that GFNs create a new kind of connectivity value that scales exponentially with N. Briefly, the number of non-trivial subsets that can be formed from a set of N members is $2^N$-N-1, which grows as $2^N$. Thus, a network that supports easy group communication has a potential number of groups that can form that grows exponentially with N.

In the first years following the deployment of the technology for the World Wide Web and privatization and commercialization of the Internet, the system became a hotbed for technical, social and business innovation that unfortunately created unrealistic economic expectations, excessive valuations of public Internet companies, and the eventual collapse of the public markets for Internet-based businesses. However Internet adoption and a mainstreaming effect continued to increase, with adopters increasingly aware of the Internet's value as an environment for many activities – information sharing and retrieval, business communication, electronic commerce, community-building and political activism.

## Netizens

Computer scientist Michael Hauben coined the term "netizen" to describe persons actively engaged in online communities, usually thought to be proponents of Internet-mediated civic engagement. Wired Magazine adopted the term, as did the magazine's online component, Hotwired. The netizen meme emerged as several groups, formal and informal, focused on computer-mediated activism. Examples:

## EFF, CDT, and Voters Telecommunication Watch

The Electronic Frontier Foundation pioneered online activism. The impetus for EFF and the first talks around its formation occurred online, via email and discussions on the WELL, primarily involving John Perry Barlow and Mitch Kapor. Barlow coined the phrase "electronic frontier" based on his observation that cyberspace communities were like the American West, not quite settled, feeling their way into local modes of governance and not quite on the radar of those "back east" or, in this case, offline. Barlow and Kapor understood the potential of the Internet and the potential for misguided law enforcement and legislation, especially if and when mainstreaming began. Later events proved them correct.

EFF evolved from a community-based organization with Cliff Figallo as director to a lobbying organization with Jerry Berman at the helm. After Berman left to form the Center for Democracy and Technology, EFF moved to San Francisco and evolved into the organization it is today, an organization providing a combination of legal support and future-focused technology evangelism.

After Berman formed CDT Jonah Seiger, a former EFF employee who moved with Berman and joined the CDT staff, began working on net.activist initiatives with Shabbir Safdar, a New York software engineer who founded Voters Telecommunication Watch (VTW). VTW, a volunteer organization that created a series of email action alerts that became models for effective online activism. The VTW alerts focused on "cyber liberties" issues like the Communications Decency Act (CDA). The alerts included everything a recipient would need to know to make an effective legislative contact. Safdar and Seiger created an online demonstration that had operators of web sites turning their web pages black in response to the CDA. This was an early and extremely effective demonstration of the Internet's political potential. The CDA was almost defeated, but passed when it was added as a rider on the Omnibus Telecommunications Act. Months of activist work followed, leading to a Supreme Court hearing after which the Court ruled that the CDA was unconstitutional.

### Geek Force

Jon Katz suggested the formation of a "geek force" as a joke at Hotwired in 1996, but readers took him seriously and a movement began to form. It was ultimately unsuccessful. Katz explains: "But this noble effort wasn't to be. It was an idea whose time hadn't come, a notion more mature than the culture it wanted to help. The posts of the Geek Force (as it came to be called) volunteers were overwhelmed by the narcissistic and mostly adolescent flamers who dominated HotWired at the time, self-styled cyberguerillas who celebrated their own free speech while enthusiastically depriving others of theirs."[210] Geek force demonstrated the potential and the fragility of Internet group-forming at the time.

## Fight Censorship

Journalist Declan McCullagh formed the "Fight Censorship" email list while still a student at Carnegie-Mellon University. The list became a rallying point for civil libertarians and free speech advocates, focusing on subjects like the CDA and the use of filtering technologies on library computers.

## Etc.

Computer Professionals for Social Responsibility (CPSR), and early group of activist techies, spawned a couple of organizations. Marc Rotenberg left CPSR to form the Electronic Privacy Information Center (EPIC), and later Audrie Krause left CPSR to form NetAction. EFF, EPIC and several other net.activist groups from around the world formed the Global Internet Liberty Campaign (GILC), an organization that focused on free speech online and unfettered access to the Internet. GILC currently lists 68 groups, which gives you an idea how online activism has grown - and many of those were on board before the mainstreaming effect kicked in.

The online activist groups that emerged during the nineties were often libertarian and generally focused on issues specifically related to the Internet: online privacy, encryption, free speech, etc. This began to change around the turn of the century, as Internet adoption became more common, and more non-technical users started doing interesting things online.

## WTO '99

When the World Trade Organization met in 1999, some anti-globalization protestors used the Internet to plan and organize demonstrations, and to discuss their positions on globalization. After the WTO meeting, groups used the Internet to debrief. The Internet aspect of the WTO protests was significant because it was an early instance

---

[210] Katz, Jon. "Post Nerds, Part II: Rise and Fall of Geek Force." *Wired News*, July 7, 1997. http://www.wired.com/news/culture/0,1284,4992,00.html.

where the Internet was used broadly for advocacy that was not tech- or network-focused. The ad hoc Direct Action Network that formed to organize protests used email and web sites as core technologies for organizing the protests, and the online Independent Media Center posted video of the protests. Internet coverage ensured global awareness of the meeting as well as the protests.[211]

## The 2000 Election

The 2000 U.S. Presidential election saw some use of the Internet leading up to election day, but when the election was contested and the contest drug on for days, the Internet became a significant platform for discussion and debate, and was widely used by mainstream media as a source of quick feedback on public opinion. CNN, for instance, conducted polls online and read email messages aloud as part of their coverage. This was an important step toward the Internet's wider adoption as a source of mainstream news and debate.

## 9/11, the war on terror, and the blogosphere

Following the September 11, 2001 attack on the World Trade Center, the number of Internet users didn't increase, and regular Internet users "they were aggressively using all the means at their disposal to get information about the unfolding crisis and make contact with their networks of loved ones and friends. That meant they were anxious consumers of TV news and restless users of the telephone even more than they used online tools," according to a study by the Pew Internet and American Life project. The project also notes that "There was much heavier use of news sites online in the days after the attack, but the overall size of the online population was slightly smaller than usual."[212] However another Pew study suggested that

> there were conspicuously more Internet users getting news online after
> September 11 than in previous periods. More than two-thirds of
> Internet users (69%) have used the Web to get news and information
> related to the attacks and their aftermath. Half of Internet users –
> more than 53 million people – have gotten some kind of news about

[211] Saracevic, Alan T. "The Net and the New Age of Activism." San Francisco *Examiner,*December 4, 1999.

[212] Rainie, Lee. "How Americans Used the Internet After the Terror Attack." Pew Internet and American Life Project, September 15, 2001.

the attacks online. Many online Americans have used the Internet to stay "on alert" for news developments by subscribing to email news updates and getting newscasts streamed to their desktops. Among those watching developments most carefully online are 33% of Internet users who have gotten information about the financial markets because of their concern about the economic impact of the terror strikes against America.[213]

Between 9/11 and the start of the Iraq War, however, Internet use escalated. According to another Pew study, reliance on the Internet was many times greater during the Iraq War than after the 9/11 attacks, with 77% of all online Americans having used the Internet in connection with the war.[214]

9/11 and the War on Terror were coincident with the appearance and early growth of the Blogosphere, and one of the first Blogosphere subspecies, the Warbloggers... conservative bloggers who expressed support for the attack on Iraq. Dave Winer defined warblogger as "a person who runs a weblog that started around, or was significantly influenced by the events of September 11, 2001." He goes on to explain its impact on the growth of the blogosphere. " Like the term "baby boom" — it accounts for an explosion of interest that was linked to a historic event, in this case, personal publishing using the Web. The baby boom was part of the aftermath of World War II. It was a return to fertility after a huge worldwide conflict that turned most adults celibate. It was hard to make babies if your honey wasn't close by. A huge worldwide conflict makes people think about survival, not reproducing. Once the fear was over, everyone made babies. It was the thing to do. Just like weblogs and Sept 11. The warblog phenomenon has many

---

[213] Rainie, Lee, and Bente Kalsnes, "The commons of the tragedy: How the Internet was used by millions after the terror attacks to grieve, console, share news, and debate the country's response." Pew Internet and American Life Project, October 10, 2001.

[214] Rainie, Lee, Susannah Fox, and Deborah Fallows, "The Internet and the Iraq War: How Americans Have Used the Internet to Learn War News, Understand Events, and Promote Their Views." Pew Internet and American Life Project, April 1, 2003.

facets, and as the echoes travel through the weblog world, it morphs and begets new weblogs covering lots of stuff unrelated to war."[215]

Blogs as we know them today started appearing in 1997, and by 2000 there were thousands of blogs and blog communities had begun to form, so what we saw post-9/11 was an acceleration of a form that was already well-established. By 2003 there was an estimated 2.4 to 2.9 million weblogs, based on Blogcount's analysis.[216] As I write this, Technorati[217] is tracking 8,272,738 weblogs, and there are many more that Technorati doesn't track, and new weblogs appearing every day. This growth in the number of blogs was accompanied by increased visibility and acceptance of blogs, some of which have developed prominent followings, approaching the popularity of mainstream media. Related tools were also appearing, such as blog search engines and indexes, syndication formats and news aggregators. A social software movement emerged among software developers and users that were focused on blogs, wikis, online discussions, etc.

*Election 2004 and Howard Dean*

The 2004 primaries and election energized many bloggers, online activists, and traditional activists who were beginning to see the potential political value of social software. MoveOn.org, which had already proved its effectiveness in catalyzing support for progressive issues and raising money via online donations, and which was influenced in the beginning by the early Internet activist campaigns spearheaded by Shabbir Safdar and Jonah Seiger, became a model for online activist and political campaign sites. The Moveon model focused on email campaigns and petitions to rally user support and encourage donations. The Howard Dean campaign sought advice from Internet activists and formed an online strategy similar to Moveon's. The Dean campaign used Meetup.com to bring supporters together, and they saw significant

---

[215] Winer, Dave. "RFC: What is a warblogger?" http://www.userland.com/whatIsAWarblogger, September 9, 2002.

[216] Wolff, Phil. "The BlogCount Estimate: 2.4 to 2.9 million weblogs." http://dijest.com/bc/2003_06_23_bc.html#105638688729256217, June 23.2003.

[217] http://www.technorati.com. Technorati is a system for searching, tagging, and aggregating weblogs.

growth in Meetup events. The combination of enthusiastic Meetups and an ability to accept online donations made Dean an early leader in Democratic fundraising. The campaign added weblogs and explored other technologies, such as "GetLocal," a system that supported users in finding Dean events near them, and Deanlink, a social network system similar to Friendster. There were also technology projects in support of Dean but not formally connected to the campaign, like DeanSpace (which later became CivicSpace) and the Dean Issues Forum. Dean's early success led other campaigns to place more emphasis on Internet technology. Though Dean lost the presidential primary, the genie was out of the bottle. The Internet was an important part of the presidential campaigns, with bloggers credentialed to attend the Democratic and Republican National Conventions .

## Activists and technology

The Internet is certain to have a growing role in U.S. and global politics following accelerated political use leading up to the 2004 Presidential Election and efforts to extend social software capabilities and free speech globally through organizations like Blogger Corps (http://bloggercorps.org/) and Global Voices Online (http://cyber.law.harvard.edu/globalvoices/). A loose coalition of activists and technologists called Activist Technology (http://activist-tech.org) met in Austin on March 16, 2005, with three general groups discussing how technology can support activism in the future. The three groups were

- Traditional activists/advocates,

- Wholistic/democratic activists, and

- Activist technologists/developers.

Advocates focus on specific outcomes, whereas wholistic or democratic activists focus more on processes for facilitating input and achieving consensus through deliberation. The two approaches have very different requirements. Advocates need technology that will present their case effectively and build support. Deliberative democracy is more difficult, especially if you're scaling up to large numbers of participants in the deliberative process. Deliberation is a process of careful consideration prior to a choice or decision, and careful consideration implies thoughtful discussion, which is difficult to scale. Deliberative Polling® is one method:

Deliberative Polling® is an attempt to use television and public opinion research in a new and constructive way. A random, representative sample is first polled on the targeted issues. After this baseline poll, members of the sample are invited to gather at a single place for a weekend in order to discuss the issues. Carefully balanced briefing materials are sent to the participants and are also made publicly available. The participants engage in dialogue with competing experts and political leaders based on questions they develop in small group discussions with trained moderators. Parts of the weekend events are broadcast on television, either live or in taped and edited form. After the deliberations, the sample is again asked the original questions. The resulting changes in opinion represent the conclusions the public would reach, if people had opportunity to become more informed and more engaged by the issues.[218]

---

[218] Fishkin, Professor James S. "Deliberative Polling®: Toward a Better-Informed Democracy." The Center for Deliberative Democracy, Stanford University. http://cdd.stanford.edu/polls/docs/summary/.

# The Revolution will be Engineered: An assessment of the present and possible future of Net-based political tools
## by Britt Blaser

There's a power grab going on in our Republic, and it isn't pretty.

I'm not talking about the constant struggle in Washington, but the powerful engagement by software experts inspired by the Dean campaign, up to their elbows in the messy process of imagining and designing a new way for political campaigns to engage voters. The Internet design and engineering community is learning how politics work and has glimpsed how it might improve. That knowledge creates an obligation on those who can make a difference. The obligation is to design accessible political choices at every level of the political process. We can only empower broad participation in politics by making participation as convenient as web browsing and Instant Messaging.

*What's the problem with politics and how might engineering help?*

### A Lever Long Enough to Suppress the World

Archimedes famously said that if you gave him a long enough lever and a place to stand, he could lift the world. Well, it works both ways. Using the long lever arm of mass media, a tiny core of politically powerful people controls the rest of the population's choices, economics and future.

Systems design is the study of how to balance inputs into and outputs from a dynamic process so that it optimally serves the needs of the highest possible number of users of the process. From a systems design standpoint, American politics is a disaster:

The Data (*official 2000 election)

# 286,196,812 Americans*

| | |
|---|---|
| **184,744,527** | non-voters* |
| **100,000,000** | voters who don't matter |
| **2,000,000** | voters who matter |
| **50,000** | political activists |
| **5,000** | political power elite |

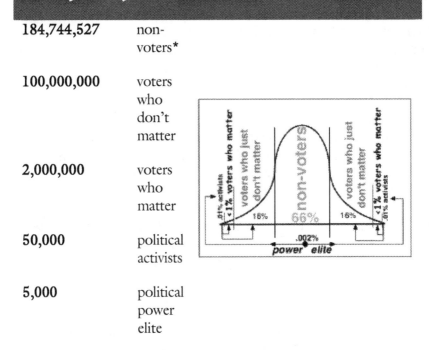

About a third of Americans vote, but most vote so consistently that their votes, needs and opinions are inconsequential. Just a few "swing" voters are the target of politicians' attention and advertising, the only voters who matter. In the 2000 election, Gore received 50.5% of the popular vote, while losing 3 states–41 electoral votes–by a total of **6,611** votes.

There's only a tiny sliver of the population zealous enough to be active in politics, and it even takes a kind of zealotry to get out and vote. I don't have the figures, but do any states have more than 1,000 full time activists? Sure, there are a lot of political hobbyists who will canvass occasionally or show up at a state convention and perform as directed, but by activists I mean those who live for or off of politics and do their party's bidding whenever asked. My working hypothesis is that there are no more than 50,000 active political foot soldiers at any one time, less than .02% of Americans. Even if you think there are double or triple the number, the fraction is still vanishingly small.

In turn, those few activists are manipulated by a tiny political elite which is probably no more than .002% of the population–5,000 politicians, lobbyists, journalists and business leaders according to Joe Trippi. Generally, Americans aren't chatting each other up to get out the vote, but rather responding to the unfolding media messages in the same passive way they might discuss episodes of *Friends* around the water cooler.

It's even worse than it appears. This tiny group of power brokers drives the agenda for a nation that the rest of the world depends upon for its very existence, in a protection-racket kind of way. This is a system that no conscientious systems architect would sign off on, but which most Americans meekly accept as how things have to be.

Paul Boutin pointed out in an enlightened Slate article that attracting new voters is the secret sauce for any winning candidate, and that's what the Dean campaign did well, though no one has the statistics to prove it. Dean's coterie of new activists were an energizing force that establishment Democrats cynically shut down as fast as they could:

> *Recent polls showed Kerry and Bush at a dead heat. But it's not so much a 50-50 split as 25-25 — half the voting-age population has failed to show up in recent elections. Bringing in new voters — if you could find a way to do it — would swing an election much more easily than converting the people who already plan to cast their ballots for the other guy.*

Real world evangelism is the part the Dean campaign didn't get right in time to empower its true believers to evangelize ever larger circles of new true believers.

**Campaign In A Box** I anticipate the emergence of an open standard and set of software tools, a campaign distro, that is available to any campaign at any level. Since all campaigns have the same challenges, but with varying populations, a single toolkit can serve all, just as MS Word can be used to write a book or a memo, or Linux can power a Tivo or Google. This integrated suite will be geared to two kinds of customers, the people running a campaign and the voters they hope to attract. As with all software and web services, the user experience is crucial. Potential candidates and their teams must be able to immediately "get" how the tools can be used and how to set their goals and message. Their potential supporters must be able to immediately "get" how this candidate improves their lot, and why and how to help the candidate serve the voters' collective self-interest.

## The 10 Step Campaign Guide, 2004

During the last half of 2003, I spent two years of my life working on the Dean campaign, but I'm not complaining. Few of the several hundred thousand Dean volunteers regret the time and energy invested. We were instrumental in launching beta socialware that worked, not perfectly, but better than expected.

The unheralded secret sauce of the Dean campaign was that, like so many web sites, it asked interested web surfers to *register* as members of the campaign. When this membership meme crossed over into politics-as-web-application, a powerful idea was born and the clear line between who was part of the campaign and who was its target changed forever:

*When supporters of a campaign register as members they become insiders*

Howard Dean's Campaign Manager, Joe Trippi, was the visionary who saw that the key to growth was to let go of the traditional command and control campaign model and put the campaign in the hands of whoever wanted to work hardest.

Was the Dean campaign a success? Conduct your own thought experiment. Imagine a survey of the 280 political races of national significance in 2004 (235 congressional races, 34 senators and 11 Governors = 5-600 campaigns). Ask the campaign manager for each of those campaigns if s/he'd like to use the socialware tools that Dean had. If the majority of your imaginary respondents say yes, the Dean campaign was a success.

## Dean-like Campaign tools you can use today

If you are a thought leader or decision maker for any campaign at any level, you should make sure your online tools are optimized because it's a more basic process than organizing in the real world. With the emergence of the Internet as a measurable force in campaigning, you can now design and maintain your message, your outreach and do it more directly than ever before. That's the good news. The bad news is that you can only control your destiny by letting your constituents control your message.

This is a summary of the online mechanisms that seemed to have worked well for the Dean campaign and ideas for the next generation of tools that seem necessary. For starters, let's review the toolkit you'll want if you're going to conduct a successful campaign in 2004. Rule 1 is to never invent software but to use off-the-shelf solutions wherever possible.

| | |
|---|---|
| **Campaign management** | Use tools like Convio's to process contributions and generate reports: |

- Web site content server
- Email grouping and targeting
- Contribution management
- Team Raising
- Event management
- Constituency data

| | |
|---|---|
| **Meetup.com** | Set up a program for your candidate at meet-up.com |
| **Campaign Blog** | Use off-the-shelf blogging software so your candidate and key staff can speak directly to your constituents and listen to their comments. |
| **Campaign Materials** | Provide campaign materials for your supporters to print at home. |
| **Viral email design** | Email is the "killer application" on the Internet. Steal from the best. |
| **P2P hierarchal linking** | Your constituents already know each other. |
| **"Get Local" tools** | Help your supporters reach out to each other in the real world. |
| **P2P policy engagement** | Give your constituents an authentic voice in ~~your~~ *their* campaign. |

| | | |
|---|---|---|
| **Voter management** | **File** | The voter file is the nervous system of the campaign |
| **Get Out The Vote** | | GOTV *is* the campaign. |

## Convio Campaign Management

This might sound like a pitch for Convio, Inc. of Austin, Texas, but it's a pitch for getting your campaign up and running as fast as possible. Convio is the system used successfully by the Dean campaign, so I'm most familiar with it.

Here in the spring of 2004, it's hard to imagine a quicker, easier and more cost effective way to get your campaign up and running than by using the systems at convio.com. Although there are competing systems (e.g., kintera.com and getactive.com), I believe that Convio is at this writing the Google of campaign management systems, and it's unlikely to be eclipsed before the end of 2004.

Here's a depiction of the Convio components:

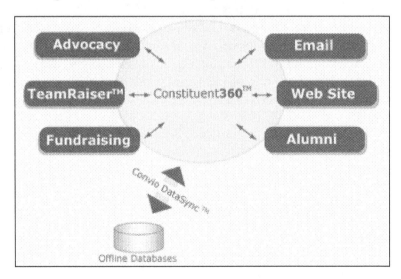

## Convio.com Services

Convio is an Application Services Provider, or "ASP". This means that it works like software you run on your computer, but it appears in your

281

web browser. That gives you a world of security and convenience. It means every authorized member of your formal or informal staff can access your campaign tools from anywhere, generate emails to constituents and every other matter that you normally need to do on paper.

(Convio's *Alumni* module looks extraneous if you're running a political campaign, but there's a great deal that campaigns can learn from any alumni office, which cannot afford to throw away any alumni the way that companies routinely discard customers by ignoring their needs.)

**DeanSpace Campaign Management** The DeanSpace project (deanspace.org), developed by volunteers, gained a lot of visibility and was widely deployed. DeanSpace is a series of modules that extend the Drupal content management system to function as a political campaign site.

There's a list of Dean sites at http://deanspace.org/sites, and an online DeanSpace guide at http://deanspace.org/development.

The virtue of DeanSpace is that it's free and supported by a small army of dedicated volunteers. At this writing, at least one campaign, Miles Nelson running for Congress in New Mexico is a DeanSpace site: http://www.nelsonfornewmexico.com. However, it is not obvious how to set up and configure a DeanSpace site. If you're going to use it, you'll need a lot of help from one of the DeanSpace volunteers or a technical person who's a fast learner.

Here's a depiction of the DeanSpace system as conceived in the summer of 2003:

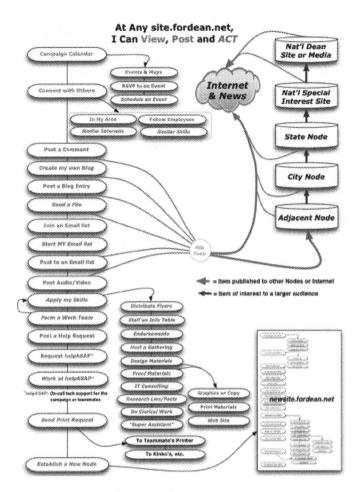

**Meetup** The power of Meetup is revealed by an anecdote: The first Meetup that Howard Dean attended was in New York. When he arrived, the waiting line wrapped around the block even though no one knew him well enough to recognize him when he arrived. Governor Dean asked a cop what the commotion was. "It's a meeting to learn about Howard Dean." Was the cop there to keep order? "Nah. I'm here to see Dean."

Here's how your Meetup will look to your constituents:

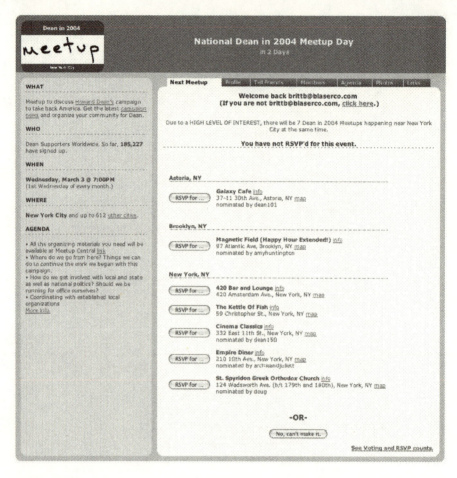

Zephyr Teachout, Director of Dean's Grassroots effort, told Baseline's Ed Cone that she could imagine the campaign without the official blog, but not without Meetup.

Every Presidential campaign sponsored a Meetup, and your campaign needs one too. Just go to http://www.meetup.com/suggest/topic to set up your monthly Meetups.

**Campaign Blog** The Dean campaign's web log put the campaign on the map, because it's a vibrant community of staff blog entries and constituent responses. Because the comments feature is turned on, anyone can comment. These comments became the community's means for blogging to each other.

284

You build an effective blog by commenting on what you are experiencing, in your own words, or saying what you want your supporters to do, worded clearly and thoughtfully.

Create your campaign blog using off-the-shelf software or a subscription-based Web service. The cost ranges from free to very low. The Dean campaign uses Moveable Type blog software, available at http://www.movabletype.org/. The official Dean blog is not hosted by Convio.

**Campaign Materials** One of Joe Trippi's favorite stories describes a handout they customized for al 50 states. As an old time organizer, Joe was blown away by the realization that a piece of campaign literature could be two things:

- Free
- Designed, produced and on the street in 1 day.

But it gets better. Within an hour, someone from Puerto Rico commented on the blog that they too deserved a customized handout. It was ready for download within 5 minutes, a level of responsiveness never before possible. When an expatriate in London chimed in, a $52^{nd}$ version was put up, earning thanks from an American in Paris.

**Viral Email Design** If you send a compelling email to a dozen friends there's a chance that three of them will forward it to another dozen friends. If the cycle continues, it becomes a viral email. The compounding math makes peer-to-peer email the most powerful tool in politics. It works because each message comes directly from an acquaintance and because it's so easy–I've already entered my friends' contact data into my computer's rolodex. It's every campaign's job to get friends' contact data from supporters and use it in an effective, responsible way. If your use of personal data is not responsible, it's probably not effective.

Most people who vote have access to email including (perhaps especially) grandparents, who love to stay connected to their families. A well-worded email message can be powerful, but it takes skill to do it right. One cardinal rule is that the message is never about money. It must be about an opportunity. Perhaps the opportunity involves an investment by your supporters, but money must never be the main point of the message.

Avoid web-based mail forms. Those are the forms in your web browser that encourage your constituent to enter the email addresses of their friends to receive your message. That seems like a great idea, since it allows the campaign to harvest new email addresses, but the problem is that the message is not from their friend, and they know it. Moreover, your constituents are accustomed to reading and forwarding email using their preferred email client software.

When you want to start a viral email cycle, send a short, urgent message to your known supporters with a link to a web page to take action. Ask your supporters to forward the message to their friends, which they can do without re-typing addresses.

If your message is compelling, they'll forward it.

If it's not compelling, why send it?

If you can't tell if a message is compelling, why be in politics?

**Peer-to-Peer Hierarchical Linking** Here's something you can do better than the Dean campaign. If your campaign catches fire, you will not be able to keep up with all the people who want to talk to you, give advice, get a job or change the world. That's a high class problem but it can degrade your efforts into a nightmare of unmanageable expectations, which is one of the limitations that prevented the Dean campaign from leveraging its passionate supporters into more votes.

If a campaign is willing to listen, *really listen*, to its supporters, it will attract friends of the supporters it engages.

**The primary driver of a campaign's success is its responsiveness to supporters**.

Any user of the World Wide Web knows that the user experience is everything. With an obsession for the customer experience, Amazon became the world's bookstore first, then a community talking about books, then a purveyor of most durable goods and now has become, literally, an operating environment for the moving of goods and money over the Internet. During this election cycle, Amazon created a service to allow its customers to "1-Click" a contribution to their preferred Presidential candidate.

To its online supporters, the Dean campaign was essentially a web service. The campaign's unprecedented success started a dialogue about the role of web services in political campaigns.

In web design, there's a lot of attention to the Graphic User Experience (GUI). Obviously you'll want to pay as much attention to design as the Dean campaign did. But campaigns depend also on their Conversational User Interface (CUI). You'll win your campaign if your CUI attracts enough new, vocal supporters who get what they seek from the campaign: an authentic voice in policy direction and the campaign's message.

The Dean campaign hit a wall at about 150,000 active, registered supporters, though four times as many were in its database. (Surprisingly, there were thousands of active supporters who chose not to get involved with the campaign's web site.) How might the campaign have scaled its conversational throughput to a high enough level that it would get the votes it needed?

The solution is to see that there's no clear dividing line between "the campaign" and "the supporters." Every campaign has volunteers working at headquarters and in the field. Are those people inside or outside the campaign? Does it matter?

**Crystal Blue Persuasion** When someone associated with the campaign is responsive to a supporter, it can be as powerful an involvement as if the supporter had engaged directly with an "official" campaign staffer.

It looks like a crystalline structure and, if those associations are updated on the campaign web site as it grows, the participants will see that their involvement is as real as a more formal campaign organization. Indeed, it might seem *more* real because of its dynamic, just-a-click-away representation, like seeing real friends in your contact file. A tool to develop such a self-propagating structure has been developed as a DeanSpace module. Here are the steps to getting your most active supporters to attract and mentor new supporters. It starts when one of

287

your supporters identifies a group of her existing contacts as potential supporters of the campaign:

Your supporter saves the selected contact records as a single text file.

The contact file is uploaded to the host DeanSpace site.

The site emails each contact with a link to their personal, online record.

The proposed new supporter follows a sequence they may halt at any time:

- Will you share your data with the campaign? If so,

- Will you make a contribution of any size? If so,

- Will you become a full member of our effort and:

- Tell us your policy preferences

- Invite your friends to join the campaign

This explicit mentorship model captures the vertical and lateral relationships among the campaign's supporters. Armed with that data, the campaign can empower its members to maintain the kind of tree structure that every organization must have to be viable and to grow as fast as people's appetite to wield real political power.

**"Get Local" Tools** One of the Dean campaign's greatest successes was its ability to inspire activism among people who had no prior interest in the political process. A key to this was the Get Local toolset hosted at its web site a kind of *ad hoc* expression of what Meetup arranges monthly. Supporters were able to find each other in their community, plan events and mutual support, be welcomed to house parties at strangers' homes, wave banners at passers-by and master those staples of retail politics, "flyering" and "tabling" – handing out flyers and sitting with literature at card tables at public events.

DeanSpace sites are also a way to organize locally, since they let your supporters find each other, become members of the campaign and reach out to their social network.

**P2P Policy Engagement** Peer-to-Peer (P2P) is an organizing force powerful enough to connect people on several continents to serve a common purpose. Other factors equal, any campaign that harnesses P2P power will defeat a campaign that does not. When supporters become members–campaign insiders–you need to give them what they want, and what they want is a voice in policy.

This was probably the Dean campaign's greatest failing. Although there were discussion forums and cross-comments on the blog, there was no systematic approach to seeking policy input from the campaign's members. It was a goal but not a priority, and there was a lot of discussion about how to so engage the campaign's members. Nicco Mele, the campaign webmaster, had reserved the domain *opensourcepolicy.org* with the expectation that it might be the right vehicle. Nicco and Mat Gross, chief blogger, and I discussed the structure at some length. I can only describe what I thought was the right solution. Until it's tried, it's impossible to know:

### People-Powered Policy Preferences

Every computer program lets you set your preferences for how it operates. Now it's time for our nation to respond to your policy preferences.

When you declare your choices in the Policy Matrix, your policy prefs are combined with those of others who have real ideas on real issues. Every night, the latest Policy Prefs data is transmitted to *your* Campaign.

The following list is alphabetical. Declare your priorities by checking the SIG box to indicate that it's important enough for you to be involved in working to give that policy area more study and weight.

| ISSUE | SIG? |
|---|---|

### Agriculture

☐ SIG

family farms• 1 ◎ ◎ ◎ ◎ ◎ ◎ ◎ ◎ ◎ ◎ 10 • corporate farming

| Comment on Agriculture | |

### Campaign Financing

☐ SIG

more reform • 1 ◎ ◎ ◎ ◎ ◎ ◎ ◎ ◎ ◎ ◎ 10 • less reform

| Comment on Campaign Financing | |

| Your Recommendations for Campaign Strategy |
|---|

### Advertising

issues ads only • 1 ◎ ◎ ◎ ◎ ◎ ◎ ◎ ◎ ◎ ◎ 10 • attack ads

| Comment on Campaign Advertising | |

### Bulk Mail and Phone Banking

volunteers only • 1 ◎ ◎ ◎ ◎ ◎ ◎ ◎ ◎ ◎ ◎ 10 • flood em!

| Comment on Bulk Mail and Phone Banking | |

*Example of explicit and generalized policy preferences*

This is scary stuff. Policy experts don't like the idea of voters like you and me–the great unwashed–actually getting involved with policy. Once the voters make their wishes explicit, the politicians may feel required to listen to the people's will, which is not their notion of leadership. However, once the campaign compiles its members' preferences, it has a database of nuanced opinion that it can use to hold the kind of conversation that the public actually seeks, rather than an inflexible message, which the public avoids. Doc Searls maintains that there's no market for messages, and it's as true for voters as for Tivo owners.

**Voter File Management** A voter file is a contact file summarizing a voter's registration record and which elections were voted in. Voter files are the nervous system of a campaign. The source data are maintained by election officials and are supposed to be reported by counties to the Secretary of State. The data can be obtained at a nominal fee directly from the Secretary of State or enhanced versions can be purchased by companies that correlate voter data with other sources to give a more complete view of the voter's likely behaviors. We can call this an *implicit* view of a voter.

But in 2003, with its accidental transformation of *supporters* into its formal *members*, the Dean campaign introduced the possibility of building an *explicit* forecast of voter behavior. We can start to imagine a movement so sweeping that a large percentage of voters become members of a particular campaign and therefore enter into a kind of contract to vote for their candidate. If you can make the movement large enough, explicit enough, it's possible that you'll know more about the outcome than the pollsters.

But it will take some experience before people get past the disappointments of the Dean campaign, where exuberance and record contributions did not translate into votes.

There are at least two DeanSpace modules to manage voter files, and a number of commercial services.

**Get Out The Vote (GOTV)** GOTV *is* the campaign. If you know who's going to support you and you know where they live, the job is to remind them to get out and vote. This is where the Internet-enabled cascade of online activity may be as powerful as putting a committed supporter in your car and driving together to the polling place.

| | |
|---|---|
| Meetup.com | Potential campaign members meet in the real world and discover their shared interests. |
| Campaign Blog | Campaign members learn what's happening and post comments that become a conversation as immediate as any other. |
| Campaign Materials | Materials printed at home reach more deeply into the community than any centralized distribution plan. |
| Viral email design | One begets three begets nine, if your message deserves it. |
| P2P hierarchal linking | When you know who recruited whom, you can let your campaign's members build your campaign structure for you. |
| "Get Local" tools | Your supporters reach out to each other in the real world. |
| P2P policy engagement | Your constituents hijack your campaign and make it *their* campaign. |

GOTV has always been a mechanical process of calling and knocking on doors–the people who physically bring others to a caucus, a primary or a polling place are often called "draggers." They have only an implicit understanding with their passenger, certainly not a meaningful meeting of the minds–there's no guarantee what their rider's vote will be. But when a community forms around a compelling candidate, they create explicit, published relationships and a mesh of interlocking expectations that can strengthen over time into tangible commitments and votes the campaign can count on.

The means to compile and document our mutual promises will be developed as they become effective as a GOTV function. Zephyr

Teachout, Dean's Director of Grassroots outreach said it best: "The campaign's out there!"

## The 2006-08 Vision

The pressure to build a 2004 Campaign In A Box is urgent and short term, a patching together of beta tools to do the best we can during this election cycle. The thrill of this dramatic transition is in glimpsing vistas never imagined; the frustration is knowing we could do so much more. A comprehensive vision for the future of populist politics requires a comprehensive vision and long term effort.

The Internet, our Great Disruptor, is woven more tightly into our choices each year. In the same way that it disintermediates bookstores and recording labels, it threatens the historic franchise of political parties and politicians and media voices accustomed to having their way with power and money, telling the rest of us how things are and how they must be. Those people will not go away quietly but they can't help being hostages to the choices made by the voters and to those best equipped to communicate with the voters.

The tools for structural political evolution will, like blogging and Google and RSS, become a constant part of our infrastructure, not the intermittent activities of campaigning and voting.

How could the nature of reporting be affected by a development effort aimed at political tools? It could because the Internet allows us to imagine such detailed attribution. I suggest that an RSS standard could help us compare the assertions in article A to those in article B and to any other RSS feeds in which, for example, the protagonist in articles A & B is also tagged as a significant actor. Any editor or reviewer could add assertion tags to a body of text, even if the author is disinclined to annotate them.

It would take a while, but some day the lack of attribution may be an impediment for serious consideration. An aid to evidentiality might be specialized RSS feeds that characterize the sources and kinds of assertions contained in an article, a service I call an Assertion Processor.

**Voter Policy Profiles and Legislative Accountability** The Policy Preferences profile described in step 8 above could be as useful for governance as for building consensus behind a candidate. Politicians take advantage of the disinterest most people feel in staying on top of their representatives. While the old saying is that we get the government we deserve, one can't escape the sense that politicians revel in a system that's impenetrable to any but the most zealous activist. Like the rest of these recommendations, I rely on the universal virtue of transparency for progress.

Suppose I have been inspired to assert my policy preferences by selecting my position on, for example, Campaign Financing:

If I declare my preference here and on a dozen other issues, I've built a profile of my personal preferences. That's the quantitative side of my declaration, but it shouldn't stop there. I'm also invited to comment on my position and I'm surprisingly likely to do so, perhaps because we've become so accustomed to typing our thoughts into emails and instant messages. Or perhaps it's not so surprising, from an educated populace tired of reading such shallow articles in the press. Naturally, a community web site eliciting comments from its participants would learn to build a web log for its respondents, and allow its participants to comment on each others entries as they're transformed into blog posts.

The profile shouldn't stop there. The **SIG** checkbox invites the respondent to join a new or existing Special Interest Group around this policy area. It means little unless the web site has a means to put its respondents in touch with each other, which is a fine-grained expression of the proven meetup model: similarly inclined people should have the means to convene in their real and virtual worlds and discover their own ways to express their political power.

While these are simply software tools to enhance collaboration, acquaintance and expression, they are also gateways into a larger world of political power. Like the skeletal HyperText Transport Protocol compounding its possibilities into a Mandelbrotian web of diversity, complexity and brilliance, so should we expect political expression to thrive in the virtual nutrients of preferences, comments, gatherings and collaborative expression.

If I and millions like me see that our preferences are expressed in combination, we no longer feel powerless. Unlike zealots, we probably don't mind being single voices among many, because most people don't seek dominance, simply parity.

If enough voters express their policy profiles, any of us can compare our profile against a meaningful sample of the populace, but it goes deeper than that, perhaps to the sinews of the body politic.

Every law expresses a policy profile, as does a proposed law or proposed amendment. A politician's voting record expresses a policy profile, as does a political party. Once we compile and aggregate policy profiles, we can compare them, and begin to understand the relationship of a politician's expressed preferences compared to those of the constituents. That's where the going might get ugly for self-satisfied manipulators of power in the absence of a clear mandate.

## The Case for Hope

The Age of Enlightenment rested on a flimsier foundation of caffeine, conversation and small printing presses. We should have high hopes for an outpouring of good sense and political power among a better educated population, leveraging a collaborative web undreamt of by even Vannevar Bush, much less Samuel Johnson.

# Deanspace, Social Networks, and Politics
## by Jon Lebkowsky

The Howard Dean campaign's groundbreaking use of the Internet and social software tools was widely publicized, though ultimately the campaign's use of the tools failed to make a winning difference in the 2004 presidential campaign. Their use has been credited for his success in achieving early front-runner status based primarily on his success in raising funds. Overdependence on the Internet was controversially blamed by some pundits for the campaign's ultimate collapse in Iowa and New Hampshire. What's undeniable is the broad impact on campaign politics: Other campaigns, including George Bush's and John Kerry's, have focused more on the Internet based on Dean's early successes, and political conversation on the Internet has gained visibility.

A volunteer project called Deanspace, which operated with little involvement or support from the Dean Campaign organization, has received too little attention for its success as an Open Source project and as a tool for building community among Dean supporters. The Deanspace Team made their first deliverables according to their schedule, created deployment and user support infrastructures, and continued to release revisions and new modules even after it was clear that Dean would not win the nomination. This is pretty remarkable for a software development project that is run totally by volunteers and completely without funds, and coordinated through online meetings in an IRC chat room.

Campaign manager Joe Trippi had a vision: social technology and networks are great tools for democracy and advocacy, and incidentally a great way to build support and raise money for a candidate with little to invest up front.

Trippi made his vision clear in a May 2003 post to the Dean for America weblog. Trippi called it "The Perfect Storm," an analogy the campaign organization carried forward into the primaries. Said Trippi, "It is a storm that has never happened before — because it could not have happened before. The forces required to come into sync were not aligned, nor in some instances mature enough prior to this Presidential campaign."

Trippi said the first step was citizen participation. "But how do these Americans find each other." he asked. "How do they self-organize? How do they collaborate? How do they take action together?" The answer was the Internet and the World Wide Web, applications like weblogs and Meetup.com, and clueful web-based political initiatives like Moveon.org. All the campaign needed at this point, he said, was "a campaign organization that gets it" and provides "the tools and some of the direction — stay in as constant communication as you can with the grassroots — two way/multi-way communication...."[219]

Deanspace fit Trippi's vision. A distributed development project that depended more on people energy than organizational energy to meet its goals, Deanspace was an attempt to create a complete web-based social networking toolkit for campaign volunteers to deploy broadly, creating many sites for different affinity groups and geographical communities. To the extent that the project was successful, it was because its proponents combined strong project commitment and clueful use of Internet communication tools (email, chat, instant messaging) for sustained communication among project participants. Though there were flaws in the project itself and in the software it produced, it was an important early convergence of social software and political campaign infrastructures. Dean campaign leaders like Joe Trippi and Zephyr Teachout were enthusiastic about the potential for Deanspace to evolve a network of localized volunteer sites supporting the Dean candidacy, and conversations peripherally related to Deanspace influenced the evolution of the campaign's software projects (such as DeanLink, a social networking software similar to Friendster, first proposed in a Deanspace IRC chat.)

The Deanspace system is built on Drupal, an open source content management platform that includes social networking features such as a collaborative "book," personalization, a role-based permissions system, authentication, blogging, syndication, and forums. These features support group-forming, collaboration, and sustained communication among local or affinity groups.

---

[219] Trippi, Joe. . "The Perfect Storm."
http://dean2004.blogspot.com/2003_05_11_dean2004_archive.html#200 303997.

This chapter discusses Deanspace in the context of emerging social software technologies, the process of building Deanspace as an Open Source project, and the relevance of Deanspace to the campaign.

## Hack for Dean

Deanspace is an Open Source project that was originally called Hack4Dean, the focus of which was to create the website toolkit that Trippi envisioned, one that could be broadly deployed to create virtual community presences for the Howard Dean campaign. One of the instigators of the project, Zack Rosen, dropped out of the University of Illinois so he could work to get Howard Dean elected. Zack discussed the project with several others, who helped tune the concept in online and offline discussions as the project was getting under way. Zack's original idea: create and distribute a set of tools that anyone with a bit of technical assistance and some degree of comfort with web tools could use to set up ad hoc Dean microcommunities on the Web, smaller communities within the macrocommunity of citizens for Dean. From these communities an autonomous campaign organization would theoretically emerge, creating a platform for the activities of hundreds of thousands of Dean supporters. Given success at this emergent group-forming, Rosen and others felt Dean supporters wouldn't need the kind of hierarchical command-and-control structure associated with traditional campaigns. Activists might plant the seeds of advocacy and watch as others took up the campaign's message and spread it through the use of the Deanspace toolkit. More practically, they would plant the seeds, spread the message, but do so in addition to a more structured political campaign.

Deanspace includes a variety of tools, such as weblogs, forums, and calendars – tools to focus on communication rather than systems for control. But the real value was going to be in linking like-minded communities and building a network that shares information, and you'd do this with RSS syndication (RSS is extended as "Rich Site Summary" or "Really Simple Syndication," among others). RSS is a relatively simple tool for sharing and distributing content through a common standard for describing content data elements (i.e. title, summary, description, etc.) so that they can be published with a common understanding about how they should be parsed and displayed. Syndication extends published content so that it reaches more readers, igniting community as content is shared and responses posted. Sites would become nodes in a network where content is shared in all directions, weaving the microcommunities together.[220]

Ultimately activists deployed over 100 sites using the Deanspace toolkit. This included one or more Deanspace sites for each state and several sites based on affinity (e.g. Catholics For Dean, Seniors for Dean, Scientists for Dean, Women for Howard Dean). Some sites were themed (Music for America, Book Tours for Dean, News for Dean). The goal of most sites was to attract more people to the campaign and keep them informed about campaign activities that were local or relevant to the affinity group represented. Deanspace was really a platform for group-forming with the assumption that the Dean campaign could grow exponentially based on Reed's Law.

## Reed's Law

Zack was influenced by David Reed's thinking about networks and group-forming, expressed as Reed's Law: which says that the utility of large networks can scale exponentially with the size of networks.[221] Reed's insight: The number of possible subgroups is $2^n$, where n is the number of participants. The growth of a social network's value is much greater than its linear growth. This is significant for political organizations that depend on numbers of adherents to establish influence. . They build support by collecting potential supporters, signing them onto mailing lists and encouraging them to give support, usually by donating money, writing letters, or volunteering time. The network view is that supporters will sign up supporters who will sign up even more supporters, so the growth through group-forming is a social network explosion, and the value is not just in the numbers here. Networking may also result in deeper engagement and what sociologist Mark Granovetter calls "the strength of weak ties.". If I was recruited by

---

[220] This description of Deanspace was captured in part from a video Lisa Rein shot at ILAW 2003 at Stanford University, which is posted at http://www.onlisareinsradar.com/archives/001562.php. [can you relate more of this description and the energy Lisa brought to the description – in some ways, the Dean energy was a collection of all these individual passions,]

[221] Reed, David P. "That Sneaky Exponential – Beyond Metcalfe's Law to the Power of Community Building." http://www.reed.com/Papers/GFN/reedslaw.html.

someone I know, I have a stronger connection to the network than I would if I was recruited via cold calling.

Reed's Law follows on Metcalfe's Law, which says that the utility of a communication network equals the square of the number of users, $n^2$. An entry in Wikipedia, a collaborative online encyclopedia, illustrates this with the fax machine as an example:

A single fax machine is useless, but the value of every fax machine increases with the total number of fax machines in the network, because the total number of people with whom you may send and receive documents increases. This contrasts with traditional models of supply and demand, where increasing the quantity of something *decreases* its value.[222]

Reed acknowledged Metcalfe's Law, but said that "many kinds of value grow proportionally to network size and some grow proportionally to the square of network size," however some scale even faster:

Networks that support the construction of communicating groups create value that scales *exponentially* with network size, i.e. much more rapidly than Metcalfe's square law. I will call such networks Group-Forming Networks, or GFNs.[223]

Reed's thoughts about group-forming is one of several drivers for a social software movement that's been growing (scale-driven, Reed would say) the last couple of years. Other influences include Malcolm Gladwell, whose book *The Tipping Point: How Little Things Make a Big Difference*[224] discusses how ideas and trends emerge from networks; Howard Rheingold, whose *Smart Mobs*[225] focuses on technologies for

[222] Anonymous, "Metcalfe's Law." Entry in Wikipedia, http://en2.wikipedia.org/wiki/Metcalfe's_law.

[223] Reed, David P. "That Sneaky Exponential – Beyond Metcalfe's Law to the Power of Community Building." http://www.reed.com/Papers/GFN/reedslaw.html.

[224] Gladwell, Malcolm. *The Tipping Point: How Little Things Make a Big Difference.* California: Back Bay Books, 2002.

[225] Rheingold, Howard. *Smart Mobs: The Next Social Revolution.* Perseus Publishing, Boulder, Colorado: 2002.

cooperation and group-forming with mobile devices; Albert-Laszlo Barbasi, whose *Linked: How Everything is Connected to Everything Else and What It Means*[226] discusses the scale-free networks underlying … just about everything, really, down to a cellular level. All of these authors talk about the emergence of ideas and actions through social networks, and how emergence is relevant to social movement and social order. Gladwell discusses "social epidemics" where ideas and behaviors spread the way disease spreads. Rheingold covers emergent group behavior among users of mobile wireless technologies, specifically, and Internet users more generally, and discusses group-forming online. Barbasi's book is a more general overview of network science, explaining network structure and relevance to complexity theory, and providing background for more effective network use. These and other books lay the foundation for a politics that conforms to network structure: individuals are nodes that are linked through hubs (communities). This political vision is relevant to grassroots politics. Grassroots political campaigns often fail, at least initially, against the organizational power of centralized political forces, however a grassroots that is both shaped and supported by powerful communication networks can in theory be both well-organized and decentralized. Groups may self-organize and create ad hoc movements. Consider the 1999 protests at the World Trade Organization meeting in Seattle: using basic Internet tools (web sites, email, immediate messaging, and chat rooms), diverse organizations produced a generally peaceful protest by 30,000 persons. The short-term protest also yielded longer-term sustained activity, such as the Independent Media Center (http://indymedia.org/en/index.shtml).

*Social Software*

These and other authors of similar works laid the theoretical foundation for developers who want to create socially relevant software and systems, systems that extend social capabilities and facilitate collaboration and cooperation. Software and networking tools have evolved in this direction all along. Consider the extent to which we use computers and computer networks to publish, share, and communicate. Email is a social technology, and so is the World Wide Web. Howard Rheingold wrote about this aspect of the technology in his 1985 book *Tools for*

---

[226] Barbasi, Albert Laszlo. *Linked: How Everything is Connected to Everything Else and What It Means.* New York: Plume, 2003.

*Thought*[227]. In 2003, Rheingold responded to a blog entry by UK blogger and social software expert Tom Coates regarding Coates' proposal of a working definition of social software with a comment on the history of social technology. Howard said that our ongoing emphasis on social software should remind us that the real capabilities of augmentation are in the thinking and communication that the tools enable, rather than the technology behind the tools. He also noted that "when a particular group of people uses social software for long enough — whether it is synchronous or asynchronous, deskbound or mobile, text or graphical — they establish individual and group social relationships that are different in kind from the more fleeting relationships that emerge from task-oriented group formation." This isn't new, it's been happening since the first email distribution lists appeared. Howard suggested that it's important to acknowledge and build on earlier work. "Something new is happening, truly, in terms of the kinds of software available, and the scale of use. But in many ways, this something new would not be happening if many people over many years had not coded, experimented, socialized, observed, and debated the social relationships and group formation enabled by computer-mediated and Internet-enabled communication media."[228]

*Deanspace: Social Network as Activist Community*

Recent social software developments are a refinement and extension of "virtual community" thinking based in part on an evolving understanding of online social networks and group-forming. The term *virtual community* was coined by Howard Rheingold as the title of his book about his experiences on and through the Whole Earth 'Lectronic Link (WELL), the seminal online conferencing system, a collection of online conversations organized as topics within conferences (which is to say discussions within forums, or conversations within high-level subject areas). With more experience, Rheingold grew circumspect about the term:

---

[227] Rheingold, Howard, *Tools for Thought: The History and Future of Mind-Expanding Technology. 2nd Revised Edition.* MIT Press: 2000. Available online at http://www.rheingold.com/texts/tft/.

[228] Rheingold, Howard. Comment posted at http://www.plasticbag.org/archives/2003/05/my_working_definition_of_social_software.shtml.

When you think of a title for a book, you are forced to think of something short and evocative, like, well, 'The Virtual Community,' even though a more accurate title might be: 'People who use computers to communicate, form friendships that sometimes form the basis of communities, but you have to be careful to not mistake the tool for the task and think that just writing words on a screen is the same thing as real community.[229]

In the original version of his introduction to the book, Rheingold writes this definition:

*Virtual communities* are social aggregations that emerge from the Net when enough people carry on those public discussions long enough, with sufficient human feeling, to form webs of personal relationships in cyberspace.[230]

As weblogs have become more popular and prominent as personal (and, increasingly, professional) publishing tools, weblog communities have formed, and these differ from traditional forums in that they are communities based on conversations that occur on public web sites, where as forums are "behind closed doors" requiring at least a login to participate. What they have in common with forums, though, is that weblog communities are communities of bloggers that have formed relationships through their online conversations, and sustained those relationships over time.

The Deanspace vision was to facilitate web communities of Dean supporters by creating a tool that can include both weblogs and forums, with the weblog posts appearing as news entries on the home page for the sites. Each site would be a node in an activist network, over which they could share content via RSS syndication.

Weblogs use RSS (an acronym variously translated as "Really Simple Syndication" or "Rich Site Summary") to syndicate content as it is published. The term *syndication* derives from the newspaper industry's practice of distributing the same content, such as a particular newspaper

---

[229] Rheingold, Howard, *The Virtual Community (Electronic version)*, "Introduction." http://www.rheingold.com/vc/book/intro.html.

[230] Ibid.

column or cartoon series, to many publications at once. Specialized applications called news aggregators allow users to subscribe to RSS "feeds" from weblogs they read regularly, so that they can track and read all of them conveniently in one place. However you can also create tools to interpret RSS content for display on a web site, which is closer to the newspaper industry's sense of the term. Deanspace does this. Administrators can capture and display syndicated content from other Deanspace sites.

Any one Deanspace site can display weblog content from many other Deanspace sites, and users can select to display either of several weblogs. It's also possible to pick up single weblog entries from other sites and include them in the front-page weblog display for your site, so that a Deanspace administrator can pick and choose news from the entire universe of Deanspace sites. Readers can post comments to weblog entries, as well, so a relatively simple content management tool is potentially a platform for robust communication within the Deanspace network.

In the context of the Dean campaign, this promise was never completely realized. The Dean campaign ended before the Deanspace network was mature enough for the network to form and conversations evolve.

*Facilitating Emergence*

Joe Trippi's idea for the campaign was to trust the people and let the campaign emerge from their efforts:

The other thing that is needed — is a campaign organization that gets it — or at least tries to get it. One of the other reasons I think this has not happened before is that every political campaign I have ever been in is built on a top-down military structure — there is a general at the top of the campaign — and all orders flow down — with almost no interaction. This is a disaster. This kind of structure will suffocate the storm not fuel it. Campaigns abhor chaos — and to most campaigns built on the old top-down model — that is what the net represents — chaos. And the more the campaign tries to control the "chaos" the more it stiffles (sic) its growth. As someone who is at least trying to understand the right mix — I admit it's hard to get it right. But I think the important thing is to provide the tools and some of the direction — stay in as constant communication as you can with the grassroots — two way/multi-way communication — and get the hell out of the way when a big wave is building on its own.[231]

This fit the Deanspace team's intention: Trippi's' thinking would tend to enable group-forming and emergence. His note about top-down military structure is significant, a description of the hierarchical, antidemocratic structure of most political campaigns. If the campaigns are run that way, what does that say about the process style of the campaigners? Activists pushing for a more democratic system can distribute the power and responsibility for the campaign among its workers and volunteers, supporting this more distributed framework this with robust communication using every tool at their disposal: weblogs and RSS, email, file sharing, forums, instant messaging, chat, teleconferences. Deanspace could be part of a toolkit that might also include other tools like Yahoo groups, various instant messaging products, IRC chat, freeconference.com (for conference calls). As Trippi suggests, this creates a somewhat chaotic environment with various challenges – fragmentation, power vacuums, information overload, etc. "*It's hard to get it right.*"

Ideally, given more time to develop, a mature and broadly adopted Deanspace could overcome some of this fragmentation by providing a complete toolkit including shared calendar, email lists, forums, blogs, and file uploads and downloads. Because Deanspace was modular, developers could create other functionalities (such as the Voterfile and Rideboard modules).

*An Open Source Project*

Deanspace was organized as an Open Source project. Open Source is more strictly a licensing concept,[232] but more broadly refers to a methodology and a set of practices for software teams that are open in the sense that practically anyone with interest and the right set of skills can participate. Successful Open Source projects include the

---

[231] Trippi, Joe. "The Perfect Storm." http://dean2004.blogspot.com/2003_05_11_dean2004_archive.html#200303997.

[232] "The Open Source Definition," http://www.opensource.org/docs/definition.php.

development of the Linux operating system, the Apache web server, and the Mozilla browser. Open source development and support are often described as community efforts, and rightly so. Communities of practice form around Open Source projects, and there is a general sense of an Open Source community that shares common practices and a common attitude of cooperation and sharing. Unlike proprietary software developers, Open Source developers publish their source code and invite enhancement. Anyone can play, undirected by any central authority and limited only by terms of the the license selected for the particular project. Open Source software development can also be described as emergent, the result of patterns of interaction within a community of individual developers that operate more or less democratically. This is similar to Joe Trippi's vision for a political campaign that emerges from the actions and efforts of self-organizing grassroots supporters. The Deanspace team worked and met openly online, therefore unrestricted by geographical constraints, and using tools similar to those that they were developing. Meetings were held in a public chat room, meeting notes were posted in public, as were all the details of the project. Decisions were made by group consensus. There were ongoing conversations via email lists and various one-to-one conversations via immediate messaging.

Rather than build a system from scratch, the team looked for a platform that could be adapted for use. They selected Drupal[233], a free Open Source platform for building dynamic web sites with content management and community features. Building onto an existing platform would save time. Drupal wasn't the only platform they considered, but the other likely candidate, Zope, would be harder for less technical users to install. Drupal was stable, well-supported by a community of programmers, modular and extensible. It also had a feature that allowed users to sign onto any site in a Drupal network. This was theoretically desirable, though it was thought to compromise security, and for that reason some site administrators disabled it.

The actual work of writing code for Deanspace fell mostly to Neil Drumm and Ka-Ping Yee, college students and proficient coders with an Open Source focus. However it's significant that the process was open

---

[233] http://drupal.org

to others who might show up and provide conceptual or technical input, add modules, and assist in installations and support.

## Does It Work?

As of January 2004, there had been almost 50 known Deanspace sites, communities built using these tools, with more on the way. Some are location based and some focus on specific demographics (e.g. SeniorsForDean, VeteransForDean, CatholicsForDean). Location-based sites may be set for a city, county, region, or state (e.g. Austin ForDean...). The Deanspace team's goal was to create an open source multifunctional web application that could be installed easily, resulting in an unlimited number of sites reaching as many confirmed or potential Dean supporters as possible. In this sense, Deanspace is an evident success: there are many sites with many users. However volunteer leaders doing actual campaign work on the ground were not enthusiastic about Deanspace because it didn't include the technology they needed. According to one knowledgeable volunteer, Deanspace was seen primarily as a technology for blogging, so other features that might be useful – e.g. the collaborative book where any site member can add content, the event calendar, forums, and a load of optional modules – were largely ignored. Campaign activists in the field didn't see the kind of application that would be useful for them, one that would capture information about specific voters, their commitments and their interests, the sort of information that helps ensure turnout at caucuses, precinct meetings, primaries and elections. There was no way to handle standard voterfiles in the original Deanspace implementation, because the Deanspace team lacked campaign experience and didn't know that voterfiles would be essential to campaign organizations. By the time a voterfile module was available, it was too late for the first primaries.

In considering Deanspace, we should also consider the difference between democracy and advocacy. The goal of a democratic activist is to give people a voice and facilitate their participation, whereas an advocate is focused on a specific result. Though tied to a specific campaign, Deanspace was about giving people a voice, about facilitating emergence of political will from within a network of nodes. These nodes, the Deanspace web sites, used a technology created to support group-forming and communication. However, despite Joe Trippi's "perfect storm" comments in support of a bottom-up, emergent campaign structure, seasoned campaigners on the ground were still depending on a more focused, predictable command and control model for the campaign. Deanspace didn't fit that purpose.

This wasn't an accident, though. Deanspace was an independent grassroots effort; it wasn't created for the campaign and wasn't designed for campaign management. Though the Dean campaign liked the software and started deploying it as a platform for state sites, it gave relatively little support and attention to the effort.

As Rosen and Drumm later commented, they didn't understand the requirements of a political campaign well enough when they started, so they failed to incorporate important customer requirements. Their goal was to create a toolkit for building political communities a network of Deanspace sites connected via RSS syndication. However this kind of network can take time to evolve and become useful. Viable Deanspace communities might form over time as participants form relationships, share experiences, and begin to have a common history, but the campaign needs were more immediate. The campaign needed a concise approach to the organization of blocs of voters committed to Dean.

As I write this chapter, Dean has no primary victories. Michael Cudahy and Jock Gill suggest that the campaign was too preoccupied with the Internet strategy, and failed to do the kind of organizing on the ground in Iowa and New Hampshire that Kerry's staff emphasized.[234] The web and social software tools have become essential parts of the political scene, but, according to Cudahy and Gill,

As astounding a tool as the Internet is, it lacks the personal and persuasive commitment- building quality a candidate gains by listening to concerned American voters in face-to-face conversations.

This may be true, but a candidate can have only so many face-to-face encounters. However a candidate, party or movement can cultivate "influentials," the ten percent of the population that provide leadership and direction for the other 90%.[235] You can reach many of these people

---

[234] Cudahy, Michael and Jock Gill, "The political is personal – not web-based." Pittsburgh *Post-Gazette.com*, February 1, 2004. http://www.post-gazette.com/pg/04032/267624.stm

[235] Berry, Jon and Ed Keller, *The Influentials*. 2003: New York: The Free Press. Berry and Keller cite empirical evidence suggesting that 10% of

via the Internet, and leverage their "personal and persuasive commitment-building" qualities. This is where software like Deanspace may have value, though we need time, thought, and empirical observation to assess its efficacy.

According to Josh Koenig, the Deanspace sites that deployed in fall of 2003 and winter of 2004 were underused. According to Josh, "there were … seemingly very few people who had enough to say on a daily basis to run high-volume Deanspace sites." The expectation that communities would form around the sites and feed the weblog on a regular basis was unrealized at all but a few sites. It could be that the users didn't quite grasp the software once it was set up, or that they underestimated the ongoing time and energy required to sustain interest.

Koenig notes that, while there was a huge upswell of grassroots support, there was comparatively little independent organizing. "Ever since the end of the summer when meetups became letter-writing sessions," he says, "the tone of the campaign shifted somewhat. In looking back, this is also when supporter growth began to slow down. I don't know if this is germane or not, but it's something I'm personally interested in trying to figure out."

In assessing whether Deanspace was successful, we also have to consider broader goals beyond this one presidential campaign. Rosen, Koenig and other Deanspace developers and proponents were keenly aware of big media and the extent to which public policy and popular belief are programmed and managed via messaging from the few corporations that own and control most of the large broadcast media channels. Joe Trippi, at O'Reilly's Digital Democracy Teach-In on February 9, 2004, said "Broadcast politics has failed the country miserably. You had no debate going into war, no debate about the Patriot Act. That debate isn't happening anywhere except on the Net." The Deanspace plan was to create a network of sites with robust communications and data-sharing capabilities, a broad platform for interaction, for discussion and debate. Though the project focused on a presidential candidate, its developers realized that this was just another step in a process that began when

Americans are early adopters with significant influence within their communities. They guide choices about products and politicians.

TCP/IP was first developed and the Internet formed. The Internet is a social tool; it connects people as nodes on a social network, and it supports social and community organization with long-term political implications. Says Koenig, "To me, the great long-term hope of what we've begun is that it will democratize the national dialogue."

## The Future of Net.Politics

The Internet has gained popular acceptance as a core technology, with over 131 million Americans using some form of Internet access[236], and 50 million with broadband access.[237] In 2000, there were over 200 million potential voters in the U.S., but only 130 million registered to vote, and only 111 million actually voted.[238] Though we could find no specific data on the percentage of registered voters with Internet access, given the numbers it seems likely that the Internet may be, or become, a significant factor in political campaigns. When we say that, though, what do we mean? The Internet is like an operating system, a platform or environment supporting many applications. Where Howard Dean's campaign was concerned, web sites like those created with Deanspace were only part of the story. Meetup.com helped Dean's campaign and others quickly organize physical meetings on a national scale. Campaign supporters used Yahoo Groups effectively to create email lists and leverage file-sharing. Campaign organizations in the field used various database tools, calendar functions, listserves, forum software etc. The Dean campaign's official web site included tools like Deanlink, a candidate-focused social network application where Dean supporters could find each other and form connections, and GetLocal, which showed events near a specific zip code. The Dean campaign was breaking new ground and working without precedent; Trippi and others understood that this mean trying many different technologies.

---

[236] *CyberAtlas,* "Traffic Patterns of 2003" (via *Nielsen Net/Ratings*), http://cyberatlas.internet.com/big_picture/traffic_patterns/article/0,,5931_3298891,00.html. January, 2004.

[237] *Nielsen/Netratings,* "Fifty Million Internet Users Connect Via Broadband, Rising 27

Percent During The Last Six Months, According To Nielsen//Netratings," http://www.nielsen-netratings.com/pr/pr_040108_us.pdf. January, 2004.

[238] U.S. Census Bureau, "Voting and Registration in the Election of November 2000," p. 5. http://www.census.gov/prod/2002pubs/p20-542.pdf. February 2002.

The Dean campaign did succeed in using Internet technology to raise money and create support and this had an obvious impact on the other 2004 Democratic presidential campaigns, even though Dean ultimately failed to translate online success into primary wins.

Is it contradictory to say that he succeeded, if he failed to win even one primary? Consider that Dean had little money and visibility at the start of his campaign, compared to other candidates — yet he raised enough money and found enough support to create front-runner buzz, and became the first presidential candidate to place Internet tools at the center of his campaign strategy. He showed other (not just presidential) candidates that the power and immediacy of the Internet is extremely relevant to their campaigns.

The resulting surge in the development of technopolitical solutions could change the way campaigns operate from now on, though the real impact is outside the campaigns, in the grassroots. Technically-proficient activists, inspired by their involvement with the Dean campaign and the lessons they've begun to learn about political process, are developing and refining technology to support grassroots efforts while the more traditional campaigns, such as Kerry's, focus more on familiar campaign strategies.

Meanwhile Deanspace has become CivicSpace, its goal expressed in the mathematics of group-forming:

# What is DeanSpace?
# by Aldon Hynes

## History

In the summer of 2003, Dean supporters with an interest in information technology started meeting online and talking about how they could use their skills to help the Dean campaign. Inspired by community-focused sites like Slashdot, IndyMedia, Kuro5hin, and Scoop, they looked for tools they could build or customize that could be used to help promote the Dean candidacy.

They wanted to create a toolkit for people without strong technical skills to use to set up powerful, interoperable websites for of information sharing and community building.

Meeting together through mailing lists, IRC chats, and experimenting with different forums, wikis, and content management systems, they decided that it would be best to build with an open source content management system as a foundation, one that would allow them to deploy distributed sites easily. These sites would be able to share and aggregate content. The sites would be built on software that could easily be extended. To the extent possible, they would use open standards for interconnectivity.

## Underlying software

After experimenting with several products, the group decided to use Drupal, an open source content management system written in PHP, a widely-used server-side scripting language. Drupal works with several different databases and can run either on Apache or Microsoft IIS servers. While there were some test sites set up using IIS with Microsoft's SQL Server, ultimately almost all of the sites were built using Apache with MySQL.

Another key goal of the project was to synchronize with its Drupal foundation and avoid forking off from the main Drupal development. When the project first started, Drupal was at release 4.1. Over the following months, release 4.2 and release 4.3 of Drupal came out. In most cases, the extensions to Drupal for DeanSpace were upwardly compatible, but in some cases, extensions required minor code revisions.

## How the components fit the goals

Drupal has many modes for creating entries. One such mode creates weblog entries. Weblogs list entries in reverse chronological order on a single page. They often allow other users to write and post comments about any entry. Called "blogs" for short, weblogs are a popular, relatively simple way to publish news or personal journals.

Drupal also allows multiple users to edit the same entries, similar to wikis. Another important aspect of wikis is the ability to use a simpler formatting language than HTML. Drupal has a Wiki module that can be used to facilitate such quick formatting. However, this module did not work as well as hoped and did not interoperate well with HTML formatting.

Drupal also supports forums, however in this context Drupal's forums didn't add enough beyond the normal blogging capabilities to be all that useful. On the other hand, Drupal's ability to both publish and subscribe to RSS feeds has proven to be very useful in supporing information-sharing by DeanSpace sites.

### Community building

Community-building was a key DeanSpace goal.. There were already some tools for this purpose deployed by the Dean campaign or volunteers, beginning with the first Dean blog, hosted on Blogspot, (http://dean2004.blogspot.com),, which came to be known as the unofficial blog. As the campaign progressed, an official blog was set up using a content management system for weblogs called MovableType. Content posted to both the official and the unofficial blog was syndicated via RSS, therefore easily accessible to users with news aggregators. Hundreds of Yahoo Groups with mailing lists were also been created, and these, if set up properly could also provide RSS feeds. Many local groups also set up their own websites.

RSS stands for either Rich Site Summary or Really Simple Syndication, depending who you talk to. It's a standard machine-readable XML format for encoding text according to the relatively simple weblog format, where content items are posted in reverse chronological order. There can be multiple content items for any given date, and each item can have a title. RSS identifies these components of a weblog item with xml tags. RSS items are published as "feeds" that can be interpreted by software packages called "aggregators." The software allows a user to aggregate RSS feeds from many sites and read them with a single interface. News aggregators provide increasingly popular functionality for tracking and reading weblogs. RSS is also a way to share specific news items with many sites; DeanSpace leveraged this capability.

The campaign was exposed like no other campaign before. Users posted many comments on the blogs, especially the official blog. In fact, it was common for the official blog to receive thousands of comments a day, and there was nothing to prevent those who would disrupt discussions, commonly referred to as trolls, from adding their distracting comments.

Among other tools, Yahoo Groups were particularly popular and effective, however, many people expressed concern about reliance on a commercial service. Yahoo Groups were effective as platforms for mailing lists, but other tools within the Yahoo Groups tool set, such as syndication and databases, were little used.

Local sites supporting Dean were often set up as static pages, and were useful in getting out general information but difficult to update.

*Easy to roll out state and constituency group sites.*

Perhaps the greatest challenge was to come up with an easy way to set up a site. The DeanSpace team wanted to make the process simple enough for someone's grandmother to create a site. The first issue in building a site is coming up with a name and registering the relevant domain, fairly straightforward for experienced technical users but potentially difficult and confusing for non-techies, including grandmothers. To help resolve the problem, the DeanSpace team registered the domain "fordean.net" so that anyone could easily set up a subdomain, e.g. "http://california.fordean.net/." Over a 100 sites were set up this way. This also saved people the expense of registering their own domains.

The next issue was who would host what sites. Many options were considered. What sites could be hosted by the official campaign? What

Federal Election laws would apply in such a case? Could a special company be set up? Could people pool money together for this? Would there be requirements about setting up a PAC or a 527, and how would these requirements affect the ability of DeanSpace sites to interact with the Dean campaign?

The Dean campaign, which had been cautious about election law issues, would host only officially sponsored state sites. Forming a PAC or 527 could prohibit communications between the campaign and website volunteers, so that idea was discarded. Ultimately DeanSpace referred volunteer site administrators to hosting services that had worked well with initial sites.

The hosting services selected were limited to those who could support PHP and provide easy access to MySQL. This ruled out quite a few hosting services, and others were ruled out for poor performance or support.

SIDEBAR: PHP is a popular general-purpose server-side scripting language often used by software developers to create applications and systems for the web. Open source software such as the Drupal content management system, which is the core of DeanSpace, is often developed for the "LAMP" platform, i.e. Linux (operating system), Apache (web server), MySQL (database system), and PHP or Perl (scripting languages). Because DeanSpace was built with PHP and designed to work with MySQL, support for both was required.

Drupal allows multiple sites to use the same set of application files on a server by creating a configuration file that specifies different databases for the different sites. One person set up a hosting account that allowed a high volume of throughput, multiple database and multiple domains. Using this account, he was able to host many DeanSpace websites in the fordean.net domain quickly easily and without any additional expense

*Easy to get non-computer people adding content.*

One of the great advantages of a DeanSpace site is that users with no knowledge of html can easily add pages,. so that state communication directors, for instance, can immediately add content up as soon as a site, as opposed to waiting for some web developer to take the content add it to the website.

However, as it becomes easier to add content, it becomes more difficult and important to determine the best way to organize that content. Drupal has many different forms that contributions can take, so there were many discussions about which forms would be the best.

As noted earlier, forum entries never gained popularity. Unless there is a fairly large population of contributors, forums can fragment the community so that it never achieves critical mass.. If all the contributors to the official blog moved over to a single Drupal space, there would have most likely been enough contributors in each forum to reach critical mass, have enough posts to keep people involved, and maintain a sense of community. However, DeanSpace itself was designed to be a collection of smaller communities, and breaking these smaller communities into even smaller units wouldn't have been beneficial. Forums would also have required support by hosts or moderators.

The most popular form of content has arguably been the blog entry. Dean Supporters were already comfortable with blogs from their experiences with the official and unofficial Dean blogs, and many Dean supporters were regular blog readers and publishers.. The blog format allows users to find easily all the posts by a single poster. Each entry often has a link to all the other entries by the same contributor In the more informal sites, this has been used to give people a sense of who the different contributors are. However, for the official state sites, the emphasis was less on individual contributors in favor of the campaign as a whole. Because of this, the Official State sites used stories instead of Blog entries.

Stories are similar to blog entries, but they're moderated by default and lack a link to other entries by the author. However, most sites haven't used moderation, except occasionally for items picked up from other sites via RSS syndication. Users of a site would rank these items, and the most highly ranked items would appear on the front page.

Another type of content is what Drupal calls a 'static page'. The only notable difference between Static Pages and other entries in Drupal is that Static Pages can be written in PHP. Since they change programmatically, static pages are actually more dynamic than other entries and facilitate having fixed links on the front page.

Events, another form of content, are similar to blog entries and Static pages but have a time associated with them and are used for promoting upcoming events..

*Use of Taxonomy.*

Once the team determined content types, there was the larger issue of taxonomy – how the content is categorized and organized – to consider.. Anyone could easily add new content, but where should that content go? For some sites, the default is to put everything on the front page, which works only if there is a small amount of content. However more content grows requires more, and better, organization.

Within the taxonomy, a user can set up different vocabularies,. each of which includes a different set of terms. The most common use of the taxonomy is to set up a 'category' vocabulary as we see in other blogging software such as Movable Type. There is also a 'location' vocabulary. Entries can be in any combination of terms from different vocabularies. For example, an item might be in the category 'fundraising' and the location 'Stamford'.

*The ability to aggregate.*

One of the most exciting aspects of DeanSpace is its ability to aggregate news, blog entries and other items from various sources online, especially where DeanSpace sites share content. This would form a network of DeanSpace sites. For example, an entry on a city site could percolate up to a state site, an entry on a state site could be propagated out to different city sites, and constituency sites could easily be tied to sites based on location. So far this kind of sharing has not evolved, but the evolution of such a network will take time,

During the Dean campaign, headquarters in Burlington published RSS feeds. DeanSpace sites could subscribe to events scheduled with the 'Get Local' tool which at the DeanForAmerica website. Also available via RSS feed from the official site were icons for DeanSpace site administrators to use.

Dean volunteers created around 2,000 Yahoo groups. Since RSS is part of the Yahoo Groups toolkit, Some DeanSpace sites aggregated relevant

Yahoo Groups news feeds, and newsfeeds from weblogs of interest to the audience for the specific DeanSpace site.

*The ability to develop additional tools*

Beyond the simple community building using tools such as blogs and RSS feeds which are core components of Drupal and DeanSpace, Drupal also provides a strong platform for developing and deploying new tools. Issues of screen layout, data access and user authentication are already handled by the core technology, allowing developers to focus on building specific tools or modules.. DeanSpace is focuses on campaign-specific contact management tools.

At the simplest level, Drupal can be configured with portable user ids. That is, a user registered at one DeanSpace site can log into any site in the network. For basic authentication this has proven useful. However, this authentication doesn't provide additional information, such as email address, or full name, and as such is limited in its functionality.

One important part of a campaign is enabling volunteers to find one another. Through FOAF, the Friend Of A Friend protocol, information about supporters from the official campaign site can be retrieved from within DeanSpace. Additional work is being done with FOAF to use it to link other Drupal based sites, and potentially other non-Drupal sites as well.

Beyond this, DeanSpace needed tools for contacting volunteers , including better email handling within Drupal, the ability to send emails to people based on grouping according to criteria such as their user roles in DeanSpace, or (for volunteers not registered with DeanSpace) data entered via a webpage or uploaded from other sources, such as Meetup participant spreadsheets.

DeanSpace developers also built tools to facilitate writing and sending letters to newspaper editors, and technology to support Get Out the Vote activities, including tools to enter voter information gathered through phone banks and door to door canvassing, and by volunteers talking with their friends, family, and neighbors. Such tools have been around for a while, but through DeanSpace tools were adapted for use anywhere over the internet, not just at campaign offices. There were also tools for virtual phone banking, and loading new voters from vCards in a viral marketing approach.

Once voters are identified, it is also necessary to get them to the polls, so developers created. rideboard software with which voters could request rides, and volunteers could offer rides.

## Beyond DeanSpace - DemocracySpace?

DeanSpace grew out of the campaign to elect Howard Dean President. However, the software could be used to support any campaign. Developers continued fixing bugs and enhancing the system after Dean dropped out of the 2004 presidential race, and the DeanSpace Team raised funds to complete development of a version 2.0 that will be much easier to install and operate.

Many of the DeanSpace volunteers have expressed interest in using this software for other campaigns., especially local races; gubernatorial races; congressional races; etc. Already a few such sites are up. The software may also be adapted for use in other countries like the United Kingdom, Austria, Canada and Hungary.

# Campaign Tools
# by Adina Levin

## Introduction

This chapter covers the tools used for political campaigns, including election campaigns and activist campaigns.

The Dean presidential campaign revealed two contradictory things about online grassroots organizing.

First, online organizing tools can be extremely powerful – they helped catapult an unknown governor of a small state into the most popular and most well-funded candidate early in the primary season.

Second, online tools and techniques are not enough to take a campaign to victory. They must be closely integrated with traditional media and face-to-face organizing.

The lessons that jumped to national prominence in 2003 have been understood by internet-savvy activists since the mid-90s. Around that time, Jonah Seiger and Shabbir Safdar collaborated on an internet campaign to oppose the Communications Decency Act, which would have imposed strict controls on internet content. They described the lessons they learned to Jon Lebkowsky, in an unpublished article at the time:

Jonah said "The political process happens in the real world, and then you have to engage in the real political process. The net works successfully only when it's integrated into an overall campaign strategy. Independent of a larger sense of what you're trying to accomplish and leveraging other forms of communication and other ways of getting your messages out to the world, the net has no *particular* advantage, except that when it's used effectively in an integrated campaign, it's the killer app. Added Shabbir, "In the real world, all that stuff only means something once you use it for something. The biggest online adhocracy in the world means nothing if nobody calls a member of Congress, nobody goes to a Town Hall meeting, nobody writes a letter. I mean a paper letter, not an email."

This chapter is written with two very different readers in mind: activists and campaign organizers, who are looking to bring innovative uses of the internet to their campaigns, and tools-builders, who are looking to adapt internet tools to activist and election campaigns. For activists, this chapter will have tips on evaluating familiar tools, and background on newer tools, like weblogs and wikis. For toolmakers, this chapter will provide background about the processes in which the tools are used, a context which is critical for successful implementation.

## Campaign Application and Campaign Tools

In order for online tools to be used successfully, they need to be integrated with the processes of campaigning. Coordinating a candidate or activist campaign involves an integrated series of processes.

- Dialog and deliberation

- Researching policies and strategies

- Educating the public and media

- Identifying supporters

- Gathering and motivating supporters

- Raising money, mobilizing action

There are tools and techniques supporting each process of these processes.

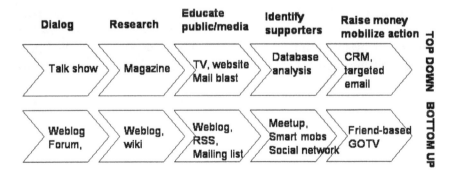

The most familiar tools for electronic organizing, websites and electronic mail, translate traditional top-down organizing tools and techniques into electronic form

- *websites* are online versions of campaign brochures and commercials.

- *campaign email* is an electronic version of print direct mail

The internet enables activists to use these traditional tactics fairly inexpensively, and with a greater level of personalization and targeting.

In addition, there are new generations of electronic organizing tools in earlier stages of adoption. These tools use the internet to facilitate "bottom up" self-organization

- *online forums, weblogs, and wikis* are used for bottom up co-ordination and communication among activist groups

- *networking services* are used for groups to self-organize, online and in person

- chat, instant messaging, and SMS enable activists to "swarm"

Traditional advocacy campaigns are hierarchical and highly structured. The techniques for using "top-down" websites and email, which fit the model well, are fairly mature at this point. Meanwhile, the techniques for using the "bottom-up" tools are still evolving as organizations ranging from the Dean Campaign to election-watchers in Kenya are pioneering techniques that take advantage of these new tools. Effective online organizing involves coordinated use of multiple tools and media. There is an emerging set of effective practices for using network tools together in conjunction with traditional media and tactics. Change won't occur in an instant. In general, change happens faster when new tools fit existing patterns, and more slowly when the tools and patterns need to evolve together.

|  | Unstructured | Structured |
|---|---|---|
| **Top Down** | Forum | Mass email  Campaign CRM<br>CMS<br>Mailing list |
| **Bottom up** | Wiki<br>SMS<br>Instant<br>Messaging | Technorati  Peer GOTV<br>Weblog  Meetup<br>Ryze, Orkut |

Assembling the tools for an online campaign takes a bit of work today. There is no single toolkit that pulls together all of the components needed for networked campaigning. Campaigns and organizers must assemble their toolsets from existing components. The interface standards to integrate tools and systems are still emerging.

Fortunately, there is a growing array of open source tools that campaigns can adapt and customize. And there is an emerging network of tools developers working on the applications, interfaces, and services required to support online campaigning.

## Website

The first campaign websites extended traditional publishing techniques to the internet, using websites to publish news and background information about a specific candidate or activist campaign.

Sites that are updated frequently or that contain more than a few dozen pages benefit from the use of a content management system (CMS). These systems automate the process of posting content, reducing the bottleneck and skill level required for a webmaster.

Content management tools vary in sophistication. Capabilities of more sophisticated content management tools include:

- personalization, enabling the targeting of content based on a user's profile

- workflow, controlling contributions based on end-user roles

- multimedia, supporting audio, video, and animated content.

In addition, some general-purpose content management systems include modules for specific purposes, such as polling, chat, forums, weblogs, etc.

Bringing in a content management system to automate a website involves more than the installation of a software package. The process of implementing a content management system includes:

- designing the site structure to fit the interests of the site's constituents (press, undecided voters, volunteers, etc.).

- setting up categories so contributed content can be organized on an ongoing basis

- analyzing and designing the content contribution workflow for the organization

- defining metrics for reporting on website success, including number of users, repeat visitors, visitor demographics, and more.

A campaign site can be used for much more than brochureware. A campaign website can enable campaign volunteers to build support for the campaign on the ground.

In the words of campaign professional Nathan Wilcox,

> Any traditional grassroots activity is more easily organized online. If a campaign has successfully clicked with the public and built a viable online supporter base, the next step is to let the grassroots organizers, and the supporters themselves, get to organizing. House parties, tabling at local elections, passing out fliers at sporting events, door-to-door canvassing, and any other sort of field activity can be promoted on your Web sites and e-mail newsletters. Supporters can RSVP online and even organize their own events. Old-fashioned door-to-door politics are back in a big way, thanks to the latest tech tools.
>
> Use your online network to organize volunteer outreach efforts to nursing homes, churches, and working neighborhoods. Ask volunteers

to distribute pamphlets and posters from the Web site to potential supporters who don't go online or don't have net access.

These processes involve using content management systems differently, with:

- sections and permissions for campaign volunteers

- the ability to upload and download materials such as sign-up sheets, posters, flyers, and videos

- CMS tools and technical support for groups of supporters to host their own websites

## CMS Tools

There are many content management systems available, including

- enterprise systems sold to corporations for hundreds of thousands or millions of dollars

- hosted services provided by application service providers

- open source systems with no software licensing costs.

Open source systems provide the "source code" free to review and customized to fit the needs of the campaign. Most open source systems are free of license charges, although providers might charge for documentation, service, and support. The typical lack of license fees and the power to customize can make open source solutions attractive to campaigns.

But the lack of license fees does not mean that an open source solution is free of cost. It takes time and skilled work to install and configure a content management system, and to customize it for the needs of the campaign. Systems also need ongoing support and maintenance, requiring skilled labor.

There are a variety of licenses with different conditions governing the user's ability to modify and redistribute the code. The GNU Public License, or GPL, is a popular license that requires users who modify the software to distribute all modifications with a GPL. Campaigns considering open source should review the license of the package to confirm that the license matches the project's objectives.

In order to use a content management tool successfully, campaign managers need to:

- involve the stakeholders who will use the system, including content creators and IT managers

- understand the types of content that will be published using the CMS, and the processes for publishing the content

- consider the skills within the organization required to maintain a system.

The evaluation process should consider the three phases of the content lifecycle: authoring, management, and publishing, as well as the business and support terms of the provider.

| CMS Selection Criteria | | |
|---|---|---|
| (adapted from How to Evaluate a Content Management System, http://www.steptwo.com.au/papers/kmc_evaluate/index.html) | | |
| Authoring | Integrated authoring environment | The CMS must provide a seamless and powerful environment for content creators. This ensures that authors have easy access to the full range of features provided by the CMS. |
| | Separation of content and presentation | It is not possible to publish to multiple formats without a strict separation of content and presentation. Authoring must be style-based, with all formatting applied during publishing. |

| | Multi-user authoring | The CMS will have many simultaneous users. Features such as record locking ensure that clashing changes are prevented. |
|---|---|---|
| | Single-sourcing (content re-use) | A single page (or even paragraph) will often be used in different contexts, or delivered to different user groups. This is a prerequisite to managing different platforms (intranet, internet) from the same content source. |
| | Metadata creation | Capturing metadata (creator, subject, keywords, etc) is critical when managing a large content repository. This also includes keyword indexes, subject taxonomies and topic maps |
| | Powerful linking | Authors will create many cross-links between pages, and these must be stable against restructuring. |
| | Non-technical authoring | Authors must not be required to use HTML (or other technical knowledge) when creating pages. |
| | Ease of use and efficiency | For a CMS to be successful, it must be easy to create and maintain content. |

| Content management | | |
|---|---|---|
| | Version control & archiving | Strict version control is necessary for legal accountability, backup and disaster recovery. A simple but powerful interface must be provided for these features. |
| | Workflow | Decentralised content creation relies heavily on a powerful workflow model, that can be easily customised, and is resilient against organisational change. |
| | Security | Adequate security levels and audit trails must be in place to protect the integrity of the content. |
| | Integration with external systems | A CMS is typically only one of a number of systems used to present information on the intranet or website.<br><br>An enterprise-wide CMS will only be successful if it can be cleanly integrated with existing business systems.<br><br>The mechanisms for achieving this must be fully documented, and based on open or industry standards. |

| | Reporting | The CMS must provide an extensive range of reports, for both users and administrators. Ideally, the system should pro- actively report on any issues that arise.<br><br>Support for customised reporting is also desirable. |
|---|---|---|
| Publishing | The publishing engine takes the content stored in the repository, and generates the final pages. While this may be a dynamic or batch process, the same basic requirements apply. Key requirements may include: | |
| | Stylesheets | Final appearance is controlled through the use of stylesheets. This provides flexibility and expandability. |
| | Page templates | Overall page layout is specified via page templates. Ideally, a non-technical interface should be provided for managing this. |

| | | |
|---|---|---|
| | Extensibility | It must be simple to integrate code "snippets" (or equivalent) to provide additional publishing functionality. The CMS must support a process of "continual improvement" in interface design. |
| | Support for multiple formats | The CMS must publish to multiple formats, such as: HTML (web), printed, PDF, hand-held (WAP), and more.<br><br>It should be possible to add support for additional formats, which will be necessary as new standards evolve.<br><br>In order to achieve high-quality in every format, it is critical that the content be separated from presentation at the time of authoring. This allows distinct stylesheets to be used for each output. |
| | Personalisation | Different information is presented based on either user profiles, or metadata in the source content. This is typically required for large "portal" websites. |

| | | |
|---|---|---|
| | Usage statistics | The CMS must allow comprehensive usage statistics to be gathered, including: most popular pages, daily usage, and search engine usage.<br><br>This information allows the success of the site to be tracked, and any usability issues identified. |
| | Accessibility | The CMS must conform to standards such as the W3C Web Accessibility Initiative (WAI). |
| | Cross browser support | The pages must be viewable in all major web browsers (Internet Explorer, Netscape, Opera, etc). Specify which browser versions are to be supported. |
| | | |
| | Speed | Page size must be limited to ensure that load times are acceptable for users. Specify the typical user access methods (LAN, modem, cable, etc). |
| Contract & business | Training | The vendor must list the training materials that exist for the CMS, and the training services that they can provide. |

| | Documentation | The CMS must be supported by adequate documentation: for users, administrators and developers. |
|---|---|---|
| | Warranty | The warranty period provided, once the software has been purchased. |
| | Maintenance agreements | The vendor must outline their preferred support arrangements, including service level agreements and upgrade processes. |
| | Resources required | The hardware, software and operating systems required by the CMS. |
| | Skills required | What skills and knowledge will be required within your organization to customize and maintain the CMS? |
| | Cost | Both the fixed costs for the CMS, and the per-user ("per-seat") costs. The latter is generally more significant for a large organization. |
| | Scalability | The load levels that the CMS supports, and the additional resources (hardware & software) required for increased usage. |

| | IT constraints | Specify any pre-existing hardware or software that the CMS must interface with, or run on. This includes specific operating systems, databases or webservers. |
|---|---|---|
| | Reference sites | The vendor must supply a number of sites where the software has been successfully implemented. These must match the characteristics of your organization. |

## Content Management Tools

Well-known providers of commercial systems targeted at political and activist campaigns include:

- Convio

- Virtual Sprockets

- CommunityZero

The more mature Open Source content management systems include:

- Drupal

- PostNuke

- Plone/Zope

- Mambo Open Source

## Email and Mass Mobilization

Internet email has proven value for notifying people and galvanizing them to action. The campaign processes for internet mailing evolved directly from print direct mail and newsletters. The campaign builds a database of constituents, and creates messages that encourage audiences to act or contribute.

There are several important differences between email and print mail:

- Email can be sent at much lower cost than print mail, providing inexpensive access to small, single-issue political organizers, as well as large mainstream groups.

- Mailings can be finely targeted more cost-effectively than print mail

- The recipient can act immediately on the subject of the mail, "clicking through" to make a donation, send a letter, sign a petition, or fill out a survey

Email-based "flash campaigns" are popular because they allow people to do something effective from their desk, in minutes. And the medium has shown impressive success.

- MoveOn.org started as a group opposed to the impeachment of President Clinton. MoveOn organized about 500,000 people over the course of the impeachment debate. Since then, MoveOn has used its list to organize flash campaigns for other issues such as media consolidation.

- The campaign opposing the Communications Decency Act in the mid-1990s mobilized 60,000 citizens to take action at critical points in the process. The CDA was passed by Congress, and was later overturned in the courts. Congress let the Court ruling stay without further legislation, because activists opposing the CDA won in the court of public opinion.

- Organizers of protests to the US invasion of Iraq used mailing lists to organize mass protests – in London, 300,000 protesters gathered on one day's notice.

Some of the most impressive results from "flash campaigning" have occurred with internet fundraising, largely using email and web.

- John McCain's 2000 presidential campaign raised $6.4 million on-line and recruited 142,000 volunteers during the primaries, the vast majority in the days and hours after his victory in New Hampshire.

- The Howard Dean campaign raised $7.5 million from 59,000 Americans in the second quarter of 2003, more money than any other Democratic presidential candidate. Close to half of Dean's fundraising came via the Internet.

The success of internet fundraising promises to reverse a decades-long trend in campaign finance, that of increased dependence on contributions by wealthy donors. In the 2004 election the majority of Howard Dean's campaign funds came from donations of less than $200. According to a USA Today op-ed on July 15, 1993, "Since the 1975 post-Watergate reforms, presidential campaigns have relied on a combination of public subsidies and high-end donors to fund their campaigns, with the proportion of large donations — $750 or more — steadily increasing. In the 1976 primary, large donations provided 18% of Jimmy Carter's private funding and 24% of Gerald Ford's. In the 2000 primary, big donors gave a whopping 74% of George W. Bush's funding and 65% of Al Gore's."

The value of online action alerts and fundraising places importance on building lists of interested constituents. The consent of recipients is extremely important to maintaining their good will. In a survey conducted in October 2002 by The Institute for Politics, Democracy & the Internet at George Washington University Graduate School of political Management, 69% of expressed reluctance to give their email, and 89% were reluctant to give a credit card number or contribute money to an online campaign, because of concerns about spam, privacy, and security.

Organizations conducting many campaigns over time gain value from analytics features that enable campaign managers to calculate the results of campaigns, and to test and optimize tactics over time. The methods are similar to those used with print direct mail, the main difference being speed. Electronic systems generate results, and reward experimentation, in batches of dozens rather than thousands, and in hours rather than weeks.

Making a solicitation online costs only 20 cents compared with $1 or more for each direct-mail or telephone solicitation, according to a McKinsey & Co. study published in May 2003. Still, only about 1% of total donations was raised online in 2002, though the Internet's share probably rose to 3% or 4% in 2003, the company says.

Suites including from vendors including Convio and Kintera help organizations maintain an online presence; manage online fundraising campaigns, and online mobilization campaigns.

For example, Consumers Union uses Convio to manage focused issue campaigns, each with its own "microsite" and action list: http://www.stophospitalinfections.org is a campaign to disclose hospital infection rates, and http://www.escapecellhell.org is a campaign to protest poor service by cellular phone carriers. The mailing lists inform interested citizens of actions they can take, and include polls and surveys to guage and engage interest. The websites have background information, and the ability to write, fax, or call congress, administrative officials, and corporations. Consumers union uses the email/web campaigns in conjunction with more traditional print and telephone communication. Convio's tools help build the polls, surveys, content, and response tools, and analyze response rates to different messages and techniques.

Since political campaigns are short-lived, and advocacy organizations are short on budget and technical staff, these applications are typically hosted.

Capabilities include

- content management/publishing for website

- personalized, demographically targeted email messages

- action alert management – enable customers to customize and send letters and petitions by email, fax, or print mail.

- Campaign management, to plan and analyze campaign results, from clickthrough rates to donations

- Constituent relationship management application to track each interaction with constituents

- Constituent database to store information about contacts

Commercial tools and services include:

- Convio

- Kintera

- Democracy In Action

- GetActive

- Orchid for Change

There are also specialized polling tools, suitable for quick-response online and in-person electronic polling.

| Tools for Polls and Surveys | |
| --- | --- |
| Source: National Coalition for Dialogue and Deliberation<br>http://thataway.org/resources/practice/hightech/polling.html | |
| **Option Technologies**<br>www.optiontechnologies.com | Polling tool for face-to-face or multi-site meetings; participants respond from PC or handheld computer |
| Sharpe Decisions<br>www.sharpedecisions.com | Collect opinions from groups using wireless keypad technology. Includes Risk Assessment, Focus Groups, Employee Surveys, Strategic and Project Planning. Multiple Choice, Rating Scale, Paired Ranking or Relationship Modeling voting |
| Site Gadgets<br>www.sitegadgets.com | Offers free polls that facilitate Web-based surveys allowing organizations to gather and analyze feedback. |

| | |
|---|---|
| SurveyMonkey<br>www.surveymonkey.com | Tools for designing online survey, collecting responses and analyzing the results. Both "basic" (free) and "professional" subscriptions available. |
| WebEnalysis<br>www.webenalysis.com/onlinepolls.asp | A free polling tool similar to PollGear but with a few more options. |
| WebSurveyor.com<br>www.websurveyor.com | Secure, do-it-yourself online surveys with ability to customize options and a unique survey-question library. |

### Group-forming – Smartmobs and Meetup

Websites and alert lists use a traditional centrally controlled process, where small numbers of campaign organizers provide action alerts and fundraising requests to a large number of supporters. The real innovation in internet campaigning comes from new tools and techniques for supporters to find each other and to organize themselves.

These tools of self-organization often bridge electronic communication with physical-world organization.

The techniques of "smart mobs" – organizing ad hoc demonstrations with email and text messaging – have become common tools of political protests. The latest tools turbo-charge older "phone chain" techniques – the difference is that recipients can be reached anywhere, organizing extends to the street and the polling place, and communication spreads through informal social networks, as activists send messages to their friends. During the protests against the WTO conference in Seattle in 1999, between 40,000 and 60,000 demonstrators from over 700 organizations used email and cellphones to mobilize protests against globalization.

- SMS text messaging, rare in the US, is phenomenally popular elsewhere in the world. In January 2001, protesters in the Philippines used text messaging to spontaneously organize protests that overthrew the government.

- In the 2003 and 2004 elections in Korea, supporters of opposition candidates swarmed on bulletin boards and SMS and mobile phone calls, on Election Day, to get out the vote and elect their candidate. In the 2004 election SK Telecom, the nation's largest wireless service provider reported that on the election-day it logged 350 million cell phone calls and 75 million text messages, a 25 % increase compared to a normal day, according to Jean K Min, reporting for Howard Rheingold's Smart Mobs weblog.

These techniques are becoming part of the election process around the world. As reported by Howard Rheingold, "elections in Kenya and Ghana were kept honest by monitors who used a network of mobile phones and radio stations; India's ruling Bharatiya Janata Party uses SMS to maintain contact with the press and voters; in South Africa, SMS registration was part of the official voter registration process."

Meetup.com provides a slower service providing online organizing tools for face to face meetings.

Meetup.com is a web-based service that lets groups organize face to face meetings that occur at the same date and time around the world. There are Meetups for Democrats and Republicans, knitters, single parents, and Mini Cooper owners. Participants can find and sign up for Meetups in their area, and be notified by email of upcoming events. Meetups help new groups organize themselves and develop a constituency, and enable more established groups to organize with no logistical effort.

The weakness of the 2003 version of Meetup is that it gave groups little control over where and when to meet, and how to communicate with each other. After a group has formed, it typically wants more control over its meetings and list. Meetup has begun to provide groups with more control – in spring 2004, the Meetup+ service provided the capability to send private messages to other members, to nominate venues to meet, to create agendas for meetings, and to create personal web pages.

Meetup-like techniques for organizing online and meeting in person are powerful ways for groups to organize. Techniques and tools for Meetups will be integrated into other campaign toolkits and custom-developed tools.

For example, The Wellstone Civic Dialog is a series of discussions that are co-ordinated online and take place in person. Participants sign up on a website (http://www.wellstone.org) to organize or attended an event or meeting. The initial Wellstone Dialogues were organized around a national reading of Paul Wellstone's book, *Conscience of a Liberal*. The program has expanded to support discussion topics of participants' choice, and to include both private and public meetings.

## Forums, weblogs, and wikis

Meetup and Smartmobs help groups assemble in the moment, but don't do much to help groups after they get together. Tools including forums, weblogs, and wikis help groups organize themselves and build a shared memory. Self-organization is a radical departure from traditional political campaigns. In the words of campaign consultant Nathan Wilcox, "This is the antithesis of the tightly controlled campaign communications model that has been the norm for at least 50 years."

## Forums and mailing lists

Forums and mailing lists are tools for conversation and collaboration. They are for conversation among the groups' members, rather than broadcast from campaign central. The forum model evolved from standalone bulletin board systems that pre-dated the internet. The more recent generations of forums were designed for the worldwide web.

Forums and mailing lists are similar. Forums are web-based, often with an email option. Mailing lists are email-based, often with a web archive, and a web-based interface to post, search archives, and administer the lists.

The forum model is an online community for discussion about a set of topics.

- Forums are used by advocacy groups for discussion and deliberation among constituents. For example, the ACLU offers online forums

discussing campaign finance and voting rights issues.
http://forums.aclu.org/categories.cfm?catid=120&zb=8680141

- During the Howard Dean campaign, "Dean Forums" were used to discuss policy. Dean supporters used the forums to post their comments, suggestions, volunteer reports, and policy ideas.

- E-democracy.org runs a lively set of forums on state and local issues in Minnesota, using the open source "Mailman" application, archived using the MailArchive service.

In order to be used effectively in political campaigns or in governance, forums need to be used in the context of a facilitated process. The process can be more or less formal, and more or less hierarchical, but should be present to ensure sustained focus and civility. One effective example is the use of online dialog by Dutch minister Roger Van Boxtel, responsible for minorities, inner cities and e-government. According to Elizabeth Richard, in a paper by the Canadian Policy Research Networks, "Van Boxtel has managed to develop a sustainable online relationship with citizens, building on the online tradition brought upon by the pioneering efforts of the Amsterdam free-net."

In the US, a variety of groups including *Web Lab*, *e-thePeople.org* and *Information Renaissance*, and America – are pioneering methods for using collaborative technology to help people engage in meaningful conversations about public issues.

http://thataway.org/resources/practice/hightech/intro.html

### Evaluation criteria

The forum format is useful for ongoing discussions, but it has notable limitations.

- It is volume-dependent. If a discussion is high-volume, participants who can't keep up will leave. If discussion is too low-volume, participants won't stay interested.

- Forums that are large and anonymous tend to attract misbehavior – viciously aggressive arguments (flamewars), and troublemakers who come to a discussion to start arguments (trolls). Moderation is needed to preserve healthy interaction.

- Forums are conversations, which by their nature tend to diverge and digress. Moderation and structure is needed in order to bring a group to agreement.

- Email and forums are good for distributing action alerts, but less-well suited for coordinating action. The group doesn't have a picture of current status. Ideas and documents proliferate in multiple versions.

Consequently, mailing lists and forums are used most effectively in conjunction with other tools that are more effective at managing attention, building consensus, and coordinating action.

Web-based forums are effective in several settings:

- when the group itself is well-known – a popular candidate or activist organization — and a website draws an ongoing stream of new and repeat visitors

- when the group is smaller and highly committed, willing to return to a website without active reminders

Mailing lists deliver messages to the recipients' inbox, and are therefore effective for active organizing, delivering action alerts, and sharing news. Mailing lists are quite sensitive to volume – high-volume lists with hundreds of postings per day will discourage participants.

Technology selection depends, in part, on the skills and technical infrastructure of the group. The simplest and easiest path may be something like Yahoo groups, an easy-to-use advertising-supported service.

Groups with access to moderate technical skills and infrastructure – including the ability to install and maintain applications on a server – have numerous free open source tools to choose from. They should consider ease of installation and administration, as well as ease of navigation and attractiveness for end-users.

High-volume forums benefit from ratings and moderation features that allow users and moderators to filter out off-topic and hostile posts, and content management features that allow users to navigate current and older discussions by topic areas, and to create customized views for their own interest. At the high end, complex forum software overlaps with general-purpose content management software and general-purpose content management tools, often including discussion board modules. High-end forum software requires a similar high level of installation, configuration, and maintenance as general purpose content-management systems.

## Tools

### Mailing lists

**Yahoo Groups**
www.yahoogroups.com

Yahoo Groups is an extremely popular, free, advertising-supported service, with tens of thousands of political mailing lists. The service has an easy-to-use web-based interface for joining and administering lists, and includes online archives, along with other, lesser-used features such as a group calendar.

**Mailman**
www.mailman.org

Open source mailing list system, written in Python with web-based administration and archiving. Requires server root access to install.

**ezmlm**

Open source mailing list system, written in C. Depends on qmail mail transport. Web administration with qmailadmin.

**Majordomo**

Venerable open source mailing list, written in some language. Web-based administration with the addition of the MajorCool utility. Harder to manage than mailman.

| | |
|---|---|
| **Listserv**<br>www.lsoft.com | Venerable proprietary mailing list, used by over 300,000 lists. Web-based administration and archive |

## Forum software

(http://www.topology.org/soft/mb.html)

| | |
|---|---|
| PHPBB | phpBB open source (GPL) message board, in HP, using MySQL, PostgresQL, MS-SQL, ACCESS databases. Flat forum structure. |
| Phorum | Uses PHP and MySQL or PostgreSQL. OSNews.com,. Tree-structured forums and message threads within each forum. Here's their list of sites running Phorum. |
| daCode | daCode. Slashdot-like BBS software which was once used for linuxfr.org. Uses PHP and MySQL or PostgreSQL. An example is this very nice French mutt site. This French Gentoo site also looks fairly good. See also their list of daCode sites. |
| Antiboard | PHP /MySQL or PostgreSQL. Customizible, designed to easily integrate into any webpage. It is multithreaded and can support multiple message boards, and also shows nested comments.'' |

| | |
|---|---|
| tForum | PHP/MySQL forum that includes many features such as easy customization, unlimited boards and categories, IP banning, e-mail notification of replies, word filtering, message preview, searching, user profiles, private messaging, polls, and much more." Made In Germany. |
| Slash | Perl/MySQL based forum software written for the popular SlashDot technology community site. Content management and forum features, with user rating sytem. |

## Weblogs

Weblogs (also called *blogs)* are easy-to-use personal publishing tools that have been adopted recently for use by activist and political campaigns. Weblog tools make posting to a website as easy as writing an email. Unlike content management systems designed for a formal editing and publishing process, requiring rounds of editing and approval, blog posting is immediate.

And unlike full-featured content management systems, which support the creation of websites with complex structures, weblogs use a simple, time-based format – the most recent posting is at the top of the page.

Weblogs have features that make them a conversational form, in a different style than web forums. Weblog systems often have comments that let readers talk back and talk to each other. And it is common for weblog entries to link to news items, or entries by other bloggers. Search services, including Google and Technorati, can make it easy to find others talking about your issue or candidate.

This simple, social form became popular among millions of individuals posting about their personal lives, interests, and careers. When they're used for a campaign, weblogs are typically written in a more personal and informal voice than formal journalism and campaign literature. They make it easy for campaigners and activists to post quickly and often – it's ideal for up-to-the minute news, fundraising results, updates from the campaign trail.

Their simplicity make weblogs suitable primary publishing tools for small campaigns. With minimal training,.non-technical users can easily post news items, The campaign can keep a site current with minimal technical burden. Items that change less frequently can be maintained as standard html or static web pages.

The immediacy, informality, and community make weblogs an effective medium for getting the word out to supporters, and, in larger campaigns, building community among supporters.. The first use of a weblog in a political campaign was by Tara Sue Grubb, a little known candidate who helped raised awareness of her candidacy by blogging. But it was the Howard Dean presidential campaign that brought campaign blogging to international prominence. The Dean campaign, having captured the interests of bloggers in early 2003, started its own weblog in June of that year. The candidate himself didn't post messages, but his campaign staffers posted about the day-to-day progress of the campaign, and quickly developed an active following.

By September, 2003, the Dean blog was getting 30,000 visits and thousands of comments per day. The blog community's enthusiasm helped to drive grass-roots fundraising. The community quickly developed a mechanism for dealing with "trolls" – people who posted inflammatory comments.

The Dean blogging community included blogforamerica.com, where the posts were written by campaign staff, as well as blogs by individual weblog supporters for Dean, including DailyKos, One Father for Dean, and several others.

While campaign blogging is best known from the Dean example, blogs can be particularly helpful for small activist groups and local campaigns. Smaller groups can use a weblog to post announcements and action alerts without delay and without technical intervention by a webmaster. For example, Environment Colorado uses a weblog to post news about environmental legislation and policy in Colorado.

Politically active citizens use weblogs to communicate about local political issues. For example, OrangePolitics.org is a group weblog about political issues in Orange County, North Carolina. It deals with nuts and bolts local issues – construction of new student housing, a local proposal for red-light cameras, and county commissioner elections.

## Evaluation Criteria

A key strength of blogging is its simplicity. Smaller groups, especially, should look for blog tools that can be used and managed by the activist team.

At a larger scale, full-featured content management systems are starting to have built-in weblog features. If a campaign is using such a CMS, it may make sense to use the native weblog capabilities – but double-check ease of use, and the presence of required features.

Handy features to look for in weblog systems include:

- comments (and the ability to turn comments off)

- support for the RSS and ATOM syndication standards

- integration with email, for posting and subscription

- easy support for multiple authors

- support for password protection, for sharing private information

It is very useful when a campaign can simultaneously post action alerts to a weblog and a mailing list. Today, it takes attentive setup to do this using the leading weblog tools. We expect it to become a standard campaign feature.

## Weblog Tools

Smaller groups can use tools designed for personal blogging including:

- Blogger

- TypePad (a for-pay hosted service) and Movable Type (free software for installation)

- Radio Userland

- BlogHarbor

- Blogware

In addition, full-featured content management systems such as Drupal and PostNuke are starting to include blogging features, along with a broad range of capabilities for managing content in a general-purpose website. Setting up a full content management system is a more elaborate and time-consuming task than starting a weblog; see the website section for details.

## Wiki

Blogs are the easiest way for campaigns to publish on the web. Wiki is the easiest way for campaign activists to collaborate. A wiki is a website where anyone can edit any page. The version history of each page is saved, so if someone makes a mistake, or vandalizes a page, the damage is easily and quickly undone.

Wikis were invented in 1995 by Ward Cunningham to support the efforts of "extreme programming" – a highly collaborative style of software development requiring very fast-turaround, rapid-co-ordination, and fast decisions. The word wiki comes from a Hawaiian word meaning "quick."

The immediacy and collaborative nature of wikis make them very useful for campaign functions requiring rapid collaboration under time pressure. The wiki form is also useful for building consensus. Unlike a mailing list or discussion forum, where each post responds to and contrasts with the next, the wiki form encourages participants to literally "get on the same page." Wikis can be used for the development of documents such as policy and procedures, grant proposals, reports, with each contributor working in their own time on the single live document.

The classic form of the wiki is entirely open to public view and editing. This form is surprisingly resilient. Wikipedia, a web-based encyclopedia with over 200,000 entries has high-quality entries produced by an army of volunteers. The community feels ownership for the content and protects it from damage.

Wikis are used effectively in collaborative civic projects such as Seattle Wireless and Austin Wireless (http://www.austinwireless.net), community portals for the deployment of wireless technology throughout the cities. The home page of the wiki keeps the community updated on what's new, individual contributors can maintain pages on their own sections of the project, and technical teams can continuously improve answers to frequently asked questions (FAQs)

There are a number of examples of wikis used for campaign and activist purposes:

- The Green Party of Canada is building its party platform using a wiki, giving citizens say in the development of policy and mission: http://www.greenparty.ca/memberzone/tiki-index.php

- CivicAction, a wiki-based guide to the organization and execution of campaigns, site put together by Kucinich activists, http://www.civicactions.org/cgi-bin/wiki.pl

- Lobbywatch is German site with a public listing of the lobbyists affecting the development of German and the European policy on issues such as health care. http://www.lobbywatch.de/wiki/wiki.phtml?title=Gesundheitsrefo rmen

A healthy public wiki harnesses community contributions, and is more flexible than a structured content management system.

Wikis can also be used with password protection, so that only members of the campaign team can see and change the pages. This makes wikis useful, lightweight tools for collaboration within a core group of campaign activists. Today, most groups rely heavily on internal email for rapid, ad hoc collaboration. Jonah Seiger describes process used to manage the CDA campaign: "We organized that entire case using internal email lists, exchanging documents, planning meetings, honing arguments, querying people for press, for specific technical or legal assistance."

However the trouble with using email in this manner is that important items get lost within inboxes, multiple versions of documents circulate, and there is no single view of status. Wikis can be used internally to bring a team literally onto the same page, to share current versions of documents, and to build a knowledge base of training material, without drowning campaign staff in email.

As this chapter was being written, the John Kerry field organizing team was using a private wiki to co-ordinate volunteer organizing in swing states. Participants kept lists of contacts and mailing lists, co-ordinated speaking and letter-writing campaigns, and were building an ongoing library of volunteer training material.

The Howard Dean campaign also used a wiki for decentralized news gathering and analysis. Every morning, between 5am and 9am, a team of 400 activists scanned news around the country and clipped news items. Each page included full text entries, a link to the source, and annotation. A small team of editors then created Issue pages that linked to the relevant clips, organized by issue.

At 9am, the campaign team would gather to plan their approach to the news of the day. This approach enabled the Dean team to:

- respond rapidly to the day's breaking news
- build a searchable library of clippings as a by-product of the day's clipping efforts
- effectively co-ordinate a nationwide network of committed volunteers

**Evaluation Criteria**

The value of wiki is the ability for activists and campaign staff to collaborate quickly and simply. However activists should be wary of wiki packages that have so many features and functions that become difficult to use.

As with other tools, consider the technical skill and time constraints of the team before deploying a wiki. For groups seeking rapid productivity, or groups without significant technical staff, hosted services can enable a team to get up and running quickly.

Features to look for include

- Notification of changes through email and RSS (so participants can get updates without continually checking the website)
- Ability to upload documents and images

- Password-protection, if you're looking to use the wiki in private mode

- Backup capability

- GUI editing, for ease of use

There are a variety of open source tools for teams with the skills and time to install and configure software.

- Usemod, the first wiki. Simple to use, and with powerful features for connecting to other public wikis

- MoinMoin, a Python-based wiki

  - OpenWiki, a Microsoft ASP-based wiki

  - Tiki, a PHP-based content management system with a wiki core

  - Twiki, with a lot of collaboration feature

  - There are also hosted services:

  - Seedwiki, a free hosted wiki service (what are their terms of use).

  - Editme, a simple hosted wiki service with GUI editing

  - Socialtext, a hosted wiki services with easy ability to manage multiple, private wikis and weblogs

### Syndication

Weblogs and wikis are great ways for campaign teams to share information and keep current on moment-by-moment campaign activities. For a busy activist keeping up with constantly-changing events in a large campaign, multiple campaigns, it becomes a chore to keep up with multiple websites.

RSS (Really Simple Syndication), the leading format for web content syndication, lets activists easily keep up with changing news at multiple sites. The website needs to publish its content in RSS format, which is a standard machine-readable XML format. Then, the activist subscribes to RSS feeds using a tool called an RSS reader or aggregator. News items automatically appear in the reader when they are updated, and disappear after they are read. The activist only receives updates to the sites she subscribed to – there is no chance of SPAM.

RSS has not yet been widely adopted as campaign technology, but it is likely to become common soon, since it is useful and easy RSS is very popular among the weblog reading and publishing community, since there are so many blogs to keep up with. Major news publishers support RSS, including the New York Times, the BBC, and Yahoo News. Government agencies have started to publish updates in RSS format. As this article was being written, the US Senate and the State of Utah have started to publish RSS feeds; we expect this to become a ubiquitous way for governments to publish news, and for active citizens to keep up.

RSS newsfeeds can also be used to connect a network of related groups. Websites are able to aggregate news stories that are posted by related sites. For example, according to Jon Lebkowsky, the Deanspace project intended to enable the Deanspace sites to share posts and feeds. At each site, an editor would be able to select from a menu of Dean-related stories around the web, and choose to publish specific posts.

## RSS Tools

It is very easy to generate RSS feeds. Most weblog tools, some content management systems, and some wikis have this ability. There is also a newer syndication format, called ATOM, that some tools are beginning to support. The distinction is not very important for campaigns or activists. Make sure that your publishing tool supports RSS, and set it up to do so. Also include an ATOM feed if your tool supports it.

There are different versions of the RSS standard, which makes publishing a bit inconvenient. To make sure that your RSS feed can be read in most readers, test the feed in validation services, including

- www.feedvalidator.org

- http://aggregator.userland.com/validator

There are a number of good, free or inexpensive RSS readers available, including:

- Web-based: Bloglines — free — *use for public workspaces only*

- Windows-based: FeedDemon — trial available, $30 price

- Windows-based: SharpReader — free

- Microsoft Outlook-based: NewsGator — 14 day trial, $30 price

- Mac-based: NetNewsWire — 30 day trial, $40 price

## Tools for Mass Listening: Google, Technorati, Daypop, Blogdex

Weblogs, wikis, and forums are great tools for activists to self-organize, allowing campaigns to benefit from the education and activism of citizens. In the words of campaign professional Nathan Wilcox, "Any candidate running in 2004 must seriously reconsider the usual messaging tactics and strategies — while polling and focus groups serve a purpose, it might be more valuable to attend a political meetup gathering or spend some time on political blogs and chat rooms looking for issues that get people engaged and speak to those concerns:

With so many more citizens talking, it is important for campaigns, and for elected and administrative officials, to use tools for "mass listening", to use the phrase of Elisabeth Richard of Canadian Policy Research Networks.

One of the challenges faced by the Dean campaign was listening to the voices of the thousands of citizens active in the blogs and forums. When Joe Trippi was asked at the 2004 O'Reilly Emerging Technology conference how the campaign considered the input of the online Deaniacs, he didn't mention ideas or policy proposals. He talked about the big red bat that was used to measure campaign contributions.

There is a new range of tools emerging on the public internet that provide a snapshot of public interest.

- Technorati is a weblog search engine that reveals which weblogs link to a given blog. An campaign site can use Technorati to find who's linking to it, to help identify supporters and opponents

- Daypop and Blogdex show the top news articles mentioned in weblogs. These tools give a quick check of the "zeitgeist", showing what masses of bloggers think about the news of the day.

- Feedster is an RSS search engine that also puts together aggregate feeds based on topics. Users can click a single checkbox to subscribe to news about George Bush, John Kerry, or some other politician or campaign of interest.

These tools will be used by activists and campaigners to surface hot topics, and integrate them into the campaign.

Mass listening tools can provide a richer perspective than polling, which captures answers to loaded, pre-defined questions. And mass listenting tools can provide access to a broader range of voices than the traditional media.

Sunir Shah, graduate student at the University of Toronto and a leading thinker about the role of the internet in collaborative discourse, comments in Meatball Wiki on the political media in Canada. "Passive observation of the political thinking of the country has always been central to crafting policy. Politicians have been reading newspapers and magazines since before confederation. However, this material represents only a very small percentage of the population, biased heavily by economic or other political aims. At any rate, it does not represent the "average citizen's opinions." http://www.usemod.com/cgi-bin/mb.pl?PoliticalAction Citizens who participate in online political forums are a subset of the electorate as a whole, but a wider section of the citizenry than those writing or quoted in the political press.

## Social Networks and Directories

In the last year, there has been an explosion of social networking services. These services provide directories of user profiles, and enable them to surf the social networks of their friends and contacts.

Tools in this category include:

- LivingDirectory

- LinkedIn

- Friendster

- Tribe

- Orkut

These services allow members to find and join groups, to participate in discussion forms; to view profiles of members and members' associates, and to post events.

LivingDirectory is intended specifically as a shared directory of progressive groups and members. Other networking services don't have a stated political affiliation.

Friendster is oriented more toward dating and personal connection, while LinkedIn focuses on business connections.

For now, campaigns and activists can look to these networks as venues for finding volunteers and supporters. Because the barrier to entry is low, the level of commitment is also low. And these services provide sparse tools to help volunteers get more involved. Over time, we expect to see more specialized networking services develop for political purposes, with tools to support in-person meetings, action alerts, and other tools. Over time, we expect to see social networking features develop within the community systems used in campaigns. For example, the Dean Campaign had developed a rudimentary directory of Dean supporters.

As social networks proliferate, we expect to see activity in standards that enable the interchange of profile data among networking services, and in privacy protocols that govern the interchange of that data.

## Social Network Analysis

As Valdis Krebs describes, political opinions and voting behavior are heavily influenced by a citizen's social network. Social network analysis tools and techniques have been pioneered in academic research and within large corporations, but have not been widely used in campaigns, according to sociologist Jonas Luster.

The traditional techniques of social network analysis used field interviewing and observation to identify the relationships in social groups, and analytical techniques to map and analyze those relationships. Now that more and more social connections occur online, there are vast and growing sets of data tracing the relationships between people. Some of these relationships are traced explicitly, in social networking services such as Friendster. And many more are traced implicitly, in the patterns of response, linking and commentary in online forums, weblogs and wikis.

These analytical tools will provide campaign organizers with the ability to understand how their issue or candidacy is being interpreted and spread within social networks, in close to real time. And they will provide citizens with greater ability to find and organize with like-minded people.

## Get Out the Vote

As described in the chapter on email targeting, activists and developers are refining applications for targeted marketing, and managing the process of fundraising among wealthy donors

Advokit is a packaged application for campaigns to support friend-to-friend get out the vote efforts, with features to support phone banking, walk lists for neighborhood visits, ride lists to rallies, and volunteer-matching. Still in development, the application will include traditional geographic and demographic targeting, and friend to friend methodologies, where a campaign volunteer identifies voters to recruit.

Indyvoter is an initiative planning using online grassroots organizing to mobilize young, progressive voters. The online application (on the drawing board at the time of this writing) enables young voters to:

- Search online voter guide for local elections

- connect with others in the region, with online directories and physical address book

- organize brunches and book clubs

- neighborhood voter registration and education

- organize get out the vote drives

CivicSpace (devel.deanspace.org at the time of this writing) is developing website applications for civic groups, based on the work pioneered at Hack4Dean, which became DeanSpace. CivicSpace enables grass roots groups to have their own sophisticated websites. Based on the Drupal open source CMS, it provides a "content management system in a box", including the features needed for campaign groups to organize themselves.

- install and configure, and customize the site

- set up weblogs, syndication, and aggregation

- threaded discussion groups, polls and surveys

- voter contact management

**Votewatch** http://www.votewatch.us/ is another, more specialized activist application. Launched during the 2002 mid-term election, The Votewatch system focuses on monitoring elections. Volunteers use handheld computers to track (what do they track) in on the day of election, and dispatch investigators to trouble spots. Statistical analysts analyze reports with an eye for anomalies related to voting equipmentand voting districts.

The application uses RSS to syndicate election-day reports to the media and concerned citizens and organizations.

- Hosted services with social networking, and meetup, giving citizens tools to organize their friends:

- Citizens Vote is a social networking application that encourages citizens ask to ask their friends to vote democratic

- Mainstream Moms against Bush (http://www.themmob.com/) provides tools for moms (and other voters) to organize meetups, host voter-writing parties for their friends. The site provides tools to print letters, flyers, postcards, tshirts, and other propaganda.

- PartyForAmerica is on online service giving voters tools to find, host, and organize house parties for progressive causes http://dev.partyforamerica.com/home.html

- National Voice is a coalition of non-profit and community groups working to maximize public participation in our nation's democratic process. They have an online database to match voluneteers and funding sources with non-profits doing voter education and registration.

- There are several early efforts to develop open source versions, including Advokit, from Pat Dunlavey, and Campaign in a Box, a project with Zephyr Teachout of the Dean Campaign.

### Privacy and security

A comprehensive treatment of privacy and security is beyond the scope of this chapter. However, there are a number of security considerations that campaigners should keep in mind when evaluating online methods and tools.

**Basic computer security.** Any network-connected computer is vulnerable to attack by random hackers. Campaigns are competitive by nature, and are vulnerable to disruption by unethical opponents. Campaigns need to deploy skilled staff to ensure that servers are protected by keeping critical software components current with security updates, using firewalls, intrusion detection, and other standard security techniques. If the campaign does not have staff to maintain the security of sensitive communication and data, reputable hosted services can be an effective solution. See *Web Security, Privacy, and Commerce*, 2$^{nd}$ Edition (O'Reilly, 2002), by Simson Garfinkel for an advanced beginner treatment of the topic.

**Private communication.** Campaigns need to balance open communication to build support, with private communication to avoid sharing tactics with competitors. Campaigns can take advantage of collaboration tools with access control, providing access to a core team, and restricting access to others.

**Protecting constituent data.** A 2003 report by Jonah Seiger of the Institute for Politics Democracy and the Internet reports that vast majority of respondents indicated that they have hesitated to provide their e-mail address (69%) and credit card number (89%) to political Web sites, citing concerns about SPAM (unsolicited email), privacy, and security. The report's suggestions include:

- Post a privacy statement

- Use standard security technologies such as SSL

- Offer visitors choice over how their data will be used

- Demonstrate a commitment that the campaign will stick to its privacy and security policies.

**Encrypted communication.** Encryption can be a valuable tool for activists who are working on repressive states, or who are working on behalf of people whose safety is at risk, such as victims of domestic abuse. For example, Human rights workers increasingly use the Internet to coordinate their actions against repressive governments. Human rights activists in Guatemala, for example, credited their use of Pretty Good Privacy (PGP) with saving the lives of witnesses to military abuses.49 Encryption is not the ultimate solution, however, as governments can outlaw its use and arrest those who do not comply.

## Evaluating tools

Each section has included tips for evaluating each category of tools. The following table, taken from an article about evaluating open source tools, is a useful summary overall.

- Does the tool do what I need 'out-of-the-box', or will it need to be customized?

- Is the user interface simple for the people who will be working with the application?

- Is there reasonable documentation and support? Does the support forum handle newbie questions well?

- Does the tool use technologies and languages we are already familiar with?

- Is there an on-line demo my users can play around with to see if the tool 'feels right' to them?

- Is the tool's programming team actively developing and maintaining the tool?

- Is the tool one of the more popular ones in its category?

## Patterns of use

This chapter has covered a plethora of tools that are useful for campaign activists using the network. Clearly, there is no single tool that addresses all of the requirements of an election or activist campaign. And there's no reason there should be. Before computers, campaign tools include postal mail, telephone, buses, trains, and walking through neighborhoods, ringing doorbells.

As the tools and methods for networked campaigning become more familiar, we are starting to see patterns for using the tools together. One such set of patterns was used in campaign by digital rights activists against the so-called "Super DMCA." This was a bill, sponsored by the

Motion Picture Association of America in numerous states, the purpose of which was ostensibly to reduce theft of services and content. However a literal interpretation of the bill would impose broad control over personal and business use of the internet. In previous years, the bill had passed quietly in seven states. In 2003, technology activists took notice.

In April, notice of a hearing on the bill was posted in Slashdot, a popular technology news site and group weblog. A number of Tennessee techies read the posting, and noticed each others' remarks in the Slashdot comments section. With just a few days notice, they organized 23 people to attend the hearing, and co-ordinated testimony against the bill. During the legislative session, the Tennessee Digital Freedom Network (http://tndf.net/) posted news and alerts on a website, and co-ordinated activity using an email network.

Activists fighting the bill in Tennessee, Massachusetts, Michigan, South Carolina, Georgia, Texas, and Florida, along with representatives of national technology policy groups used the internet to co-ordinate. The activists set up a mailing list to co-ordinate opposition across the states, and held regular conference calls, supported by online chat.

State-based groups sent email action alerts with links to the action alert systems from national EFF and Public Knowledge, and in response activists sent letters and faxes to their local legislators.

The activist groups used combinations of electronic and traditional methods.

- In Texas, the activist group used a weblog and mailing list to post alerts to members

- A private wiki was used to draft and store fact sheets, which were delivered by fax and in personal visits to legislators' offices

- Personal relationships were used to reach out to high-tech manufacturers whose consumer electronics businesses would be harmed by the bill

- A mailing list call for volunteers was used to organize a team of 8 volunteers, visited each of the 150 members of the Texas House of Representatives on Memorial Day weekend

With coordinated opposition, the bill was defeated in six states in 2003.

Diagram of tools for different purposes.

## Trends

In recent years, activists have been experimenting and pioneering techniques for using network tools in activist campaigns. Out of the details of these efforts, we can see and predict a number of trends and themes.

- **Presence.** Over time, we'll see richer tools for immediate communication and more sophisticated use of these tools. More campaign processes will involve co-ordination among people who are mobile and always-connected, facilitating rapid response at the high speed of an active campaign.

- **Integration.** Today's disconnected software tools will be integrated into suites, and pluggable at interface points.

- **Aggregation.** Activist groups will be able to aggregate content and bring together activist networks to combine forces on larger goals. Online tools will support traditional processes of coalition building.

- **Connection to traditional campaign process.** One of the challenges in the early days of networked campaigning has been a gap between the technical savvy of toolmakers and the process savvy of traditional activists. This gap will be bridged, resulting in effective processes for using network tools in effective campaigns.

- **Mass listening.** Activists need to adapt their traditional campaign processes to campaign effectively using networks. Over time, we'll see better tools and techniques for mass listening – identifying ideas and themes in the net-discussion, and using deliberative processes to inform decisions. These techniques for mass listening are a technically augmented version of a skill that talented organizers have had for years – the ability to listen to people, and synthesize a common approach.

- **Connect to the physical world.** The Canadian paper on "Lessons from the Network Model for Online Engagement of Citizens" has an important caution for networked organizers: *Don't mistake email for organizing.* An action alert is not an organization. If you want to build a lasting political movement, at some point you'll have to gather people together. The Internet is a useful tool for organizing, but it's just one tool and one medium among many that you will need, and you should evaluate it largely in terms of its contribution to larger organizing goals. Do the people you reach through Internet alerts move up into more active positions in your movement? Do you draw them into conferences, talk to them by phone, meet them in person, become accountable to them to provide specific information and answer questions? If not, why do you keep reaching out to them?

- **Bottom-up campaigning.** The overall theme of this book is bottom-up campaigning. Every new generation of technology changes culture, and is assimilated into culture. The new style of networked campaigning will be assimilated into traditional campaign processes. Activists won't think about "e-campaigning" as a separate subject – they'll think about campaigning, communicating online and in person. At the same time, the properties of the network will transform campaigning. The internet's ability to enable many to many communication will break the stranglehold of the mass media, and create a return to an older world of grassroots campaigning.

# The Authors

## Joichi Ito

Joichi Ito is Vice President of international and mobility for Technorati, which indexes and monitors blogs and the Chairman of Six Apart Japan the weblog software company. He is on the board of Creative Commons, a non-profit organization which proposes a middle way to rights management, rather than the extremes of the pure public domain or the reservation of all rights. He is also serving a three year term as board member of Internet Corporation For Assigned Names and Numbers (ICANN) for a three year term starting December 2004. He has created numerous Internet companies including PSINet Japan, Digital Garage and Infoseek Japan. In 1997 Time Magazine ranked him as a member of the CyberElite. In 2000 he was ranked among the "50 Stars of Asia" by Business Week and commended by the Japanese Ministry of Posts and Telecommunications for supporting the advancement of IT. In 2001 the World Economic Forum chose him as one of the 100 "Global Leaders of Tomorrow" for 2002. He has served and continues to serve on numerous Japanese central as well as local government committees and boards, advising the government on IT, privacy and computer security related issues. He is currently researching "The Sharing Economy" as a Doctor of Business Administration candidate at the Graduate School of International Corporate Strategy at Hitotsubashi University in Japan. He maintains a personal weblog where he regularly shares his thoughts with the online community.

## James F. Moore

James F. Moore is a business and technology strategist who wrote the best seller The Death of Competition: Leadership and Strategy in the Age of Business Ecosystems (HarperBusiness, 1996) and a McKinsey Award winning Harvard Business Review article "Predators and Prey: A New Ecology of Competition." He is the former Chairman and Chief Executive Officer of GeoPartners Research, which he led from 1990 to 1999. He earned a doctorate in Human Development (clinical developmental psychology) from Harvard in 1983, where he conducted research on cognition and expert practice, and worked closely with C. Roland Christensen, one of the founders of modern business strategy. Jim continued his research as a Post-doctoral Fellow in Organizations at Stanford in 1983-84, and as a Senior Research Associate at the Harvard

Business School in 1984-85. He attended Williams College (Massachusetts) and earned his undergraduate degree from The Evergreen State College (Washington) in 1975.

## Clay Shirky

Clay Shirky divides his time between consulting, teaching, and writing on the social and economic effects of Internet technologies. His consulting practice is focused on the rise of decentralized technologies such as peer-to-peer, web services, and wireless networks that provide alternatives to the wired client/server infrastructure that characterizes the Web. Current clients include Nokia, GBN, the Library of Congress, the Highlands Forum, the Markle Foundation, and the BBC.

In addition to his consulting work, Mr. Shirky is an adjunct professor in NYU's graduate Interactive Telecommunications Program (ITP), where he teaches courses on the interrelated effects of social and technological network topology — how our networks shape culture and vice-versa. He has written extensively about the internet since 1996. Over the years, he has had regular columns in Business 2.0, FEED, OpenP2P.com and ACM Net_Worker, and his writings have appeared in the New York Times, the Wall Street Journal, the Harvard Business Review, Wired, Release 1.0, Computerworld, and IEEE Computer. He has been interviewed by Slashdot, Red Herring, Media Life, and the Economist's Ebusiness Forum. He has written about biotechnology in his "After Darwin" column in FEED magazine, and serves as a technical reviewer for O'Reilly's bioinformatics series. He helps program the "Biological Models of Computation" track for O'Reilly's Emerging Technology conferences. Mr. Shirky's writings are archived at shirky.com, and he currently runs the N.E.C. mailing list for his writings on networks, economics, and culture.

## Mitch Ratcliffe

For more than 15 years Mitch Ratcliffe has chronicled and participated in the development of the Internet. He spent his early days on The W.E.L.L. In the 1990s, he covered networking, privacy and cryptography for MacWEEK, and was the editor of Digital Media, the first publication to explain how the Internet would really work. By 1996, he had launched Internet/Media Strategies and was starting and investing in companies for SoftBank, consulting with leaders like America Online, Audible, EarthWeb, Time Warner, Personify, and many others. ZD Net brought him on to lead their Year 2000 coverage for the two years leading up to Y2K In 1999, he took on the content development for ON24, the financial news network-where he co-authored the business plans and built the editorial and content teams from their launch. He left in 2001, when I/MS partnered with The Petkevich Group, a San Francisco merchant bank focusing on healthcare and information technology.

## Steven Johnson

Steven Johnson was Editor and founder of Feed, a pioneering Web publication. He is currently a columnist on Discover Magazine, and the author of Emergence (2002).

## Ken White

Ken White, the administrative director of the Chaordic Commons, has worked for much of his career on democracy, community-building, and opportunity. A graduate of Harvard University's John F. Kennedy School of Government's mid-career program, he has worked with nonprofits for 15 years. Most recently, he was the executive director of Common Cause Massachusetts, a citizen-led organization dedicated to building truly representative government. Prior to that, Ken was the director of communications for the Annenberg Institute for School Reform and Coalition of Essential Schools, and held similar posts with Oxfam America and the Institute for Defense & Disarmament Studies. Ken has also been a consultant to numerous nonprofits on growth and strategy issues, and was formerly a journalist.

## Valdis Krebs

Valdis Krebs is a management consultant and the developer of InFlow, a software based, organization network analysis methodology that maps and measures knowledge exchange, information flow, communities of practice, networks of alliances and other networks within and between organizations. Clients such as IBM, TRW, Raytheon, Aventis, Cardinal Health, CapitalOne, Centers for Disease Control [CDC], Lucent Technologies, Hiram Walker, Shell, ACENet, CWRU-REI, Rubbermaid, Sempra Energy, Deloitte Touche Tohmatsu, Jaakko Poyry, PricewaterhouseCoopers, Booz-Allen & Hamilton, KPMG, University of Michigan Business School and many others use his software and services to map and measure networks, flows, and relationships in organizations, communities, and other complex human systems. His work in organizational network analysis has been covered in major media including Discover Magazine, Business 2.0, New York Times, Wall Street Journal, USA Today, CNN, Entrepreneur, First Monday, Optimize Magazine, Training, PC, ZDNet, O'Reilly Network, Knowledge Management, Across the Board, Business Week, HR Executive, Personnel Journal, Forbes, FORTUNE, MSNBC.com, HR.com, Release 1.0, and several major newspapers around the world.

Valdis has undergraduate degrees in Mathematics & Computer Science, and a graduate degree in Organizational Behavior/Human Resources and has studied applied Artificial Intelligence. He has given invited talks on organizational networks at UCLA Anderson School, Michigan State University School of Labor and Industrial Relations, Weatherhead School of Management - Case Western Reserve University, Cleveland State University, University of Michigan Business School, Kellogg School of Management - Northwestern University and the University of Latvia.

### Ross Mayfield

Ross Mayfield is CEO and co-founder of Socialtext, an emerging provider of Enterprise Social Software that to increase group productivity and develop a group memory. SocialText was the first company to adapt wikis (group-editable websites) and weblogs for enterprise use. Prior to SocialText, he was VP of Marketing and Business Development at a Fujitsu spinout developing telecom software. Before that, he co-founded RateXchange (AMEX:RTX), the leading B2B exchange for telecom where he served as VP of Marketing, then COO and finally President. He is a former advisor and speechwriter to the President of Estonia.

### David Weinberger

Dr. Weinberger taught philosophy at New Jersey's Stockton State College for five years. (He has a Ph.D. in philosophy from the University of Toronto.) During this time he maintained his steady freelance writing of humor, reviews and intellectual and academic articles, publishing in places as diverse as The New York Times, Harvard Business Review, Smithsonian, Alfred Hitchcock's Mystery Magazine and TV Guide. In 1985, he began working for Interleaf, an innovative start-up with new ideas on how to create and structure documents. At

Interleaf he helped launch the industry's first document management system and its first electronic document publishing system, years ahead of the Web. He left Interleaf after 8 years, as VP of Strategic Marketing.

He founded the one-person strategic marketing company, Evident Marketing, in 1994 and within two years counted among his clients a wide variety of companies, including RR Donnelley, Intuit, Sun Microsystems, Esther Dyson's Release 1.0 and CSC Index.

In 1995-96, he was VP of Strategic Marketing at Open Text, after which he returned to consulting, writing and speaking, helping to found a couple of dot-coms, and serving on industry and company boards. He was co-author of The ClueTrain Manifesto and author of Small Pieces Loosely Joined, both influential works. During the 2004 presidential campaign, he was Senior Internet Advisor to the Howard Dean campaign, consulting on Internet policy. In 2004 he was made a Fellow at Harvard's prestigious Berkman Institute for Internet & Society.

## danah boyd

An information management PhD student at the University of California, boyd focuses her research on how people negotiate their presentation of self in relation to varying social contexts, including social software like Friendster.

## Philip J. Windley, Ph. D.

Philip J. Windley is an Associate Professor of Computer Science at Brigham Young University where he teaches courses on digital identity, interoperability, web services, middleware, and programming languages. Phil is also a frequent author and speaker on these topics and writes a blog at www.windley.com. Prior to joining BYU, Phil spent two years as the Chief Information Officer (CIO) for the State of Utah, serving on the Governor Mike Leavitt's Cabinet and as a member of his Senior Staff. Before entering public service, Phil was Vice President for Product Development and Operations at Excite@Home and Chief Technology Officer (CTO) of iMALL, Inc. an early leader in electronic commerce.

## Jon Lebkowsky

Jon Lebkowsky is CEO of Polycot, an innovative team of Internet technology experts with broad experience creating and managing information systems for businesses and nonprofit organizations. An authority on computer-mediated communications, virtual communities, and online social networks, he has worked as project manager, systems analyst, technology director, and online community developer. He was cofounder and CEO of one of the first virtual corporations, FringeWare, Inc. He is currently President of EFF-Austin, a cofounder of the Open Source Business Alliance, the Austin Wireless City Project, and the national Social Software Alliance, and advisor for the annual South by Southwest Interactive conference. He serves on the Advisory Board for the University of Texas Science, Technology, and Society Program. A longtime Internet activist, he is co-editing a book on technology, democracy, and advocacy, and served on the organizing committee for O'Reilly's Digital Democracy Teach-In (February 9, 2004). He recently completed a year-long engagement with IC$^2$ Institute at the University of Texas, where he managed Wireless Future, a project that produced a major economic development report as well as a national wireless track within South by Southwest Interactive. He contributes to weblogs at weblogsky.com, smartmobs.com, worldchanging.com, ob4.org, greaterdemocracy.org, and austin.metblogs.com. He has written about technology for many publications such as Mondo 2000, 21C, Whole Earth Review, Fringe Ware Review, and the Austin Chronicle.

### Adam Greenfield

Adam Greenfield worked as lead information architect for the Tokyo outpost of Razorfish, and has been a rock critic for SPIN Magazine, a coffeehouse owner in West Philadelphia, a San Francisco bike messenger, a medic at the Berkeley Free Clinic, the editor of a free magazine in Seattle, a PSYOP sergeant in the US Army Special Operations Command, and director of new media development for a now-defunct dotcom. He graduated from NYU with an honors degree in Cultural Studies, and has traveled widely in Europe, South America, and Asia.

### Ethan Zuckerman

Ethan Zuckerman's main affiliation is with the Berkman Center for Internet and Society at Harvard Law School, which is sometimes described as a "do-tank", a think tank for folks who effect change as well as study phenomena. He's working on a number of projects there, including Research on the Global Attention Gap, Blogging in the Developing World, and Digital Democracy.

He co-founded <u>Geekcorps</u>, an international non-profit organization that transfers tech skills from geeks in developed nations to geeks in emerging nations, especially entrepreneurial geeks who are building small businesses - a Peace Corps for geeks. Ethan was also a co-founder of Tripod.originally a content provider that became a leading host of user-created content before selling the company to Lycos.

## Roger Wood

Roger Wood wasn't using his civil rights [enough], anyway.

From his home turf in the Washington DC area, he has worked in and around the business of music and technology since the late 1980's, exploring approaches to make performers more economically viable and

restore value to the audience experience. He helps talented performers reap direct economic benefit from their work and is working on an infrastructure to remove some inefficiencies from the experience economy. He is currently assembling a touring dance, music, arts and education project from pieces of culture around the world.

When not instigating trouble, he is a performance photographer and embraces the challenge of capturing moving targets under strange lights between awkward expressions.

Roj is still reconsidering his career at the institution.

## Britt Blaser

For 33 years, Britt Blaser has been forming companies and organizing projects to seize opportunities dimly glimpsed by others. The first half of his career was in real estate development in Colorado, in mountain resorts and along the Front Range. In 1986-92 he was the angel investor and later President and CEO of <u>Dynamac Computer</u>, the first authorized Macintosh clone. In 1992-4, he co-founded the Trust Company of Washington in Seattle. For the last decade he's advised clients on a range of increasingly technical projects.

Classically educated and descended from a family of writers, Britt's explored many corners of the American experience: Patrol Leader, Colorado Outward Bound School (climbed five of Colorado's 14,000 ft. peaks); USAF combat pilot in Vietnam (awarded 2 Air Medals and 3

Distinguished Flying Crosses); ski instructor; Trustee and Development Director, Colorado Academy (Colorado's largest independent school); Trustee, Colorado Children's Chorale; Author, Xpertweb peer-to-peer reputation protocol; Senior Advisor for Internet Strategy for the Howard Dean Campaign; Senior Architect for web strategy, Spirit of America; Widely read blogger at "Escapable Logic" (http://www.blaserco.com/blogs).

He recently founded and now serves as CEO of Open Resource Group, LLC, developer of a comprehensive content management system for spontaneous community-forming. The architecture and user orientation are based on lessons learned from the Dean campaign and the Spirit of America project. Clients are communities that want to grow and organizations seeking to inspire a dynamic community around their efforts.

### Aldon Hynes

Aldon was very involved working as a volunteer in the Howard Dean's 2004 Presidential Primary campaign. In particular he has set up several DeanSpace based websites, and moderated several mailing lists. Aldon's political activities recently involved working as campaign manager for his wife's run for State Representative. He contributes to several blogs, has had articles published on a wide ranging set of topics from hedge fund technology to group psychology of internet communities and has presented research at conferences on the Dean Campaign's use of the internet. Aldon served as Director of Technology for the $2 billion hedge fund, S.A.C. Capital Advisors, from 1997-2000. In that role, Aldon held primary responsibility for all aspects of information technology supporting the firm's primary high-volume, short-term equity trading strategy as well as fixed income, international, statistical arbitrage, risk arbitrage, currency and commodity trading strategies. From 1992-1997, Aldon was Vice President of the Union Bank of Switzerland with responsibility for developing technology for desktop trading systems, servers and internet applications for the bank's North American business unit. Aldon developed the structuring system for collateralized mortgage obligations at Shearson Lehman beginning in 1987 and was appointed Head of Mortgage Technology at Smith Barney in 1989. Prior to his move to Wall Street, Aldon consulted as a systems developer for a number of Fortune 500 companies including

AT&T, Bell Labs, IBM and Exxon. Aldon studied Philosophy at the College of Wooster.

## Adina Levin

Adina Levin has over 13 years of experience in strategic marketing and product planning in a variety of emerging high-tech markets. At Vignette Corporation, a leading provider of Internet content management software, Levin served as Senior Director at Corporate Strategy, a role that included product strategy and planning, marketing strategy and operations, and management consulting in the areas of mergers, acquisitions, and distribution. Prior to Vignette, Levin was co-founder and partner in Fastwater LLP, a research and consulting firm focusing on ebusiness marketing and business metrics. Prior to Fastwater, Levin served as senior consultant in the Document Software Strategies group at CAP Ventures, where she specialized in emerging Internet collaboration and publishing technologies. At CAP Ventures, Levin also managed a major multi-client study on the Future of Paper analyzing the ways that electronic media will transform the ways that business and individuals will use paper and print. Before joining CAP Ventures, Levin tracked the markets for traditional and digital publishing for seven years at BIS Strategic Decisions where she designed, managed, and authored numerous market research studies. Levin currently serves on the Board of Directors of Campaigns for People, a non-profit working for campaign finance reform in Texas, and is a member of the Advisory Board for the Electronic Frontier Foundation, Austin